Learning
.NET MAUI

*Unlock the potential of .NET MAUI
for Cross-Platform app development*

Aleksei Starkov

www.bpbonline.com

First published: 2023

Published by BPB Online
WeWork
119 Marylebone Road
London NW1 5PU

UK | UAE | INDIA | SINGAPORE

ISBN 978-93-55518-804

www.bpbonline.com

Dedicated to

My beloved wife:

Ekaterina

&

My Son **Stepan**

About the Author

Aleksei Starkov is a seasoned software developer with over 10 years of experience in the tech industry. After 5 years of working on industrial automation projects that shaped his work ethic, he has been specializing in .NET, Xamarin, and MAUI since 2017. Aleksei's deep understanding of these technologies has been honed by participating in developing multiple commercial projects of different sizes and working for various software companies, from startups to large enterprises. In his free time, Aleksei spends time with his family and enjoys riding a motorcycle.

About the Reviewer

Anton Tereshko, a seasoned, certified software developer, holds a degree in Computer Software Engineering. His extensive career, spanning over eight years in the software development sector, includes three years of demonstrated leadership. He has proficiently led and streamlined the development processes for application services across numerous large-scale businesses operating in complex sectors such as medicine, transport & logistics, and insurance, utilizing his expert knowledge of MAUI, Xamarin, .NET, Flutter, and Microsoft Azure technologies.

Embracing the rise of AI/ML technologies, Anton is actively engaged in the development of applications featuring artificial intelligence. He holds a certificate in Azure Cognitive Service and continues to advance in this direction. In addition to his software development accomplishments, Anton is a serial entrepreneur, having co-founded multiple technology startups.

Acknowledgement

I want to express my deepest gratitude to my family for their endless support and encouragement throughout this book's writing, especially my wife Ekaterina and my son Stepan.

I am also grateful to the team of BPB Publications for their guidance, expertise, and professionalism. It was a long journey, with valuable participation and collaboration of reviewers, technical experts, and editors.

I would also like to acknowledge the valuable contributions of my colleagues, teammates, employers, and clients, who have taught me much and shaped me professionally.

Finally, I would like to thank all the readers who have taken an interest in my book.

Preface

In its time, Xamarin, the predecessor of .NET MAUI, played a crucial role in establishing a sustained trend for cross-platform GUI applications. Business owners, managers, and engineers were captivated by the opportunity to write code once and run it on various platforms and devices, all while leveraging the power of .NET.

When creating my first application with Xamarin, I used only official documentation and some blog posts from experienced colleagues. Time passed, and I worked on many different apps. Some of them I built alone, and for others, I worked as part of a group with more than 20 engineers. This book was born out of my desire to share my knowledge, passion, and experience to help others grow faster in their journey through the world of .NET MAUI.

In writing this book, my goal has been to provide as much useful theoretical and practical knowledge as possible to prepare you for work on real-world commercial projects while minimizing any confusion about the purpose of what you're learning.

Throughout the book, you will refresh your knowledge about .NET and C#, learn about the fundamentals and internals of .NET MAUI, its features, and how to use them to build real-world applications with custom UI and high-quality codebase that are reliable and easy to maintain. You will also learn about best practices and design patterns on the path through the mixture of theory, practical examples, and coding tasks.

This book is intended mostly for developers without commercial Xamarin and .NET MAUI experience and want to learn how to build GUI applications targeting different platforms and devices. However, it would also be helpful for developers with Xamarin experience who want to switch to .NET MAUI and improve their skills in building robust and reliable cross-platform applications.

Welcome aboard; our .NET MAUI adventure begins! I hope you'll enjoy it. See you on the other side.

Chapter 1: Getting Started with .NET MAUI - covers a .NET MAUI environment setup. The chapter introduces Visual Studio 2022 and the NuGet package manager.

Besides, this chapter shows how to create the blank application from the predefined template, and explains platform-specific debugging details and the anatomy of the .NET MAUI solution.

Chapter 2: Upskill Essentials of C# - covers the most important .NET and C# topics knowledge of that are crucial for understanding upcoming chapters. The chapter introduces the concept of modern .NET and explains numerous areas, including data types, Object-Oriented Programming, memory management and generics, and more.

Chapter 3: Exploring .NET MAUI and Its Features - covers the fundamentals of .NET MAUI, starting from the history of Xamarin to how MAUI works. It explains such crucial topics as main .NET MAUI classes, HostBuilder, and application lifecycle. This chapter is where the reader gets familiar with managing application assets and starts creating their first MAUI application.

Chapter 4: In and Out of UI Development - allows the reader to learn fundamental concepts related to user interface implementation. The chapter addresses the main challenges while creating applications targeting different platforms and devices. Within this chapter, the reader also learns the fundamental UI controls, layouts, binding and navigation mechanisms while constantly developing the application from the previous chapter. One of the main areas covered by Chapter 4 is the XAML declarative markup language mainly used in MAUI to describe the user interface.

Chapter 5: Layering with MVVM - specializes the application architecture explaining MVVM, Inversion of Control, addressing in-app navigation challenges, and more. It also covers the usage of third-party dependency injection containers, embedding the NoSQL database, and local persistent storage creation.

Chapter 6: Deep Dive into UI Design - covers more complex areas of UI development. Within this chapter, the reader turns its application into a multilanguage one that handles different color schemes and visual states reacting to data changes. This chapter is where the application UI appearance and behavior become more polished and sophisticated thanks to custom animations, custom controls, and a new group of built-in controls and features.

Chapter 7: Essentials and Community Toolkit - explains extremely helpful libraries nearly every commercial application uses. One of them introduces a bunch of useful, commonly used classes created by the community, like converters, behaviors, and AsyncRelayCommand. The other introduces support for unique operating systems and platform APIs like Text-to-Speech, Gyroscope, or Secure Storage.

Chapter 8: Accessibility - covers the important topic of accessibility support. The chapter addresses the most popular accessibility issues and explains the tools and APIs provided by operating systems and .NET MAUI to make the application more accessible.

Chapter 9: Native Interactive Features with Shell and Blazor - introduces alternative approaches to .NET MAUI application development. During this chapter, the reader will turn its application into a Shell application learning the differences between the classic approach and Shell. Additionally, they will learn methods to optimize Shell for real-world commercial projects. Besides, this chapter covers Blazor Hybrid applications, their concept, anatomy, and superpower.

Code Bundle and Coloured Images

Please follow the link to download the
Code Bundle and the *Coloured Images* of the book:

https://rebrand.ly/2b1m6y2

The code bundle for the book is also hosted on GitHub at **https://github.com/ bpbpublications/Learning-.NET-MAUI**. In case there's an update to the code, it will be updated on the existing GitHub repository.

We have code bundles from our rich catalogue of books and videos available at **https://github.com/bpbpublications**. Check them out!

Errata

We take immense pride in our work at BPB Publications and follow best practices to ensure the accuracy of our content to provide with an indulging reading experience to our subscribers. Our readers are our mirrors, and we use their inputs to reflect and improve upon human errors, if any, that may have occurred during the publishing processes involved. To let us maintain the quality and help us reach out to any readers who might be having difficulties due to any unforeseen errors, please write to us at :

errata@bpbonline.com

Your support, suggestions and feedbacks are highly appreciated by the BPB Publications' Family.

Piracy

If you come across any illegal copies of our works in any form on the internet, we would be grateful if you would provide us with the location address or website name. Please contact us at **business@bpbonline.com** with a link to the material.

If you are interested in becoming an author

If there is a topic that you have expertise in, and you are interested in either writing or contributing to a book, please visit **www.bpbonline.com**. We have worked with thousands of developers and tech professionals, just like you, to help them share their insights with the global tech community. You can make a general application, apply for a specific hot topic that we are recruiting an author for, or submit your own idea.

Reviews

Please leave a review. Once you have read and used this book, why not leave a review on the site that you purchased it from? Potential readers can then see and use your unbiased opinion to make purchase decisions. We at BPB can understand what you think about our products, and our authors can see your feedback on their book. Thank you!

For more information about BPB, please visit **www.bpbonline.com**.

Join our book's Discord space

Join the book's Discord Workspace for Latest updates, Offers, Tech happenings around the world, New Release and Sessions with the Authors:

https://discord.bpbonline.com

Table of Contents

CHAPTER 1
Getting Started with .NET MAUI

Introduction

Let us imagine an enthusiastic mechanic who builds a car in the early 1900s in a backyard. They do it right on the ground under the open sky without precise tools, ergonomic toolboxes, and bright lights. Needless to say, ensuring the speed and quality of work requires significant efforts in such conditions.

Programmers from the 70s and 80s were in pretty similar situations. They had to use a set of separate hardware and software tools to write, compile, and debug the code they wrote.

Because of the same reasons why mechanics eventually moved from dusty backyards to shiny workshops, developers ended up with **Integrated Development Environments** (**IDE**). The first IDE was created by *Anders Hejlsberg*, engineer of *Borland Ltd.*, in 1983 featuring an integrated code editor and compiler for the first time.

Microsoft Visual Studio is a modern IDE loved by millions of software developers around the world. It provides numerous handy development tools and features and supports multiple development platforms and frameworks. Since Microsoft Visual Studio is an official free IDE for the .NET **Multi-Platform App UI** development framework (**MAUI**). The main task of this chapter is to help you learn how to establish an MAUI developer environment on both Windows and macOS operational systems, take a look around, and run the blank project of an MAUI application.

Structure

In this chapter, we will cover the following topics:

- Visual Studio 2022 installation
- Visual Studio 2022 for Mac installation
- Creating .NET MAUI project
- Let's make it alive
- Visual Studio IDE overview
- Anatomy of .NET MAUI solution
- NuGet package manager

Objectives

After going through this chapter, an essential set of development tools will be established, making your virtual workplace ready for work on MAUI projects. Besides, you'll be familiarised with the fundamentals of the Visual Studio IDE, MAUI project structure, and NuGet package manager.

Visual Studio 2022 installation

To install Visual Studio 2022 for Windows, go to the official website, that is, **https://visualstudio.microsoft.com/downloads/**, and download the free community version of Visual Studio 2022. At this stage, you might notice that there are three trims of Visual Studio:

- Community
- Professional
- Enterprise

The main idea here is 'the larger the team and project, the more likely it is that a more advanced version of IDE is needed'. The community version is an appropriate choice for students and individual developers. It contains all essential tools and functionalities, and it's free.

The tool you have downloaded is a Visual Studio Installer. It's an answer to the need to have a single place to manage installed Visual Studio versions and modules of each installed version:

Figure 1.1: *First launch of Visual Studio Installer*

Since Visual Studio is a modular IDE that allows the creation of various kinds of software products, you can select only the modules you need to make it as lightweight as possible. *Figure 1.1* represents the modules selection step of the installation wizard:

Figure 1.2: *Selecting the MAUI module*

Let's scroll it down and select **.NET Multi-Platform App UI development**, as shown in *Figure 1.2*. There are two important things you should pay attention to.

The first thing is the **Preview** version used. This book is being written in May 2022 and MAUI is still unavailable for the regular version of Visual Studio. So, if the regular version of Visual Studio you downloaded doesn't contain the MAUI module, go to **https://visualstudio.microsoft.com/vs/preview/** and download the preview version of Visual Studio. However, it is believed that MAUI would have been included in stable Visual Studio 2022 before this book goes on sale.

The second thing is the **Xamarin checkbox** you might notice under the **Installation details** section. It's optional, but it is recommended to select it. In the later chapters, we will touch on the differences between Xamarin and MAUI. So, it might be helpful to play around Xamarin project for better understanding. You might probably not know what Xamarin is and how it relates to MAUI. We will talk about it in *Chapter 3, Exploring .NET MAUI and Its Features*.

Now, we are ready to click **Install**. Make sure you have a stable internet connection during the installation process:

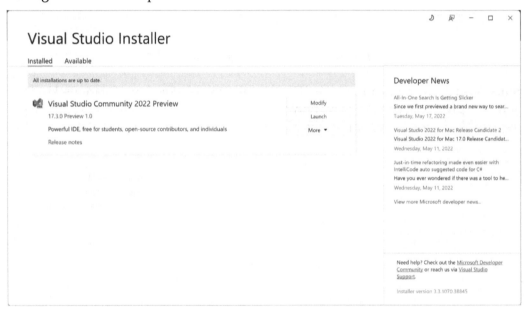

Figure 1.3: *Visual Studio Installer with installed Visual Studio 2022*

Figure 1.3 shows what the Visual Studio installer should look like after the installation. Call the installer from time to time to check if some updates are available. Besides, you can add or remove specific modules from the menu hidden under the **Modify** button.

The next step to take right after Visual Studio installation is checking the Android SDK Manager configuration. The Android SDK Manager helps developers control and update the installed native Android development tools, such as Android Emulator, build tools, drivers, and SDKs, to target different versions of the Android platform.

Launch the Visual Studio and choose **Continue without code.** Then, go to **Tools** > **Android** > **Android SDK Manager**, as shown in *Figure 1.4*:

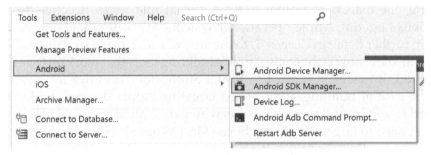

Figure 1.4: Visual Studio tools menu

Right after you have launched the Android SDK Manager, it might offer you to repair and reinstall SDK and SDK tools to make sure the latest versions are installed. Click the **Repair** button and follow the instructions.

General advice: Keep the SDK of the last two versions of Android installed. It's not a rare situation when you are forced to target the previous version of Android instead of the latest one because some other parts of your infrastructure, like the CI/CD pipelines of a build server, are not ready yet to work with the latest version of Android SDK. So, having a previous one hundred percent reliable version of SDK might be useful.

Figure 1.5 shows what the SDK manager should look like when it's configured and ready for work:

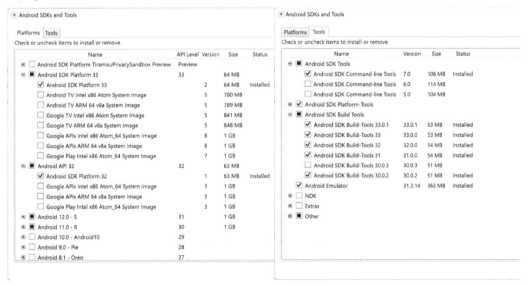

Figure 1.5: Final look after Android SDK installation

Visual Studio 2022 for Mac installation

In general, the macOS computer plays a crucial role when it comes to building applications targeting Apple operational systems. We will talk about the building process in further detail in *Chapter 3, Exploring .NET MAUI and Its Features*. The thing you need to know now is that only Apple's building tools that work on Mac machines are required. It means you can use Visual Studio for Windows for development, but in the case of building applications targeting Apple devices, a Mac machine connected to a PC is still needed. This is why most Xamarin and MAUI developers who don't need to target Windows choose MacOS-based computers as workhorses.

So, the first step on the path of arranging your macOS environment is Xcode installation. It is highly recommended to install Xcode before Visual Studio because the Visual Studio installation tool is looking for installed Apple SDKs and Xcode during the installation process, and it makes all the necessary configurations related to them automatically. Installing Visual Studio before the Xcode may cause issues with application building.

Xcode is an Apple's IDE used to develop software for macOS, iOS, iPadOS, watchOS, and tvOS. This is a fully native tool to create applications using Swift or Objective-C languages, but most importantly, it contains all the building tools we need to turn our cross-platform MAUI code into a native application. Besides, it has several cool debugging tools that might be really helpful sometimes.

Installation of Xcode is as simple as the installation of any application from the App Store. Find Xcode in App Store, as shown in *Figure 1.6*, and click the **GET** button; macOS may ask you to provide your system password or fingerprint during the installation process:

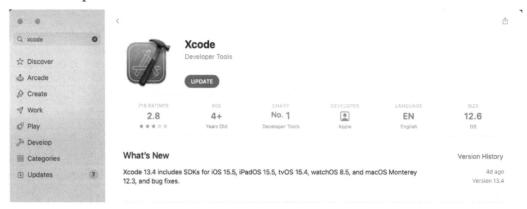

Figure 1.6: Xcode IDE in the App Store

To install Visual Studio 2022 for Windows, go to the official website, which is **https://visualstudio.microsoft.com/downloads/**, and download Visual Studio 2022 for Mac. Here, the situation is pretty similar to that of Visual Studio for Windows. Since the chapter has been written in May 2022 and the regular version of Visual Studio 2022 for Mac is not available yet, use Visual Studio 2022 for Mac RC (Release Candidate). However, the stable version of Visual Studio 2022 for Mac will mostly have been made available before this book goes on sale:

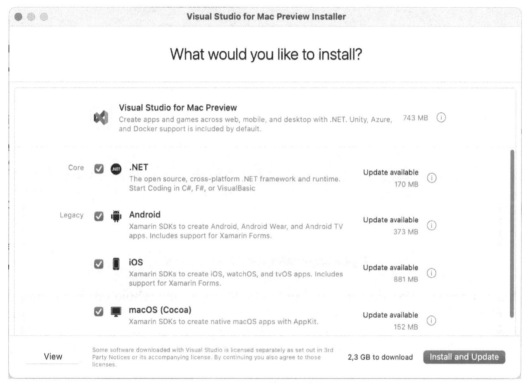

Figure 1.7: Visual Studio for Mac installer

Select all modules as shown in *Figure 1.7*. Then, make sure you have a stable internet connection and click **Install and Update**; macOS may ask for the system password during the installation process.

Wait a bit until all the required components are downloaded and installed. *Figure 1.8* shows Visual Studio 2022 for Mac that is ready to go:

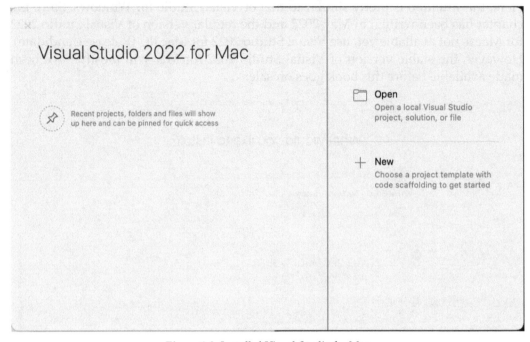

Figure 1.8: Installed Visual Studio for Mac

When it comes to configuring Android SDK Manager, the whole process is pretty similar to the ones we have already followed for Windows. The only significant difference is in the place where the SDK manager is. To configure and update Android SDKs, go to **Visual Studio** > **Preferences** > **SDK Locations** > **Android**.

Creating .NET MAUI project

Now, it looks like you are ready to create your first .NET MAUI solution. This process looks pretty much the same for both Windows and Mac.

First of all, launch the Visual Studio application and click the **Create a new project** button. Here, you will find numerous project templates from simple console applications and unit test projects to class library and GUI application projects. You will have an opportunity to use each of them in your career. However, for learning MAUI, we will mainly use MAUI project templates.

As you can see in *Figure 1.9*, there are two ways to find MAUI templates: search bar and drop-down filters. You can put **Maui** in the search bar or select the **MAUI** project type. Use whatever way you like, select the **.NET MAUI App** template and press the **Next** button:

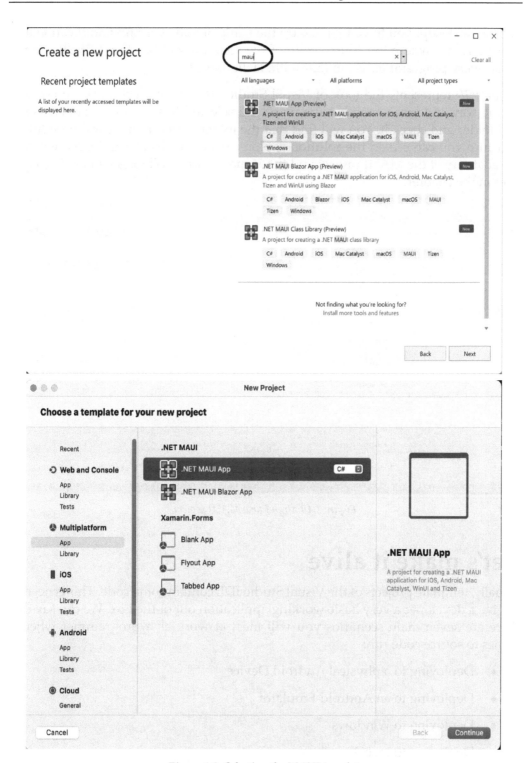

Figure 1.9: *Selecting the MAUI template*

For the next step, you have to make up the name of your very first application and select a folder where the source code of the solution will be stored. We'll use the name every programmer is familiar with: Hello World.

Figure 1.10 represents the look of Visual Studio after the project has been created. By the way, did you remember the place you selected to store project data? Go to that folder and check it. You will find that the folder structure matches the solution structure you can see on the solution explorer panel of Visual Studio. No worries, the anatomy of the MAUI project and the Visual Studio toolboxes will be discussed later in the chapter:

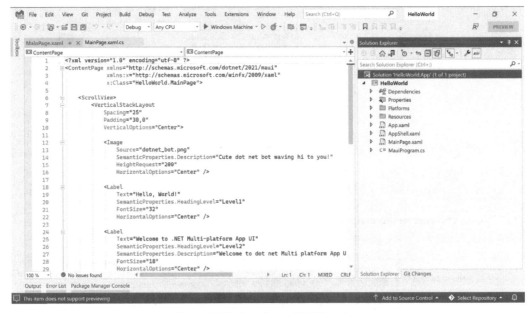

Figure 1.10: Brand new MAUI project

Let's make it alive

Usually, template projects of the Visual Studio IDE contain some code. This is needed to give a developer a very basic working application out of the box. We can say that there are seven main scenarios you will meet at work as a programmer when it comes to source code run:

- Deploying to a physical Android Device
- Deploying to an Android Emulator
- Deploying to Windows
- Deploying to macOS

- Deploying to iOS simulator using Visual Studio for Mac

- Deploying to an iOS simulator using Visual Studio for Windows

- Deploying to an iOS physical device

The first thing that should be done in terms of deploying an application to an Android device is activating the development mode and developer options menu. Unfortunately, the way of doing this might differ between Android versions or even models of phones with the same Android version. So, you must learn how to turn development mode on for your Android device. On some Samsung devices, for example, you must go to **Settings** > **About Device** > **Software Information** and tap the android build number seven times to activate the **Developer Options** menu. Once the developer's menu has been activated, take the following steps:

1. Switch USB debugging on and connect the device to your computer.

2. Android will ask to allow USB debugging for your computer. Select **Always allow from this computer** if you don't want to see this dialog window again, and press the **Allow** button.

3. Android may also ask for permission for USB file transfer. Select **Yes**:

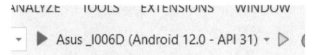

Figure 1.11: Run button

Right after performing the connection, the deploy target will be changed automatically, as shown in *Figure 1.11*. If not, open the deployment targets list drop-down menu by clicking on the small grey arrow placed between two green play buttons and select your device. Usually, the device deployment target contains the manufacturer's brand name or device model name. However, in the case of some manufacturers, it may have no meaningful label indicating a specific device brand or model.

It is now ready to perform the very first launch of a .NET MAUI Application. So, press the bright green play button with a device deployment target label on it. The first deployment may take a few minutes. You can track the progress by looking at the bottom status bar of Visual Studio. As a result, you will see the blank template application running on your device. Congratulations!

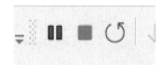

Figure 1.12: Stop debugging button

To stop running, just press the red **Stop debugging** button, which is shown in *Figure 1.12*.

This process for Visual Studio for Mac hasn't been described as it looks exactly the same and has no Mac-specific steps.

The main difference between deploying to an Android Device and an Android Emulator is the necessity to configure the Android Emulator. The whole configuration process looks the same on Windows and Mac. So, launch the Visual Studio and go to **TOOLS** → **Android** → **Android Device Manager** (**Tools** → **Device Manager** in case of Visual Studio for Mac) and press the big **New** button:

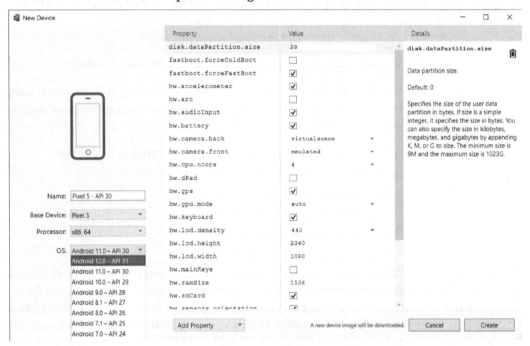

Figure 1.13: *New Android Emulator creator window*

As you can see, the Android Emulator creator allows a developer to control a wide range of emulator parameters, such as display parameters, SD-card size, RAM size, and camera image source. It might be useful for your future work. For the purpose of this book, default emulator settings are just fine. So, select the latest Android platform version and press the **Create** button in the New Device window, as shown in *Figure 1.13*. The required components will be downloaded and installed:

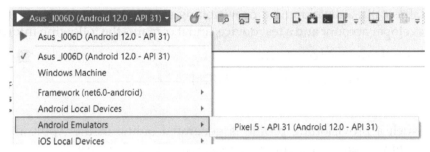

Figure 1.14: Selecting Android Emulator as a deployment target

Once the Android Emulator is installed, you will be able to select it as a deployment target, as shown in *Figure 1.14*. Visual Studio restart might be needed to make the Android Emulator option show up.

In case you want to deploy your application to Windows, you need to just select the Windows Machine option; this is also visible in *Figure 1.14*.

Let's now look at how to deploy the application to iOS. As discussed earlier, a computer with macOS is needed to build Apple targeting application. So, let's launch Visual Studio for Mac and create the same blank multiplatform HelloWorld application using the corresponding MAUI template:

Figure 1.15: Starting application panel of Visual Studio for Mac

As you probably already noticed, the panel responsible for selecting the deployment target and initiation deployment procedure looks slightly different on Mac. Looking at *Figure 1.15*, you can guess that Mac Machine (**My Mac**) is selected as a deployment target by default. So, try to run the Hello World application on your Mac.

Since iOS simulators are delivered along with Xcode, no additional configuration is needed. Moreover, a closed ecosystem of Apple with strictly regulated nomenclature of devices enables Apple to deliver not generic emulators, but simulators of specific devices, including iPod and iPads. So just select the device simulator you wish as a deployment target and try to run the application on it. Click on the currently selected deployment target to open the drop-down menu (**My Mac** target in the case shown in *Figure 1.15*).

This is a good moment for a brief explanation of an Apple-specific thing, which is the Provisioning Profile. Every application you want to install on an iOS device has to be approved and signed by Apple first. However, before sending an application for Apple review, it should be tested on a device for multiple reasons, like device-only bugs or performance issues. To enable this, a development provisioning profile is required. Basically, a development provisioning profile acts as a bridge between an Apple developer account and a test device, and it contains the following information:

- Apple Developer certificate
- List of test devices identifiers (UDIDs)
- AppID

Usually, such a provisioning profile is generated online in the Apple Developer account control panel. And here, a problem occurs because Apple Developer Program's annual subscription isn't free. However, there is a way to generate a short-term free provisioning profile using Xcode. Such a free development provisioning profile has limitations. For example, provisioning for most Apple application services like Apple Pay, Push Notifications, or iCloud is not possible. Despite that, there's good news. Since this book is not about using advanced iOS-specific features but about the MAUI framework, a free provisioning profile will be enough. So, let's deploy our Hello World application to an iOS device.

First of all, modify the **ApplicationId** of the MAUI project by editing the **HelloWorld.csproj** file. This ID is used as a **BundleId** and must be unique according to Apple rules. So, change it to **com.learningmaui.helloworld**, as shown in code snippet below:

```
<!-- Display name -->
<ApplicationTitle>HelloWorld</ApplicationTitle>

<!-- App Identifier -->
<ApplicationId>com.learningmaui.helloworld</ApplicationId>
```

Next, launch the Xcode IDE and create a new iOS project. The idea is to make Xcode create a local signing developer certificate for your Apple ID and Xcode Managed development provisioning profile for **BundleID (ApplicationId)** of our Hello World application:

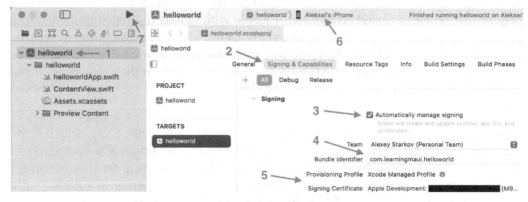

Figure 1.16: Creating Xcode project

Take a look at *Figure 1.16*. Once the Xcode project has been found, go to its settings and take the following steps:

1. Select the root node of the project.

2. Go to the **Signing & Capabilities** tab.

3. Make sure **Automatically manage signing** is turned on.

4. Make sure the bundle identifier is `com.learningmaui.helloworld`.

5. Make sure the **Provisioning Profile** as well as **Signing Certificate** was created by Xcode.

6. Next, choose your iOS device as a deployment target.

7. Press the **Run** button.

Your iOS device will show you the following alert: Untrusted Developer. It means iOS prohibited installing an application signed with an unknown certificate because it doesn't know whether this certificate may be trusted. To resolve this, you have to go to **Settings → General → VPN & Device Management → Developer App: Apple Development** (not trusted) and press the **Trust** button. Trusting will allow any app signed by your developer certificate to be installed on this device. Now, press the **Run** button again and deploy the Xcode blank app to the device.

Congratulations! Now you can select your device as a deployment target in Visual Studio and deploy your MAUI application to the device.

One more topic that should be described within the making alive topic is using Mac for builds only. Some developers prefer using the Visual Studio for Windows. Fortunately, MAUI covers this scenario as well. Since we have already installed all essential tools on Mac, the only thing that should be done is pairing Visual Studio for Windows to Mac. Here's how to do that:

1. Make sure your Mac is on the same network as your PC.

2. Open the **Sharing** settings of your Mac and enable the **Remote Login** feature.

3. Then, launch Visual Studio for Windows and go to **TOOLS → iOS → Pair to Mac**. Pair to Mac tool will discover your Mac automatically, showing its name. If not, press the **Add Mac** button to reach the Mac machine using its IP address.

4. Press the **Connect** button, provide the credentials of your Mac user, and wait until Visual Studio configures all the required tools.

Congratulations! Now, you can use the full power of Visual Studio for Windows, while Mac performs all work of building a native application.

It's worth noticing that Windows and Mac are paired using SSH protocol. It means you can also pair with a Mac machine over the internet by applying appropriate settings to your network infrastructure and adding Mac via its external IP address. The static external IP address is highly recommended for this approach.

Visual Studio IDE overview

As you might notice, the Visual Studio IDE is a powerful tool that can accompany a developer in many areas of software development. However, capabilities differ between platforms. For example, Visual Studio for Mac doesn't support the classic .NET Framework, **Universal Windows Platform (UWP)**, Python, and developing SQL databases. On the other hand, the standalone Visual Studio for Windows can't build applications targeting Apple operational systems like macOS or iOS. However, when it comes to .NET MAUI and .NET Core applications, capabilities are comparable. So, it's mostly about personal preferences or development team agreement on what platform to use for work.

You already learned how to create a project, how to configure Android-related things, and how to select the deployment target and run the application. However, regardless of whether you're an experienced Visual Studio user, it's worth making an overview of our workplace. The Visual Studio 2022 for Windows is used for the purpose of this book, but all panels and tools we'll talk about might easily be found in Visual Studio for Mac too. Take a look at *Figure 1.17*:

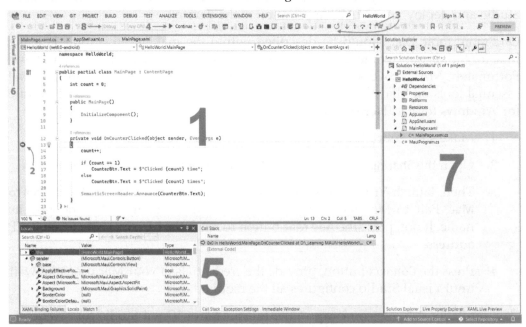

Figure 1.17: *The main window of Visual Studio 2022 for Windows*

The following list describes all areas highlighted in Figure 1.7:

- The code editor (1) is the heart of an IDE. A text editor changes its look depending on the language you use. Besides, the text has a set of tools to speed up code writing, like code formatter and IntelliSense code completion tools. The behavior of helpers changes depending on the programming language, individual settings, or rules defined for a particular project.

- A breakpoint (2) is essential for debugging. It enables you to pause the code execution in a place you wish to check variable values or run the program step by step to track its behavior. *Figure 1.7* is a screenshot of such a paused state of execution.

- Debugging toolbar (3) enables a developer to control program execution. You can pause a program execution, perform control of step-by-step execution, or rerun the program.

- You are already familiar with the launching toolbar (4). It's responsible for the selection deployment target when the execution is not run yet. When the application runs, the toolbar is transformed to give a developer additional debug controls like the continuation button and hot reload manager button (the hot reload feature will be described in the subsequent chapters).

- In most cases, the bottom panel (5) is used for displaying different kinds of information, like logs and error messages, or to display debugging information, as shown in *Figure 1.7* above. It is worth noting that we are talking about the default arrangement of elements now. Basically, you are free to configure your own workspace by turning on and off particular views and toolbars, and by placing them wherever you like.

- Live Visual Tree (6) is another important debugging tool. Sometimes, especially when you need to debug a huge application with dozens of custom UI controls, views, subviews, and so on, it might be helpful to take such a helicopter view look on a tree of visual elements of an application.

- Solution explorer (7) represents the solution elements tree. In most cases, the solution tree structure matches the solution folder structure on a disk. We will take a closer look at the application solution structure in the next section.

- The solution configuration selector (8) allows a developer to select a mode that will be used to run the application. In most cases, two kinds of configurations are used: Debug and Release. The list of available options might be changed or extended.

Anatomy of .NET MAUI solution

Figure 1.18: .NET MAUI solution tree

A .NET MAUI application includes several components. Every component is just a file that contains some code, configuration, or resources.

The root solution element represents a ***.sln** file. It contains text-based information about what projects are in a solution and whether there are relations between them. Our HelloWorld application contains only one project, but big applications that have advanced modular architecture might have dozens of projects.

The HelloWorld project is next in a hierarchy of the solution. It is represented by the **HelloWorld.csproj** file. Basically, a ***.csproj** is an XML file that contains everything needed to build a project. It contains information about files included in the project and specific settings for them, special instructions for the compiler, build configurations, configurations of the application icon and splash screen, project metadata, references to other projects and third-party plugins, and so on.

The **Dependencies** node contains information about references to other projects, external libraries, frameworks, and NuGet packages.

Despite the fact that almost everything in .NET MAUI is cross-platform, there are cases when platform-specific code is essential just because of unavoidable differences between platforms. So, the **Platforms** directory contains platform-specific code, configurations, and assets. Here is a place to put a code based on the native platform API. At a build time, the builder only includes the code and assets that belong to the selected platform.

The **Resources** folder stores different essential things that are used in code, such as images, fonts, icons, definitions of colors, and styles. While fonts, images, or AppIcon are self-explanatory resource names, you might be confused by **Raw**, **Colors**, and **Styles**. A raw resource is any resource of any format that you can embed into your application. Suppose you want to display some *.pdf file to a user. This is where the Raw type of resource comes into the picture. When it comes to styles and colors, those resources will be covered in *Chapter 4*, In and Out of UI Development.

Now, put a hat of a pioneer on and explore the solution. Try to find where image resources are used.

Hint: Try to open such files like ***.csproj** in a text editor.

NuGet package manager

Another tool that almost every .NET developer uses daily is a NuGet package manager. It's hard to imagine software that doesn't use third-party libraries. Almost no one reinvents the wheel by writing their own loggers, JSON serializers, or Application Programming Interfaces (API) to enable an app to communicate with an external device. Your company can even have its own private libraries containing some unique business logic used by different kinds of applications and supported by a separate team located in another country.

In the case of an external device, whether it is a barcode scanner or an ultra-modern complex medical device, the producer delivers a ready to use library. A developer, in turn, includes the library in a project to consume the code library contains. Everyone wins. The customer gets a fast and convenient way for device integration, and the producer gets a satisfied customer and control over the correct use of the device communication interface. When it comes to more commonly used libraries like loggers or UI components, the general idea is the same: getting a reusable code library to maximize the productivity of software developers and minimize final product cost and the amount of time needed to release the product.

In the world of .NET, such libraries are called **Dynamic-link libraries** (DLL). Everything goes fine while there are a small number of external library dependencies in a project, but the situation changes as the number of dependencies increases. The source code of a project starts consuming more and more space. Someone needs to take care of the whole logistics related to updating libraries. Someone needs to check what version of a library is compatible with other parts of the project. Such external dependency problems are known as **Dependency hell**. This is the point where the NuGet package manager appears. Its user interface is shown in *Figure 1.19*:

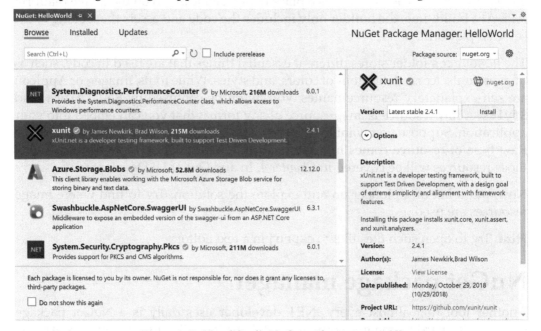

Figure 1.19: Visual Studio NuGet package manager UI

A NuGet package manager is a **software as a service (SAAS)** solution designed to provide an automated, easy-to-use, and consistent way to manage external library packages. It doesn't resolve all kinds of dependency, but it automates a huge amount of routine related to dependency management. Let's look at the most important features of NuGet from the perspective of the developer's daily routine.

- The NuGet package manager has a huge central package repository called NuGet Gallery behind it. NuGet Gallery includes hundreds of thousands of packages created by Microsoft and packages made by independent companies, small groups of enthusiasts, or even single developers.

- Every package might be installed for free because NuGet only provides a package management mechanism. However, some packages might just not work without the payment being made. In most cases of paid libraries, you will be obligated to initialize the plugin with some unique key. Probably the most obvious example from the MAUI world is paid UI components libraries. Imagine a company that creates complex UI components like charts, calendars, and so on. Sometimes, such components take more than a thousand hours for development, testing, and bug fixing. Don't forget about follow-up maintenance. So, it might be easier to buy lifetime access or a subscription to the appropriate UI component library. As a customer, you get a secret token related to your account that should be used in the code of your application to make a plugin work.

- If a package you install depends on some other packages, NuGet will take care of those down-level dependencies automatically. What if two or more packages you installed depend on different versions of the same widely used package? Suppose you use the logger package and REST API client package, both of which use the JSON serialization plugin, but the logger uses v1.1 and the REST API client uses v.1.2. In such a case, NuGet does all the dirty work to determine which version of the JSON serialization plugin should be installed to meet the requirements of both.

- NuGet package manager notifies developers about a new version of an installed package.

- Since Visual Studio has a built-in NuGet package manager UI module, it's super easy to install, uninstall, and update NuGet packages in projects.

- NuGet helps save space on your local machine and GIT repository because actual DLLs are not stored along with your project's codebase. Therefore, even routine daily manipulations with a remote GIT repository become smoother, especially when the connection is slow.

Conclusion

You are free to use Windows or macOS to create cross-platform .NET MAUI applications. The only thing you need to be aware of is its limitations. A Mac machine is needed to build an application that targets Apple devices, and PC is needed to run an application on Windows. You will need an Apple developer program membership to test Apple services-related features like Push Notifications or Apple Pay, but you need no paid account to develop and test other features.

A basic .NET MAUI template solution includes one project with a **Platforms** folder in it for platform-specific code, resources, and configuration. Besides, it has predefined folders for different kinds of resources.

The NuGet is the modern tool that provides a mechanism to deliver and consume reusable libraries and a huge NuGet gallery. The built-in NuGet Package Manager makes its usage easy and comfortable.

The next chapter will get you through the essential concepts of .NET and C#, covering important topics like inheritance, polymorphism, memory management, objects, events, and more. See you in the next chapter!

Points to remember

- Both PC and Mac support .NET MAUI application development.

- Keep the SDK of the last two versions of Android installed.

- A Mac machine with Xcode installed is required to build applications targeting Apple operating systems.

- A short-term free Apple provisioning profile can be generated using Xcode without an Apple Developer program subscription.

Questions

1. What is an IDE?

2. What is the Android SDK manager?

3. What is Apple's development provisioning profile necessary for?

4. How can we pair PC and Mac to build applications targeting Apple operating systems?

5. What is the *.csproj file needed for?

6. What is the Live Visual Tree about?

7. What modern tool is used to deliver reusable external libraries?

Join our book's Discord space

Join the book's Discord Workspace for Latest updates, Offers, Tech happenings around the world, New Release and Sessions with the Authors:

https://discord.bpbonline.com

CHAPTER 2
Upskill Essentials of C#

Introduction

As you already know, the framework is called .NET Multi-platform Application UI, and it uses C# as the main programming language. Such a mix of names and keywords may seem confusing. So, before we deep dive into the cross-platform framework itself, it's important to get familiar with the technology stack MAUI is based on.

Indeed, both the C# and the whole .NET platform topics are huge, and it's impossible to cover them comprehensively in this chapter. Besides, there are many excellent thick books about C# and .NET covering them in detail. This chapter is not meant to replace complete C# and .NET guides; the main purpose of this chapter is to give people who are new to .NET a wide look at the basics of the .NET platform and C# programming language and provide a recap of some of the important topics to people familiar with .NET.

This chapter would be helpful in multiple ways. First of all, this book expects C# knowledge or at least experience of commercial development with other programming languages, so it's important to cover some fundamental topics before describing advanced MAUI-specific things. The second reason is that you'll get a better understanding of what is going on under the hood when a .NET application is executed. Finally, it's completely fine if you will be getting additional questions while getting through the book. Having knowledge from this chapter, you will be able to formulate your questions more accurately and therefore, get more precise answers faster.

Structure

In this chapter, we will cover the following topics:

- .NET 6
- C#
- Value types
- Reference types
- Classes and objects
- Class members
- Memory management
- Garbage collector
- Strings
- Interfaces
- Inheritance
- Access modifiers
- Polymorphism
- Generics
- Delegates
- Events
- Anonymous methods
- Async Await and TPL
- Exception handling
- IDisposable
- Coding style

Objectives

This chapter will provide a brief history of the .NET platform to understand the how and why of .NET being where it is today. A significant part of this chapter is taken for describing fundamental concepts and technical solutions like components of .NET, typing system, and memory management. Additionally, the chapter covers crucial topics of C#, which are essential for the further learning process and real commercial projects.

.NET 6

.NET started in 2002 when the Microsoft .NET Framework v1.0, C# v1.0, and Visual Studio .NET 2002 IDE were released. With a .NET Framework, Microsoft provides an environment to create and execute Windows applications and web services. Let's look at what the modern .NET Framework consists of.

FCL

The FCL or Framework Class Library is a comprehensive object-oriented collection of tested reusable types that enables a developer to accomplish a wide range of programming tasks, from common operations like string manipulations or mathematical calculations to specific scenarios like implementing **Graphic User Interface (GUI)** or sending HTTP requests. In practice, it means fewer efforts and time are needed to create various kinds of applications.

CLR

CLR or Common Language Runtime is the heart of the .NET Framework runtime environment. It's a virtual machine that runs code and manages the life cycle of the executed .NET applications written in any .NET compatible programming language (that is, VB.NET, C#, or F#). The code that is run under the Common Language Runtime control is called Managed Code. There are five main components of CLR:

- **Common Type System (CTS)** is responsible for converting the data type system of each .NET programming language into a common CLR understandable format. The CTS includes two kinds of types: **Value Types** and **Reference Types**. Those kinds of types will be described further in this chapter.

- **Common Language Specification (CLS)** is a set of rules that all .NET compatible programming languages must follow. Since .NET allows different parts of a program to be written in different languages, following CLS ensures that those parts of the program can communicate with each other.

- **Common Intermediate Language (CIL)** is a bytecode language that CLR executes. When you hit the **Build** button in Visual Studio, whatever .NET compatible programming language you used, the language-specific compiler generates a set of CIL instructions and metadata from your source code.

- **Just In Time Compiler (JIT)** converts CIL instructions during the runtime into machine codes specific to the machine a program is executed on. This happens on a requirement basis before the CIL code can be executed, so only the required parts of the CIL code are compiled into machine code. The parts of CIL that were already compiled are stored so that they are available for subsequent calls.

- **Garbage Collector (GC)** serves as an automatic memory manager. It means that it's the responsibility of the garbage collector to remove data that is not used anymore and allocate memory for the new data.

If you Googled anything about creating applications with .NET, Xamarin, or MAUI, you probably met a kind of a strange mess of .NET names, such as .NET Framework, .NET Standard, .NET Core, and just simply .NET 5/6. If so, it's normal if you were surprised and confused. The good news for you is that almost every .NET developer who tries to figure out what .NET is comes across it sooner or later. To unravel this tangle of names and understand why they came out, we will make a timeline that covers the most important milestones between 2002 and 2022, paying special attention to MAUI-related details.

2002 – .NET Framework 1.0

The first version of .NET Framework for Windows was released.

2004 – .NET Framework 1.1, Mono 1.0

The first version of the Mono project led by software engineer Miguel de Icaza (Vice President of Developer Platform at Novell, Inc) was released. The main idea was to implement Microsoft's new .NET Framework development platform on Unix-like platforms.

2006 – .NET Framework 3.0, WPF Framework

The WPF Framework was released as part of a new major version of the .NET Framework. It offered a new way to build Graphical User Interface applications. WPF introduced a new XML-based programming language (XAML) that later became an integral part of Xamarin and MAUI. Many developers worldwide working with desktop and mobile GUI applications have been considering XAML the best way to implement a graphical user interface.

2011 – Xamarin Co.

After Novell was bought by Attachmate and the new owner decided to layoff significant part of Mono project workforce. Miguel de Icaza and Nat Friedman wanted to save promising technology and develop successes the mono team had with mobile platforms and Mac. So Miguel and Nat founded Xamarin.

2014 – .NET Core announcement

During the end of 2000s, a lot of things were being changed in the computer world. Broadband internet connection was becoming common, changing businesses around the world. Interest in cloud computing was growing, along with companies' desire to use .NET and C# but to not depend on Windows-based infrastructure to run internet services. Finally, thanks to the efforts of Apple, the smartphone was turning from a device for geeks to an everyday essential for millions of people. All these factors led to the announcement of the cross-platform relative of the .NET Framework called .NET Core.

2016 – .NET Core 1.0 and .NET Standard 1.0 release. Xamarin Inc. acquisition by Microsoft

2016 was a year of big changes. The first version of cross-platform .NET Core was released. While .NET Core is a reworked modern cross-platform variation of .NET with lots of architectural and performance improvements, it doesn't offer a cross-platform UI framework. That is why Microsoft acquired Xamarin based on Mono, which allowed users to create cross-platform UI applications. There was also another issue. Although some part of codebase could be shared between the .NET Framework, Xamarin, and the .NET Core, the compiled binaries could not. For example, the .NET Core application runtime that is running on a Linux machine can't rely on a library compiled as a .NET Framework library to be run on a Windows-only machine.

Now, let's imagine the situation when your innovative "413 Oversize Logistics" transportation company has libraries with business logic. Most likely, millions of dollars were invested to write and test all this code, including labor of developers, testers, business analysts, managers, and other company members. Additionally, your clients' businesses depend on the stability of that code. It's pretty much obvious that you would wish to apply your bulletproof business logic libraries to a dispatcher's Windows desktop application, web API runs on Linux, the iOS application for truck drivers, and an application for warehouse personnel who use Android-based tablets. However, as we learned earlier, you can't just create .NET Framework or .NET Core library and use it everywhere. It means business logic libraries have to be copied, adapted, and maintained separately to be consumed by the .NET Framework app, the .NET Core app, the Xamarin.iOS app, and the Xamarin.Android app. Sounds like a failure of the whole movement to the cross-platform environment. The need for unification was obvious.

Of course, Microsoft understood that and released the .NET Standard (*Figure 2.1*) 2 months after .NET Core had been released.

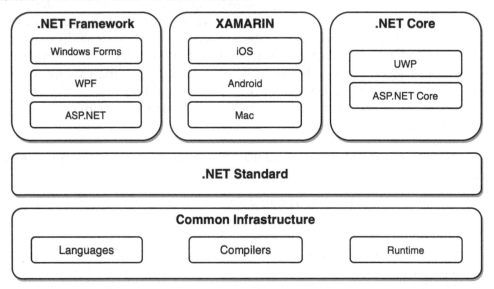

Figure 2.1 *.NET-based platforms in relation to .NET Standard*

The .NET Standard is not one more .NET platform. .NET Standard is an API specification that defines what different .NET platforms must implement to be .NET Standard-compliant. In other words, the .NET Standard guarantees a code that a binary targeting .NET Standard is compatible with all .NET platforms that follow the .NET Standard. So, the same .NET Standard library with a business logic inside can now be consumed by Windows desktop .NET Framework applications, .NET Core web API, and Xamarin applications.

2020 – .NET 5

Although .NET Standard worked pretty well and allowed users to put out the fire of .NET platforms compliance, it still felt like a temporary solution on the way to real unification. According to the article of Immo Landwerth from devblogs.microsoft. com, .NET Standard had three problems:

- **New features' standardization** required too much effort. The idea of the .NET Standard was that it standardized only the existing APIs of .NET platforms. However, starting from .NET Standard 2.1, new features had to be added to .NET Standard. It meant the API of each .NET Standard-compliant platform had to be reviewed regarding such an API of a new feature. Those reviews were necessary to make sure the new API doesn't break the constraints of different .NET platforms. And those reviews were so laborious that it was impossible to release new versions of .NET Standard frequently enough. As a result, some features were just lost because of the cost of processing every single feature. To solve this issue, such reviews were supposed to become a part of feature design rather than afterthought action.

- **Cross-platform version compatibility** was still a problem; take a look at *Figure 2.2*. Since each .NET platform has its own release plan and APIs implementations, it's just impossible to ensure that a specific version of the .NET Standard contains as many as possible APIs and is compatible with each version of each platform. So, you would have trouble trying to use v2 of the .NET Standard library that provides access to the most number of APIs, along with application targeting .NET Core 1.0. The only way to solve it was creation a common platform that has a single versioning strategy (this getting the same version number) and provide unified implementation where all parts are built on the same foundation:

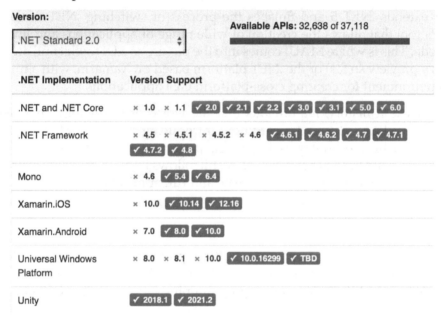

Figure 2.2: dotnet.microsoft.com/platform/dotnet-standard

- Since the engineers had to make compromises designing the .NET Standard, it **exposes some platform-specific APIs**. Sometimes, it led to situations when the code compiled and appeared to be ready to run on any platform, but it suddenly threw runtime errors.

Despite the problems the .NET Standard had, it was a successful first step on the road to making .NET unified and cross-platform. So, the .NET 5 was another step. Technically, it had to be named .NET Core 4 because it was the role of .NET Core to become a cross-platform version of the .NET. However, by calling it .NET 5, Microsoft tried to achieve a few goals. First, they wanted to put an end to the confusion in minds of developers caused by naming. And since number 4 was already booked by .NET Framework, they decided to go straight to 5. Some people joked that Microsoft is faithful to their traditions, referring to Xbox generations' naming. Finally, by dropping Core/Framework, they highlighted a whole new era of the .NET that becomes a unified cross-platform environment for every kind of application from Windows desktop to mobile and IoT apps.

Looking deeper, it is worth saying the .NET 5 was a combination of .NET Core and .NET Standard, removing the complexity around .NET Standard and providing a single codebase supporting desktop apps, mobile apps, websites, etc. without an additional superstructure.

2021 – .NET 6, MAUI Preview

.NET 6 extends .NET 5 and finishes the process of switching .NET to the cross-platform tool that allows the creation of wide range of applications and libraries to share code. This is where MAUI comes into the picture as a UI toolkit and an integral part (as a preview so far) of the .NET platform based on Xamarin, with a mission to be an environment for creating cross-platform GUI applications.

Looking back at history, it's obvious that the world of technology changed a lot and .NET was being changed accordingly, introducing support for the newest web, mobile, and hybrid technologies, improving performance and its inner architecture. However, it would be fair to say that .NET still follows its main principle of providing a modern, complete environment to create and run applications.

C#

As we already know, .NET supports multiple programming languages. However, the most popular one is C# (pronounced "C-Sharp"). Moreover, if you try looking for lists of the world's most popular programming languages, the C# is on each of them.

If you remember, Andreas Hejlsberg was mentioned as the creator of the first IDE. This Danish-origin engineer is deservedly considered one of the most famous IT personnel in history because of the products he created or participated in the creation of. In 1995, Sun Microsystems released its Java programming language, and the Java Virtual Machine revolutionized the world of software development with the "Write Once, Run Anywhere" concept and capabilities of Java language. Needless to say, Java's popularity was growing rapidly.

Being a well-known top-level engineer, Andreas joined Microsoft in 1996 as an architect for the Visual J++ language and WFC (Windows Foundation Classes). J++ and WFC were Microsoft's attempts to bring Java closer to Windows OS, promising better performance and access to Windows-native technologies. Those efforts, and both technical and non-technical reasons led to a decision of creating a completely new programming platform from scratch. So, Andreas Hejlsberg became the chief designer of the C# programming language and a key participant in the .NET Framework project in 2000. As a result, a brand new general-purpose, object-oriented, type-safe programming language was born.

To reveal the reasons for the popularity of C#, it's important to consider a few aspects that are tightly linked to each other. First, let's look at *Figure 2.3*, which demonstrates the areas where C# can be used as the main programming language nowadays:

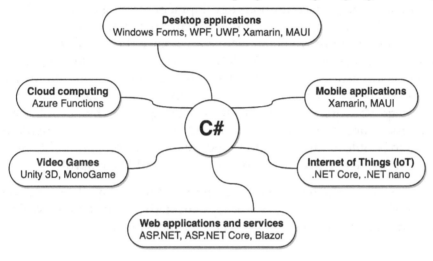

Figure 2.3: Areas of use of the C# language

What does it mean for developers?

Imagine you are a person who speaks English only, and you decided to learn how to build awesome winter houses. Both Finnish and Canadian schools are perfect choices. But I'm pretty sure that the Canadian approach will be much easier because you already know the primary tool of knowledge transfer, which is the language. That is the English language in this case. So, switching from desktop applications development to video games development, you have a lot of area-specific things to learn, but you don't need to learn a new programming language.

What does it mean for business?

As a business owner, you reduce the cost of development and better optimize the workflow of your company by choosing Microsoft's technology stack for each part of your product. Do you remember our "413 Oversize Logistics" transportation company that shares libraries between different software? To complete the picture, assume that the transportation company infrastructure uses cloud Azure services and IoT solutions to track loads and trucks, and you will get advanced enterprise-level infrastructure fully based on the Microsoft ecosystem, .NET platform, and C# language. There is one more beneficial thing here. The more professionals in your company who are passionate about the same technology, the more opportunities for experience exchange and interchangeability you have, which makes your company stronger and more reliable. Apart from this, when a talented professional you don't want to lose decides to make a career change and switch from let's say mobile development to cloud development, you can offer them such an opportunity without losing the talent.

Finally, C# is a language in continuous development reacting to market changes and the demands of the developer community. The current major version of C# is 11. Tons of new features and improvements were added since the initial release. Although each new feature does not become widely popular, such attention to programming language development is looked at rather positively by the community. However, it's a double-edged sword. Sometimes, while reading "what's new" of a new version of the language, you might catch yourself considering some change or improvement as non-necessary and non-beneficial. That said, as a developer, you should learn all new things to be able to understand the code of other developers and to recognize a place in your future practice where this new thing could be helpful.

Thereby, C# is a powerful modern programming language supported and constantly updated by Microsoft. Along with the ecosystem of Microsoft and the .NET platform, C# is a good choice for both developers and business owners.

Value types

Every computer program consists of data and instructions to manipulate the data. Every single entity of the program contains some elementary numeric data. A button drawn on the screen has the following parameters: width, height, border width, and corner radius. A name of a customer that might not even be displayed on a screen but is processed in a business logic algorithm also has at least one numeric parameter, which is text length:

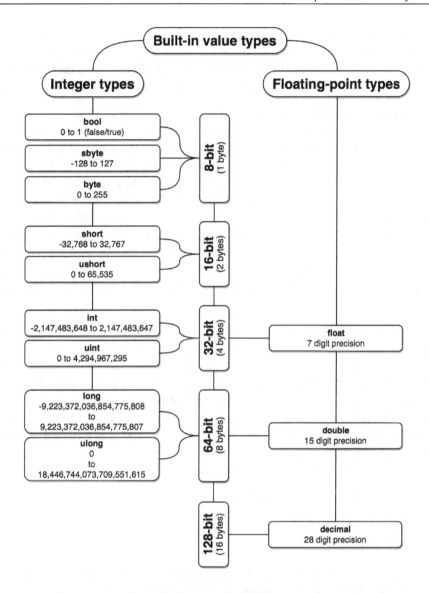

Figure 2.4: *Built-in value types in relation to occupied memory space*

Figure 2.4 shows the built-in value types in C# and the memory space each of them takes. The most popular integer type is int because of a set of interrelated reasons. First, it covers most cases when an integer variable is needed, thanks to its capacity. Second, by using **int** everywhere, you eliminate the need for type casting. The fewer unnecessary operations, the fewer bugs and lesser runtime processing costs. Finally, it occupies a reasonable amount of memory space considering these reasons.

However, sometimes other integer types are necessary. For example, trying to handle some binary communication protocol, you will find yourself working tight with arrays of **bytes**. On the other hand, the capacity of the int type is definitely not enough to display the world's population number, which is almost 8 billion people.

Figure 2.4 shows the **bool** type that is supposed to occupy only one bit but takes an entire byte (8 bit) instead. Because of historical reasons, the byte is the smallest addressable unit of memory in many CPU architectures since the 70s. Moreover, it has become the standard across the computer industry as the smallest chunk of information. For example, you can't save 9- or 7-bits long files on a hard drive or send exactly 3 bits over a network. However, C# does offer tools to work with data on a level of bits when you need it. Sometimes the possibility of extracting or inserting values of specific bits might be useful. For example, working with a low-speed serial data transfer protocol on a level of bits enables you to pack states of 32 discrete sensors into 4 bytes. Without such packaging, it would take 1 byte per sensor, that is, 32 bytes. Eventually, it makes a difference when a network contains a big number of devices.

The key thing about floating-point types of values is the more bits the type occupies, the more bits are available for the fractional part, and therefore, the more precise number (with more decimal places) you get. The most popular floating-point type in .NET world and in the MAUI in particular, is double. For example, the height and width of the button mentioned earlier have the **double** type. When it comes to the **float** type, in MAUI, it can be met pretty often in the case of working with platform-specific APIs and the **GraphicsView**. The most common use case for the **decimal** type is financial calculations, where precision has the highest priority. The following code snippet shows how different floating-point types are defined.

```
float singlePrecisionNumber = 6.2f;

double doublePrecisionNumber = 6.2d;

decimal decimalNumber = 6.2M;
```

Pay attention to the suffixes **f**, **d**, and **M** you might notice in the code snippet above. It's important to use them to declare **float**, **double**, and **decimal** variables, respectively. Every fractional number without a suffix is treated by the compiler as **double**:

```
int var1 = 3;        //Defining "var1" with value 3

int var2 = var1;     //Defining "var2" by copying the value from the
"var1"

var1 = 7;            //Changing the value of "var1" to 7

Console.WriteLine("Result:");
Console.WriteLine($"Var1 value: {var1}");
Console.WriteLine($"Var2 value: {var2}");
```

Console output:

```
Result:
Var1 value: 7
Var2 value: 3
```

Another important thing about value types is the way they behave when you copy them. As you can see in code snippet above, when you try to assign number 3 from **var1** to **var2**, it's just copied to another place in a memory allocated to store the value of **var2**. So, nothing happens when you assign 7 to the **var1**. The result of the program execution is expectable: **var1** is 7, **var2** is 3. However, it's important to describe this to show a significant difference between behaviors of value and reference types.

Reference types

There are five built-in reference types:

- The object type;
- The string type;
- The delegate type;
- The record type;
- The dynamic type;

The first three types will be covered in detail further in this book. For now, let's talk about the **dynamic** and the **record** types. Usually, it's considered a bad practice among the .NET community to use dynamics. The **dynamic** type was introduced in C# 4.0, mainly to make it easier to work with COM objects like Microsoft Word documents and dynamic-typed languages like Python. The dynamic keyword asks the compiler to avoid compile-time type checking for a particular variable. Normally, compiler checks whether the type of the variable matches the type of a value that is being assigned to it and throws an error if you try to reach something that a type doesn't contain. When the dynamic type is applied, the compiler avoids this check, so the type is recognized dynamically at runtime.

So, a variable of the **dynamic** type might contain everything until the code is run. You can assign a number to a dynamic variable and then try to get a number of chars from this variable as if it were a text, and the compiler will accept it. Alternatively, you can map the JSON data received from the back-end REST API server to a dynamic variable without creating a corresponding type. It might seem like a magic panacea that reduces the amount of code to write. However, when your application becomes bigger than the simplest proof of concept, it turns into a time bomb because every small mistake or oversight leads to a potential crash of an application in runtime. No one will tell you that user data received from the back end doesn't contain a middle name anymore, or a text variable was changed to a numeric one and doesn't contain a number of chars anymore.

Another reason to not use dynamic type for cross-platform MAUI applications is that there is no rule that every operating system must support runtime code generation; iOS is a perfect example. The iOS kernel prevents an application from generating code dynamically. Reflection API functionality is also limited on iOS. So, the best practice regarding the **dynamic** type when you work on a MAUI application is to avoid using the **dynamic** type.

Unlike value types, a classic reference type variable like class or string doesn't store its value directly. It stores the address (reference) of another place in a memory that holds the data (objects). It gives you an opportunity to share access to the same set of data with different parts of an application by creating a few references to the same entity. Moreover, it helps optimize memory usage when it comes to complex data sets.

A reference type variable can be compared to a remote control of a TV, as shown in *Figure 2.5*. It's not the TV itself, but it provides an access to the TV. Also, the same TV can be controlled by multiple remote controls:

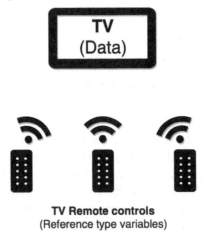

Figure 2.5: TV and remotes representation of reference types

Following this analogy, imagine that you have a huge collection of invoices a user can manipulate with. There is no need to copy the entire heavy-weight collection to pass it to a different module of an application and make a synchronization after the copy of the collection was modified. It's enough to create a new reference and pass it to the place where it's needed.

Now, let's look at the code snippet belowwhich shows how it works in practice. Let's imagine we have a class called TV that contains a property of type int called

VolumeLevel. As a first step, we create an object of class TV with the initial volume level 10 using the **new** keyword and assign it to a reference type variable **tv1**. So, the **tv1** variable is a remote control for the actual TV somewhere in memory. As a next step, we copy it to **tv2**. So, the **tv2** is a second remote control of the same TV. As you can see, **tv2** returns the same volume level, which is 10. So far so good. Then we change the volume level to 15 using **tv1**. Now you can see that, unlike the value type, copying the reference type variable value doesn't copy an actual object but references to it, because now both **tv1** and **tv2** return volume level 15, which is the volume level value of the same TV.

```
Console.WriteLine($"Creating the TV and a reference to it");
TV tv1 = new TV { VolumeLevel = 10 };
Console.WriteLine($"'tv1' volume level is {tv.VolumeLevel}");


Console.WriteLine($"Copying the TV reference to tv2…");
TV tv2 = tv1;
Console.WriteLine($"'tv2' volume level is {tv2.VolumeLevel}");


Console.WriteLine($"Changing the volume level of tv1…");
tv1.VolumeLevel = 15;


Console.WriteLine($"'tv1' volume level is {tv1.VolumeLevel}");
Console.WriteLine($"'tv2' volume level is {tv2.VolumeLevel}");
```

Console output:

```
Creating the TV and a reference to it…
'tv1' volume level is 10
Copying the TV reference to tv2…
'tv2' volume level is 10
Changing the volume level of tv1…
'tv1' volume level is 15
'tv2' volume level is 15
```

The **record** type is a quite new reference type introduced in C# 9. Unlike other reference types, records use value-based equality. For example, while two variables of a class type are equal when referring to the same object, two variables of a record type are considered equal when they contain the same data. Being immutable reference types by default, records might be useful as a data bag for the set of data that has no behavior and is unlikely to be modified (that is, **Data Transfer Objects**). A record type is covered in fewer details since it's not a significantly popular type so far, and it's not used in code examples of this book.

Classes and objects

Class and Object are basic concepts that Object-Oriented Programming is based on. Technically, a **Class** is a custom reference type. For instance, the TV from the earlier example is a class we created to show how the reference type variables behave when you copy them. On the other hand, a class might be considered a blueprint for an object (see *Figure 2.6*).

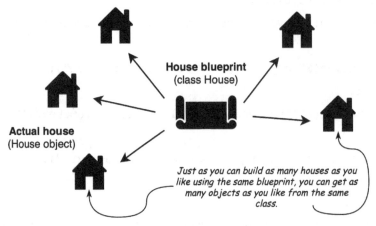

Figure 2.6: Blueprint analogy

Class and **Object** are basic concepts that Object-Oriented Programming is based on. Technically, a **Class** is a custom reference type. For instance, the TV from the earlier example is a class we created to show how the reference type variables behave when you copy them. On the other hand, a class might be considered a blueprint for an object (see *Figure 2.6*).

To create the actual object of a class, the **new** operator is used; it creates a new instance of a type.

Class members

As you might notice, Classes are based on principles of real-world entities. Just like real-world entities, they can contain information and perform actions. There are the following class members:

- **Fields** are variables that keep some information. They may have a value type or a class.

- **Constants** are fields whose values are predefined at compilation time and can't be changed in runtime.

- **Methods** are actions that a class can perform. A method can take parameters from its caller and return some result of execution. A method that doesn't return a result is marked by the void keyword.

- **Constructors** are methods that are called during object creation. They're mainly used to initialize the data of an object.

- **Finalizers** are methods that are called when an object is about to be removed from memory.

- **Properties** are methods that behave like fields. A property provides `init`, `get`, and `set` accessors and enables a class to provide a public way of getting and setting values while hiding implementation or verification code.

- **Events** enable objects to notify other objects about some changes. For example, the `Button` class has a `Click` event to call the event handler method when a button has been clicked.

- **Indexers** enable an object to be indexed similar to an array.

- **Nested types** are declared within another type. For example, you can declare the `SmartHome` class inside the `Home` class to ensure that only the `Home` class uses it and prevent other classes of a program from using it.

Memory management

Value type values and **Reference** type values are stored in RAM but in different ways because of performance reasons. Despite the process of memory management being automated, it's good to know what happens under the hood if the quality and performance of applications are important for you.

There are two places where data can be stored: Stack and Heap. In fact, the Heap is split into two heaps: **Small Object Heap (SOH)** and **Large Object Heap (LOH)**. LOH is used for objects bigger than 85,000 bytes because of performance reasons related to the SOH fragmentation issue. The Stack is responsible for keeping track of what's executing in code by stacking data as boxes stacked on the floor one on top of the another. It's populated by data as a program executes. Stack is a LIFO (Last In First Out) data structure. When a method is called, new data is added to the stack one by one. After the method is executed, the data is released. The **Heap** is different; it doesn't keep data in a strong order, providing anytime quick access to data:

While reference types are always allocated on the heap, value type data can be stored on both stack and heap, depending on the way the value type was declared. *Figure 2.7* shows two classes, **Program** and **House**.

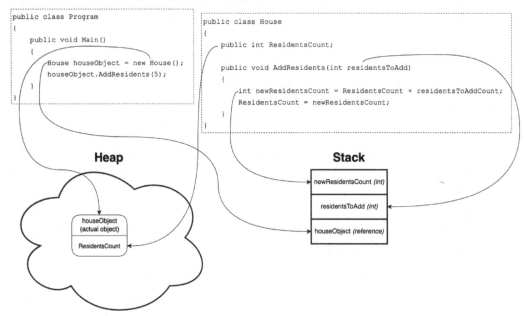

Figure 2.7: Stack and Heap

The **Program** class contains the **Main** method that is the entry point of an entire application, and the **House** class is just some class that contains a number of residents, and the **Method** adds the given number of new residents to the resident counter of a **House**.

- The actual **houseObject** is stored in the Heap because it's the object of reference type **House**.

- The reference to the **houseObject** object is stored in the **Stack**.

- Despite being a value type, the **ResidentCount** is stored in the Heap. However, it's not stored in a random place on the heap, but along with its object, which is **houseObject**.

- The **houseObject** reference is stored in the **Stack**.

The **residentsToAdd** argument and the **newResidentsCount** variable are also stored in the **Stack**.

Garbage collector

As we learned earlier, the **Garbage Collector (GC)** serves as an automatic memory manager, allocating and releasing memory for the needs of an application.

It has several benefits for developers. First of all, it frees developers from manual handling of the allocation and release of memory, minimizing the chance of a memory leak. Next, it increases memory management efficiency. And finally, it provides memory safety by making sure an object cannot try to occupy the memory allocated for another object.

When an application creates the reference type object, memory is allocated for it. When the garbage collector detects that an object is not needed anymore (it has no reference pointing to it), the garbage collector releases the memory allocated for that object. Since there is no strong order of objects stored in the Heap, GC launches a memory compaction process when the amount of freed (but fragmented) memory is large enough. During memory compacting, the GC relocates objects using freed memory spaces and updates object references. In the case of big objects, such a relocation is too expensive, so they are stored in the **Large Object Heap** (**LOH**), which is not compacted.

In the context of cross-platform development, it's worth noting that under-the-hood garbage collection processes might differ between platforms. So, it might be useful to check some platform-specific things regarding garbage collection, especially if you dive deep into writing platform-specific code using Android, iOS, or Mac native APIs.

Strings

The built-in string type is a kind of specific one. In C#, the **string** keyword is an alias for the **String** class, which contains a collection of characters. It means every time a text surrounded by double quotes is assigned to a string type variable, a new String object is created. String type is indexable, so the specific char of a string can be accessed by index (but in read-only mode) like an element of an array. Just like every other class, **String** contains properties and methods to perform operations on strings.

String objects are immutable. It means they can't be changed after they've been created. Remember that every time string is modified somehow, a new string object is created and an old one is released:

```
string str1 = "Initial text";
string str2 = str2;

str1 = "New text";

Console.WriteLine($"Str1 value: {str1}");
Console.WriteLine($"Str2 value: {str2}");
```

Console output:

```
Str1 value: New text

Str2 value: Initial text
```

The code snippet aboveshows another consequence of immutability. Although **str1** and **str2** keep references, the value of **str2** stays the same after **"New text"** is assigned to **str1**. This is because once **"New text"** is assigned to **str1**, the new object is created; and since that moment, **str1** keeps a reference to that brand new **"New text"** object.

String operations are very well optimized. However, in scenarios when a string needs to be modified many times, string operations can affect performance. Because of that, the **StringBuilder** class was added to the .NET class library. **StringBuilder** doesn't create a new object in memory each time a string needs to be modified. Instead, it dynamically expands memory to accommodate the modified string. Use the **ToString()** method to retrieve a string from the StringBuilder object.

Interfaces

What is the most obvious thing different vehicles must share to make the average driver enable to drive them? The steering wheel-based control principle is a suitable example. If a vehicle has a steering wheel, then pretty much everyone knows how to use it to get to a supermarket, whatever body shape, number of axles, or weight a vehicle has. Besides, it doesn't matter to the average driver how exactly steering works under the hood of a particular vehicle from a mechanical perspective. An interface serves this function in C#. It ensures that every class that has made a commitment to follow an interface implements all the functionalities it declares. Otherwise, the compiler throws an error, reminding that interface implementation is mandatory. Let's try to code this:

```csharp
public interface ISteeringWheelControl
{
    int CurrentVehicleSteeringAngle { get; }

    void TurnSteeringWheelLeft(int steeringAngle);
    void TurnSteeringWheelRight(int steeringAngle);
    void StraightenSteeringWheel();
}
```

An interface is declared in a similar way to a class. Use the **interface** keyword instead of the class keyword for interfaces. Three functions are essential for steering wheel control: turn the steering wheel left and right until the wheels of a vehicle reach the desired angle and straighten a steering wheel to go straight. So, the **ISteeringWheelControl** interface defines three methods to make these actions and a property to store the actual vehicle wheels steering angle:

```
public class SportsCar : ISteeringWheelControl
{
    public int CurrentVehicleSteeringAngle { get; private set; }

    public SportsCar()
    {
        Console.WriteLine("Activating innovative AI-based assistants");
    }

    public void StraightenSteeringWheel()
    {
        Console.WriteLine("Straighten wheels using servomotors");
        CurrentVehicleSteeringAngle = 0;
    }

    public void TurnSteeringWheelLeft(int steeringAngle)
    {
        Console.WriteLine("Turning wheels left using servomotors")
        CurrentVehicleSteeringAngle = -steeringAngle;
    }

    public void TurnSteeringWheelRight(int steeringAngle)
    {
        Console.WriteLine("Turning wheels right using servomotors")
        CurrentVehicleSteeringAngle = steeringAngle;
    }
}

public class MagicCar : ISteeringWheelControl
{
    public int CurrentVehicleSteeringAngle { get; private set; }
```

```csharp
    public SportsCar()
    {
        Console.WriteLine("Magic Crystal Activation");
    }

    public void StraightenSteeringWheel()
    {
        Console.WriteLine("Straighten wheels using the magic power");
        CurrentVehicleSteeringAngle = 0;
    }

    public void TurnSteeringWheelLeft(int steeringAngle)
    {
        Console.WriteLine("Turning wheels left using the magic power")
        CurrentVehicleSteeringAngle = -steeringAngle;
    }

    public void TurnSteeringWheelRight(int steeringAngle)
    {
        Console.WriteLine("Turning wheels right using the magic power")
        CurrentVehicleSteeringAngle = steeringAngle;
    }
}
```

As a next step, with code from above, we declare two car classes: **SportsCar** and **MagicCar**. As you can see, the constructors of classes initialize different things. While **SportsCar** activates its innovative AI assistants, **MagicCar** activates the magic crystal. Moreover, the ways in which those cars perform actual steering within class methods also differ. **SportsCar** uses servomotors, while **MagicCar** uses its mysterious power:

```csharp
public class Driver
{
    public string Name { get; }

    public Driver(string name)
    {
```

```
        Name = name;

    }


    public void DriveSupermarket(ISteeringWheelControl
steeringWheelControl)

    {

        Console.WriteLine($"{Name} is starting a trip to a
supermarket");

        steeringWheelControl.TurnSteeringWheelLeft(45);

        steeringWheelControl.StraightenSteeringWheel();

        steeringWheelControl.TurnSteeringWheelLeft(30);

        steeringWheelControl.TurnSteeringWheelRight(50);

        steeringWheelControl.StraightenSteeringWheel();

        Console.WriteLine($"{Name} has arrived at a supermarket");

    }

}
```

Finally, a driver who knows the route to a supermarket and is skilled enough to drive a vehicle with a steering wheel is needed (code snippet above). And here's the thing: by passing an argument of the interface **ISteeringWheelControl**, we ensure a driver that he or she can use any vehicle to get to a supermarket as long as this vehicle has a steering wheel (implements **ISteeringWheelControl**):

```
public class Program

{

    public static void Main()

    {

        Driver driver1 = new Driver("Veronika");

        SportsCar sportscar = new SpoortsCar();

        driver1.DriveSupermarket(sportsCar);

        Console.WriteLine();


        Driver driver2 = new Driver("Dave");

        MagicCar magicCar = new MagicCar();

        driver2.DriveSupermarket(magicCar);

    }

}
```

Console output:

```
Activating innovative AI-based assistants
Veronika is starting a trip to a supermarket
Turning wheels left using servomotors
Straighten wheels using servomotors
Turning wheels left using servomotors
Turning wheels right using servomotors
Straighten wheels using servomotors

Veronika has arrived at a supermarket
Magic Crystal Activation
Dave is starting a trip to a supermarket
Turning wheels left using the magic power
Straighten wheels using the magic power
Turning wheels left using the magic power
Turning wheels right using the magic power
Straighten wheels using the magic power
Dave has arrived at a supermarket
```

The code above shows how it all works altogether. The program creates two drivers of type **Driver** and different cars for them. Veronika drives a sports car, while Dave drives a magic car. As you can see, despite different cars, both Veronika and Dave are able to reach a supermarket, thanks to the **IStearingWheelControl** interface that forces cars to implement a familiar driver class way of steering.

Inheritance

Inheritance is a way to program real-world-like processes based on hierarchies. It means child classes (also called derived classes or subclasses) acquire the features and behaviors of a parent class (also called base class). Add : **[BaseClassName]** after the name of a derived class to inherit some base class, as shown in *Figure 2.8*. In C#, class can inherit only one base class and implement multiple interfaces:

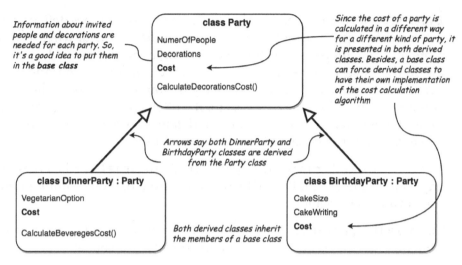

Figure 2.8: Inheritance diagram

Notice that the **Party** class seems to not derive any class since it doesn't have :
[BaseClassName] after the class name. It's not true. In C#, classes that don't derive
any class explicitly, derive the object class implicitly. So, object class every time is on
the top of an any hierarchy of classes.

There are several benefits that inheritance brings:

- It reduces code redundancy.

- It provides code reusability.

- It increases reliability and decreases required maintenance efforts.

- It makes code more structured and readable.

Access modifiers

As you might notice, classes and class members of code examples in this chapter are
marked with the **public** keyword, which is an access modifier. Access modifiers are
used to define the visibility level (or access level) for **classes**, **methods**, **fields**, and
properties. Let's consider the access modifiers that C# has:

- The class member marked as **private** is accessible for the members of the
  same class only. It's helpful when you need to make some internal logic of a
  class inaccessible from outside the class.

- **Protected** is like a private, but it also makes a class member accessible for
  a derived class.

- The **public access modifier** provides access for all other classes.

- **Internal** is an access modifier that limits the access to types defined within the current project assembly. This access modifier is useful when you have more than one project in a solution and wish to make some code accessible inside the project where it's defined. Another example is libraries. When you create a reusable library, most likely it would have classes that a client application should not have access to. It's often considered a good practice to use the internal access modifier as a default choice instead of the public when you have more than one project in a solution.

- The type or member marked as **protected internal** can be accessed by any code in the assembly in which it's declared, or from within a derived class in another assembly.

- The **private protected** type or member can be accessed by types derived from the class that is declared within its containing assembly.

Polymorphism

Polymorphism in C# is an ability of classes to implement different members with the same name.

Method overloading is the first kind of polymorphism. It gives classes the ability to define multiple methods that take different parameters. The code snippet below shows an example of method overloading.

```
public class Cart
{
    private List<Product> _products = new List<Product>();

    public void Add(Product productToAdd)
    {
        _products.Add(productToAdd);
    }

    public void Add(Product[] arrayOfProductsToAdd)
    {
        _products.AddRange(arrayOfProductsToAdd);
    }
}
```

Suppose you work on an online ordering application that has the **Cart** class to keep the products a user is chosen to buy. Thanks to polymorphism, you can provide the ability to add a single product or a few products at a time by overloading the **Add** method. The compiler chooses the correct option by the type of parameter passed to the method.

Another kind of polymorphism is tightly related to the **virtual** and **override** keywords.The following example shows a hierarchy of classes that use overriding.

```csharp
public abstract class Party
{
    public int NumberOfPeople { get; } = 10;

    public virtual decimal Cost => NumberOfPeople * 5m;

    public abstract void HaveFun();
}


public class DinnerParty : Party
{
    public override void HaveFun()
    {
        Console.WriteLine("Eating, Drinking, Talking");
    }
}


public class BirthdayParty : Party
{
    public decimal CostOfCake { get; } = 20m;

    public override decimal Cost => NumberOfPeople * 5m + CostOfCake;

    public override void HaveFun() => Console.WriteLine("Cake eating");
}
```

The **Cost** property is marked as **virtual**. It means that the **Cost** property has a default implementation, but it allows overriding of the implementation by derived classes. There are a few more things here that need to be commented on. For the purpose of the example, the **NumberOfPeople** property is predefined. The **Cost** and the **NumberOfPeople** are also properties that have getters only. In the case of properties and methods that execute only one expression, the lambda operator (**=>**) helps make code more compact. Another interesting thing here is the abstract method **HaveFun()**. An abstract method is one that has no implementation. However, it's an obligation of derived classes to have an implementation of an abstract method. Since an abstract class has no implementation, the instance of a class that has an abstract member makes no sense. So, such a class must be marked as an abstract. An object of an abstract class can't be created. Abstract classes are for deriving only:

```
DinnerParty dinner = new DinnerParty();

dinner.HaveFun();

Console.WriteLine($"Cost of the Dinner Party: {dinner.Cost}");

Console.WriteLine("");

BirthdayParty birthday = new BirthdayParty();

birthday.HaveFun();

Console.WriteLine($"Cost of the Birthday Party: (birthday.Cost}");
```

Console output:

```
Eating, Drinking, Talking
Cost of the Dinner Party: 50


Cake eating

Cost of the Birthday Party: 70
```

The code above shows overriding in action. As you remember, the **DinnerParty** class inherits **Cost** property as is, so the result of getting the value of the **Cost** property is 50. The **BirthdayParty**, in turn, overrides an implementation of the **Cost** property, bringing another formula to calculate the value. So, the **Cost** property of the **BirthdayParty** class returns 70.

The **virtual** keyword can be used to modify a class's method, property, event, or indexer.

Generics

Generics is one more important feature of C# that helps increase codebase reusability, reliability, performance, and type safety. Generic means it is not specific to a particular type. A generic type is declared by specifying a type parameter in angle brackets after a type name, for example, **MyCustomType<T>**, where **T** is a type parameter.

C# allows users to define generic classes, interfaces, fields, methods, properties, events, delegates, and operators.

We already used a generic type earlier considering polymorphism. As you might remember, we used the **List<Product>** type to store the products a user adds to the **Cart**. It doesn't matter for the **List<T>** class what data is kept inside because the manipulations it is able to do with the data are not dependent on type of that data. Consider a librarian who takes care of the preservation of books. It doesn't matter to the librarian what a book is about when it comes to cleaning them. So, making the list generic allows writing type-independent code, reducing the amount of code to write and maintain. Besides, generics shift the burden of type safety from a developer to the compiler. There is no need to take care of data type correctness because it's enforced at compile time. Moreover, there is no need for type casting that might cause runtime errors.

The type parameter can be constrained if needed by using the **where** keyword, for example, **class Garage<T> where T : ISteeringWheelControl**. Constraints inform the compiler about the capabilities a type argument must have.

Delegates

Delegate is a reference type that represents a reference to a method. So, when a delegate type variable is called, the method that this variable references is invoked. A delegate's declaration specifies a signature of a method it's able to refer to:

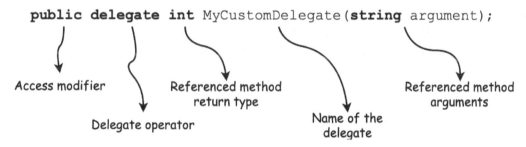

Figure 2.9: Declaration of a delegate

One of the most popular applications of delegate is the callback pattern. Callback enables a class **A** to ask class **B** to make an action defined in class **A**. Besides, class **B** determines how this action (method) should look (method signature).

Let's get back to the car analogy for a minute. The dashboard of every car has a **Check Engine** control lamp. Some advanced cars can also show error codes that might be told to a mechanic to get quick advice via phone. The program below demonstrates how a callback based on a built-in **Action** delegate works.

```csharp
public class Car
{
    public Action<string> EngineErrorDetected { get; set; }

    public void RunEngine()
    {
        //Statements to start the engine
        //Some error detected
        Console.WriteLine("Car -> Engine error detected");
        EngineErrorDetected?.Invoke("Error E899");
    }
}

public class Driver
{
    private Car _carToDrive;

    public Driver(Car carToDrive)
    {
        _carToDrive = carToDrive;
        _carToDrive.EngineErrorDetected = OnCarEngineErrorDetected;
    }

    public void DriveHome()
    {
        _carToDrive.RunEngine():
        //Statements to drive home
    }

    private void OnCarEngineErrorDetected(string errorCode)
    {
        Console
            .WriteLine($"Driver -> Calling a mechanic to say about
```

```
{errorCode}");
    }
}


public class Program
{
    public static void Main()
    {
        Car carToDrive = new Car() ;
        Driver myDriver = new Driver(carToDrive):
        myDriver.DriveHome();

        Console.ReadKey();
    }
}
```

Console output:

```
Car -> Engine error detected
Driver -> Calling a mechanic to say about Error E899
```

There are two classes: **Car** and **Driver**. The **Car** class has the **EngineErrorDetected** property of the generic delegate type **Action<T>**, where **T** is used as a type of a referenced method argument. The **Driver** class accepts an object of the **Car** class. Here, we deal with a responsible driver that wants to be up to date with things that happen to the car. So, the driver assigns a reference to the **OnCarEngineErrorDetected** method to the **EngineErrorDetected** delegate variable of a car. Trying to drive home, the driver object calls the **RunEngine** method of the car object. However, the car object detects an engine error and calls the **EngineErrorDetected** delegate passing an error code to it as a parameter. Since the **EngineErrorDetected** delegate keeps the reference to **OnCarEngineErrorDetected**, it's called, and the driver handles it by calling a mechanic.

Pay attention to a question mark in the middle of the **EngineErrorDetected?. Invoke ("Error E899")** expression. This question mark is a null check. Since the car object knows nothing about the class it's used by, it's worth checking whether **EngineErrorDetected** keeps a reference. Calling a delegate variable that doesn't keep a reference leads to a runtime error and a crash of an application. Here, null check ensures that the delegate variable will be called only if it keeps a reference to some method.

Events

Although callback based on the delegate variable is extremely useful, it's able to keep only one reference. What if we would like to build a car that can notify not only a driver but also a mechanic and a manufacturer to increase customer service and help find a solution as soon as possible. This is where events come into the picture.

Events in .NET follow the observer design pattern. An event is a notification based on a delegate and sent by an object (publisher) to notify other objects (subscribers) about something.

Let's modify the program from the previous example, as shown below, to enable a car to notify multiple subscribers about engine fault:

```
public class Car
{
    public event EventHandler<string> EngineErrorDetected;
    public string SerialNumber { get; }

    public Car(string serialNumber)
    {
        SerialNumber = serialNumber;
    }

    public void RunEngine()
    {
        //Statements to start the engine
        //Some error detected
        Console.WriteLine("Car -> Engine error detected");
        EngineErrorDetected?.Invoke(this, "Error E899");
    }
}

public class Driver
{
    private Car _carToDrive;

    public Driver(Car carToDrive)
```

```
    {
        _carToDrive = carToDrive;
        _carToDrive.EngineErrorDetected += OnCarEngineErrorDetected;

    public void DriveHome()
    {
        carToDrive.RunEngine();
        //Statements to drive home
    }


    private void OnCarEngineErrorDetected(object sender, string errorCode)
    {
        _carToDrive.EngineErrorDetected -= OnCarEngineErrorDetected;
        Console
            .WriteLine($"Driver -> Calling to a mechanic to say about
{errorCode}");
    }
}

public class CarManufacturer
{
    public Car CreateCar()
    {
        var brandNewCar = new Car("826");
        brandNewCar.EngineErrorDetected += OnEngineErrorDetected;
        return brandNewCar;
    }

    private void OnEngineErrorDetected(object sender, string error)
    {
        Car brokenCar = (Car) sender;
        Console.WriteLine($"CarManufacturer => Car #{brokenCar.
SerialNumber}: engine error - {error}");
    }
}
```

As you can see, **EngineErrorDetected** has become an event of the **EventHandler<string>** delegate. **EventHandler<T>** is a generic built-in delegate that specifically represents an event handler method. Type parameter **T** is used here as a type of the second parameter of an event handler method.

The type of the first parameter according to the definition of the **EventHandler<T>** delegate is always object. It's needed to pass a reference to a publisher object as a parameter to event handlers of subscribers. Such a trick is possible thanks to the implicit conversion of types. For reference types, an implicit conversion always exists from a class to any one of its direct or indirect base classes or interfaces. Since every class is eventually derived from the object class, such an implicit conversion is legal.

The **Driver** class now uses the addition assignment operator (**+=**) to attach an event handler (**OnCarEngineErrorDetected**) to the event and the subtraction assignment operator (**-=**) to unsubscribe from the event:

```
public class Program
{
    public static void Main()
    {
        var carManufacturer = new CarManufacturer();
        var carToDrive = carManufacturer.CreateCar():
        var myDriver = new Driver(carToDrive);
        myDriver.DriveHome();


        Console.ReadKey();
    }
}
```

Console output:

```
Car -> Engine error detected
CarManufacturer => Car #826: engine error - Error E899
```

Driver -> Calling a mechanic to say about Error E899

The **CarManufacturer** class (see the code above) is responsible for creating cars and reacting to errors that cars send to it. The **CreateCar()** method creates a new instance of the **Car** class and passes a serial number to its constructor. As you remember, the **Car** class passes a reference to itself, calling the **OnCarEngineErrorDetected** event. Although the **Car** object was converted to the object type, it's still a **Car** object. So, it can be easily converted back to the **Car** type explicitly and assigned to the **brokenCar** variable. Thanks to a reference to a sender object (**Car**), we have an opportunity to get a value of a **SerialNumber** property. As a result, once the **Car** object raises event, handler methods of all subscribers are run. **CarManufacturer** writes a message about the error of car #826, and the **Driver** calls a mechanic.

Another new thing you might notice here is a **var** keyword. It's not related to events, but it's important to make a short side note about it. The var-typed variable is an implicitly typed local variable (declared at method scope) where the type is determined by the compiler. The following declarations are equivalent:

```
var carManufacturer = new CarManufacturer();

CarManufacturer carManufacturer = new CarManufacturer();
```

The **var** type is widely used by C# developers around the world because it makes the code simpler and more readable.

Anonymous methods

Anonymous methods are methods without a name, just a body that is assigned to a delegate:

```
public void SomeMethod()
{
    Action<string> delegateVariable = WriteToConsole;
}

private void WriteToConsole(string argument)
{
    Console.WriteLine(argument);
}
```
→ *Classic method*

```
public void SomeMethod()
{
    Action<string> delegateVariable = delegate (string argument)
    {
        Console.WriteLine(argument);
    };
}
```
→ *Anonymous method*

```
public void SomeMethod()
{
    Action<string> delegateVariable = (argument) =>
    {
        Console.WriteLine(argument);
    };
}
```
→ *Lambda expression*

Figure 2.10: Named method vs anonymous method vs lambda expression

Since anonymous methods have no name, they can't be reused. So, they are used where creating a new named method is an unwanted overhead. *Figure 2.10* shows three ways to do the same thing. While the classic named method differs from the anonymous method and lambda expression by the ability to be reused, there is no significant difference between the anonymous method and the lambda expression. Lambda expression here is a shortcut that is converted by the compiler into an anonymous method. De facto, the lambda expression is the most popular way to declare an anonymous method because of its simpler and elegant look. When it comes to best practices, it's not recommended to declare anonymous methods with numerous lines of code, since it usually makes the code less readable for other developers. So, it's better to declare a classic named method for the complex logic.

Async Await and TPL

In C#, any method we normally create is synchronous by default. However, a UI application where all methods are synchronous has a significant problem. Since the whole application is executed synchronously in a single thread, UI gets blocked when some time-consuming action is executed, leaving end users with a bad user experience. Imagine an application making an HTTP request to get data from a remote host. When such an operation is executed synchronously in the main thread of an application, the UI freezes until data is retrieved and processed. Unresponsiveness of UI and lack of indication for time-consuming operations are things users usually hate. Asynchronous programming solves this problem, as the application can continue other work (for example, handling UI) while waiting when a time-consuming operation executed in another thread finishes. Consider the following asynchronous method:

```
public async Task<string> DoHardWorkAsync()
{
    Console.WriteLine("This is executed syncronously");
    var result = await Task.Run(() =>
    {
        Console.WriteLine("Doing hard work in another thread");
        //..Time-consuming computations...
        return "Time-consuming computation has finished";
    });
    return result;
}
```

The method is executed synchronously until the **await** keyword is met. Once **await** is met, it launches the time-consuming computation in another thread using the tread pool of the **Task Parallel Library** (**TPL**) while promising to return the result. The **Task<TResult>** and **Task** classes typically returned by asynchronous methods are those promises. When the task finishes (with a result in the case of **Task<TResult>**) the infrastructure behind the **await** keyword chooses a thread to resume the remaining code in the **DoHardWorkAsync** method, that is, after the **await** keyword. This explanation of the async await mechanism is quite simplified but conveys the main idea.

As you might notice, all magical things are done by the **await** keyword. The **async** keyword tells the compiler that the method contains at least one await keyword. So, a method without await but marked as async is executed synchronously.

The **Task Parallel Library** (**TPL**) is an extensive set of types and APIs that was built to make asynchronous programming simpler and more effective. It's built around **Task<TResult>** and **Task** classes and the Thread Pooling concept. Since asynchronous programming and multi-threading are some of the biggest C# topics, it's highly recommended to reach out to C# specific literature to learn about them in depth.

Exception handling

An exception is an error arising during the execution of a program. Exceptions are represented by classes. There are several built-in exception types in .NET. Exceptions are derived from the base **Exception** class and are used to react to critical issues that make it impossible to continue program execution. Division by zero is a classic example of such an issue. For the need of an application, custom exception types might be created. C# provides a try-catch exception handling tool. The following code snippet shows how it can be used.

```
try
{
    // statements that may cause an exception
}
catch (OutfMemoryException memoryEx)
{
    // specific exception handling block
    // to be executed in the case of OutofMemoryException only
}
catch (Exception ex)
{
    // general exception handling block
```

```
    // to be executed in the case of any exception
    // since Exception is a base class for all exception classes
}
finally
{
    // statements to be executed whenever an exception is thrown or not
}
```

Try-catch mechanism is based on four keywords:

- The **try** is a block where statements that may cause an exception have to be put.

- The **catch** is a block where exception handling code is put. For example, it might be making some logging.

- The **finally** block is optional and is used to execute statements, regardless of whether or not an exception is thrown. For example, if you make a request to the remote server to retrieve some data and provide the user with an indicator of progress, it must be hidden anyway no matter of retrievement result.

- The **throw** keyword is used to throw an exception when it's needed.

IDisposable

The Garbage Collector handles the memory management of most objects. However, sometimes applications use operating system or low-level APIs and services that can't be released by the Garbage Collector. It's called unmanaged resources. For example, when the object of a class that initiated the network connection is not needed anymore, GC removes this object from the memory. But the operating system has no idea that network connection can be closed. To release such an unmanaged resource, the **IDisposable** interface must be used.

IDisposable contains the **Dispose** method, which must be used by the client class to release all unmanaged resources, as follows:

```
public class MyCustomType : IDisposable
{
    //My custom type class members


    public void Dispose()
```

```
    {
        //Unmanaged resources release and clean up
    }
}
```

The recommended way to call the **Dispose** method by client class in C# is by using statement block or declaration. Consider the following methods that are equivalent:

```
public void PrintFile(string filePath)
{
    //Using declaration
    using var reader = new StreamReader(filePath);
    var fileContent = reader.ReadToEnd();
    Console.WriteLine(fileContent);
}

public void PrintFile(string filePath)
{
    //Using block
    using(var reader = new StreamReader(filePath))
    {
        var fileContent = reader.ReadToEnd();
        Console.WriteLine(fileContent);
    }
}
```

The **using** statement calls the **Dispose** method of the **StreamReader** object when it goes out of scope, so we don't need to remember to call the **Dispose** method manually anymore. Besides, both using forms ensure that **Dispose** is called even if an exception occurs.

Coding style

Usually, the coding style is considered as a set of guidelines used by a group of developers to keep the codebase easy to read. Although this set of rules might differ between companies or even departments of the same company, there is a starting point, that is, two articles from official C# documentation:

- https://docs.microsoft.com/en-us/dotnet/csharp/fundamentals/coding-style/identifier-names

- **https://docs.microsoft.com/en-us/dotnet/csharp/fundamentals/coding-style/coding-conventions**

In addition to the rules described in the articles, it's worth pointing out a few things based on the author's experience:

- **Always use access modifiers**: Although classes and class members declared without access modifiers get default ones implicitly, it's considered a good practice to add access modifiers explicitly everywhere. Explicitly stating access modifiers improves readability. The developer reading your code should focus on business logic, architecture, and performance, not be trying to remember what the default modifier is in a given situation.

- **Don't use public fields**: Use properties instead. Public fields bring no benefits but expose the internal state of a class without any control. With property, you can specify different access restrictions, validations, or multithread support easily by getter and setter building a consistent public API of a class. Besides, .NET is built in a way that assumes you'll use properties for your public data members.

- **Use underscore prefix for fields (for example, `private string _userName;`)**: This improves readability because it makes it easy to distinguish a class field from a local variable of a method.

- **Always use the `Async` suffix for methods that return `Task` or `Task<T>`**: Such a suffix lets other developers know that your method is an asynchronous one by just looking at IntelliSense autocomplete.

Conclusion

C# and .NET have come a long way from a Windows-only platform to constantly developing advanced cross-platform environments. C# became one of the most popular programming languages being used in different areas, from desktop applications to video games. C# is an object-oriented programming language with a set of built-in data types where reference types are always stored in the **Heap** managed by the garbage collector. Mechanisms of inheritance, such as polymorphism, provide a strong fundament for building applications of each size, while particular features of a language, like **Events**, make it attractive compared to competitors.

The next chapter will focus on the fundamentals of .NET MAUI, covering topics like the differences between Xamarin and MAUI, the life cycle of an application, dealing with application assets, and more.

Points to remember

- A compiler generates a set of Common Intermediate Language CIL instructions and metadata from your source code.

- Just In Time Compiler (JIT) converts CIL instructions during the runtime into machine codes specific to the machine a program is executed on.

- Garbage Collector (GC) serves as an automatic memory manager, allocating memory for the new data and releasing data that is not used.

- A value type variable keeps value, while a reference type variable keeps a reference to an object.

- An object can be referenced by multiple variables.

- Class is like a blueprint for objects.

- String type is a reference type that behaves like a value type because of immutability.

- The StringBuilder class should be used when text needs to be modified multiple times.

- Every class that has made a commitment to follow an interface must implement all functionalities that the interface declares.

- A class that doesn't inherit another class explicitly inherits the **Object** class implicitly.

- In C#, a class can inherit only one base class and implement multiple interfaces.

- Access modifiers are used to define the visibility level (or access level) for classes, methods, fields, and properties.

- Generics help increase codebase reusability, reliability, performance, and type safety.

- Delegate is a reference to a method.

- An event is a notification sent by an object (publisher) to notify other objects (subscribers) about something.

- The **IDisposable** interface must be applied to release unmanaged resources.

Questions

1. Why was .NET Core created?

2. What is .NET Standard?

3. Why is using dynamic type considered a bad practice?

4. Is string a reference type?

5. What is the difference between private and protected access modifiers?

6. What is the difference between overriding and overloading?

7. How does the event mechanism use delegates?

8. Are anonymous methods class members as well as named methods?

9. What is an exception?

Join our book's Discord space

Join the book's Discord Workspace for Latest updates, Offers, Tech happenings around the world, New Release and Sessions with the Authors:

https://discord.bpbonline.com

CHAPTER 3

Exploring .NET MAUI and Its Features

Introduction

Just like a foundation of a house cannot be built without knowledge about materials, tools, and construction processes, an application cannot be built without an understanding of the concepts and fundamental elements every application stands upon.

The best way to understand this and all the subsequent chapters is by following instructions and getting tasks done. Make sure you have access to the repository that accompanies this book since it is referenced multiple times in the second part of the chapter. It is also highly recommended not to just go through sections one by one but to take breaks, playing around with the code we will work on.

All software products, even the most popular ones, have multiple bugs, and .NET MAUI is not an exception. Since .NET MAUI is still in active development, it is recommended to check the **Issues** section of the official .NET MAUI repository (**https://github.com/dotnet/maui/issues**) in case something is not working as expected. In most cases, the issue you are facing is already known, a workaround is already found, and developers plan to fix it in an upcoming release. Otherwise, it is worth creating an issue ticket to help the .NET MAUI team make the framework more stable.

Structure

In this chapter, we will cover the following topics:

- Why did cross-platform development come up?
- History of Xamarin and Mono
- What does .NET MAUI change and why?
- Where are Renderers?
- Handlers
- Building an app: from shared code to a native application
- Application life cycle
- Exploring App.xaml.cs
- HostBuilder pattern
- MauiProgram.cs
- MAUI application life cycle events
- Platform-specific life cycle events
- MessagingCenter
- Dealing with image resources
- Application icon
- Splash Screen
- Fonts

Objectives

In this chapter, we will be working tight with .NET MAUI and the cross-platform development conception. The chapter can be logically split into three parts. The first part covers the concept of cross-platform development; the history of Xamarin, which can be treated as the father of .NET MAUI; and the main differences between Xamarin and MAUI.

The second part explains the fundamentals of .NET MAUI and .NET MAUI applications. We will talk about how a cross-platform code becomes a native app, building process specifics, application life cycle, and so on.

In the third part of the chapter, we will start creating your first cross-platform .NET MAUI application from the ground up.

Why did cross-platform development come up?

The cross-platform way of creating **Graphical User Interface (GUI)** applications is relatively new. The classic approach says an application must be implemented separately for each platform it is supposed to work on, using platform-native development tools. That way has its own benefits, such as easier and full access to platform-specific capabilities, no additional intermediate frameworks, and no risk of lowered performance. That is why companies go classic approach even today when working on applications that are highly depend on platform-specific features and platform-native look and feel. Especially when it comes to specialized business-oriented desktop applications. However, there is a price to pay here. The same features must be implemented by different teams in different programming languages from scratch to provide support for different platforms. Besides, additional management efforts are needed to make sure the product roadmaps and development teams are synchronized. So, the development, maintenance, and management costs might be high. However, historically, there was not enough demand for unifying GUI and to stop writing the same business logic code multiple times until the mobile applications and cloud computing market skyrocketed.

A few things became obvious by the end of the first half of the 2010s. First, the way customers used their smartphones, along with market competition, led to a steady trend of fully custom user interfaces mostly unified across the platforms. Second, the high market competition required faster and cheaper delivery. So, the idea of having a shared codebase for each mobile platform became popular enough to motivate people around the world to develop and apply cross-platform solutions. The desktop application market was, of course, also transforming during that time, but mostly under the pressure from the web applications side. So, it was the mobile app market that drove the growth of cross-platform GUI frameworks. Besides, in the second half of the 2010s, even big corporations that can easily afford to create applications in a classic way started using mature cross-platform frameworks like Xamarin to unify the technological stack and speed up development.

Today, .NET MAUI allows sharing up to 95% of a codebase. The percentage tightly depends on the number of platform-specific APIs that must be used. For example, because of significant differences between the ways iOS and Android handle push notifications, some amount of platform-specific code needs to be written.

Cross-platform development advantages

- **A single technology stack** makes project management much easier. In the case of MAUI, it also enables the usage of compatible .NET libraries common to multiple company products.

- **A single codebase** to implement and maintain drastically reduces the cost of development and maintenance.

- **Faster product delivery** makes a business more flexible and more responsive to market needs.

Cross-platform development disadvantages

- **An additional layer** of cross-platform framework code also brings the framework's possible bugs and performance issues with it.

- **There is a dependency on updates**. Usually, it takes some time for framework development teams to provide access to brand-new features added to a particular OS.

- **Constraints** are part of the process. Despite the tremendous efforts of framework creators, a cross-platform framework might not always support every single platform-specific feature.

History of Xamarin and Mono

A free and open-source .NET Framework compatible framework called *Mono* was announced on July 19, 2001. A talented Mexican-origin engineer and co-founder of *Helix Code* (later renamed Ximian) *Miguel de Icaza* saw the potential of a Windows-oriented .NET Framework to become cross-platform. Since the *Ximian* was bought by *Novell* in August 2003, Mono v1.0 was released in June 2004 under *Novell's flag*. The progress was impressive. Mono v1.0 allowed the creation of applications for *Linux, Solaris, MacOS X, Windows,* and various *Unix* systems. It included C# compiler, implementation of the **Common Language Infrastructure** (**CLI**), class libraries, execution system, and other important components like Gtk# (bound gtk+ toolkit) for creating Graphical User Interface, providers for all popular databases, and more. Mono was also able to run many of the existing .NET software, for example, NUnit (unit-testing framework).

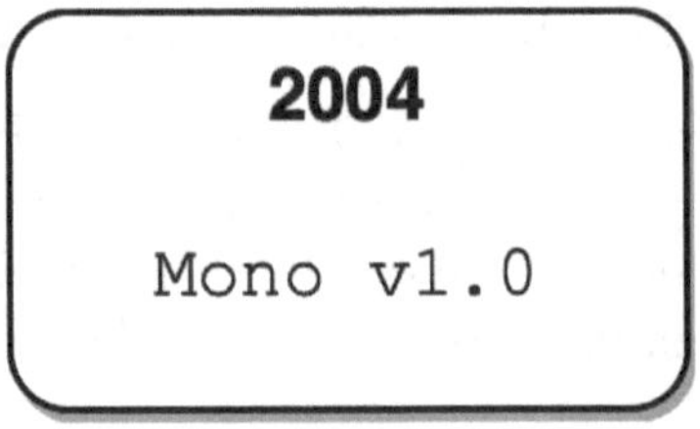

2004

`Mono v1.0`

Figure 3.1: Year 2004

Four years passed between the release of Mono's first and second versions. During that time, the Mono team was fixing issues, improving performance, and adopting new versions of the .NET Framework. Mono v2.0 was released in October 2008 as a major milestone. It delivered lots of Microsoft Compatible APIs and new or updated Mono APIs. There are a few novelties that are important to mention. Starting from Mono v2.0 it supports embedded SQLite database that is often the default choice for mobile applications .

Figure 3.2: Year 2008

Another notable feature that appeared in Mono 2.0 was Mono Linker. A linker is a tool that helps significantly reduce the size of the compiled library or an application. The size of a ready-to-install application is especially important in the case of mobile devices since they often retrieve applications via a low-speed cellular connection even nowadays. It is a common situation when some large library is added to the application to use only a few classes. So, there is no need to pack the unnecessary code of a library, increasing the size of the application. The linker checks what features are used and removes parts of libraries that are not used by your application.

Two years after the original iPhone had been released, in September 2009, the Mono team released MonoTouch, which was later renamed to Xamarin.iOS. It is a Mono-based framework that allows the creation of C# and .NET-based applications for iPhone, iPod, and iPad devices. The important part of Xamarin.iOS is libraries that bind the native Apple's Cocoa Touch APIs. Thanks to accessing those libraries, Xamarin and MAUI allow capabilities for extending cross-platform features to be delivered by Xamarin.Forms and MAUI:

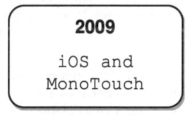

Figure 3.3: Year 2009

In the fall of 2010, the SGen garbage collector was released as a part of Mono v2.8, replacing the Boehm garbage collector. The Sgen generational garbage collector provides much better performance in managing memory, which is crucial for mobile devices:

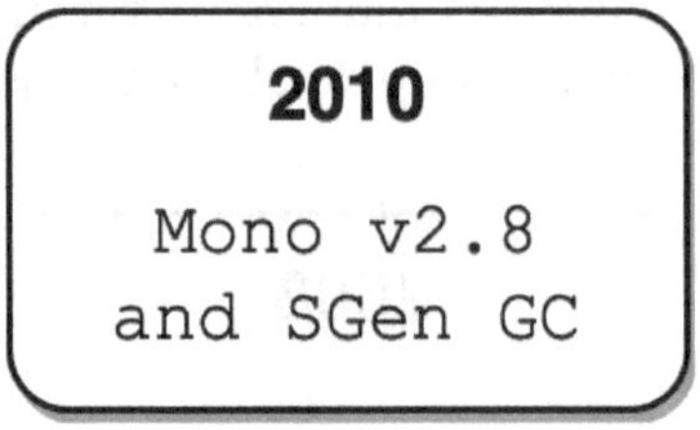

Figure 3.4: Year 2010

Xamarin.Android (formerly known as Mono for Android) was introduced in April 2011. It followed the principles of Xamarin.iOS offering Mono runtime, .NET class libraries, SDK tools, and libraries that bind the native Android APIs. Thereby, Xamarin provided a solution that allowed the sharing of business logic code between mobile platforms, while UI had to be implemented using platform-specific APIs:

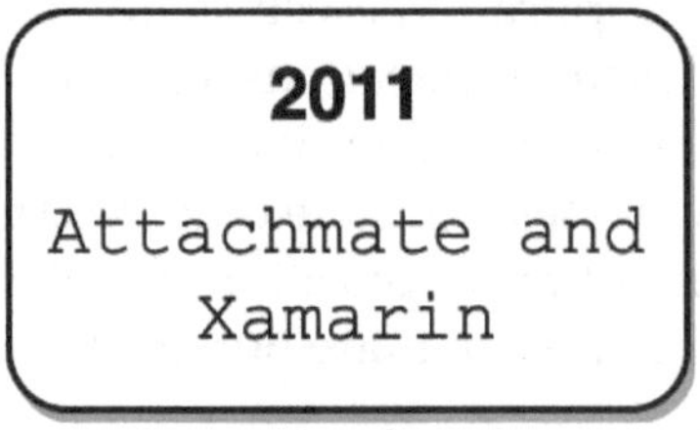

Figure 3.5: Year 2011

After the Attachmate Corporation acquired *Novell* in April 2011, Attachmate announced massive layoffs. The future of Mono was a big question. Trying to save Mono, Miguel de Icaza and Nathaniel Friedman founded the Xamarin company. A significant part of the original Mono team moved to Xamarin to continue the support and development of Mono. Xamarin decided to direct the main vector of efforts on mobile platforms, macOS, and Windows. It was supposed to become a complete solution enabling the creation of cross-platform applications for all the most popular platforms.

The next major milestone was May 2014, when Xamarin.Forms was released as part of Xamarin v3. Xamarin.Forms increases the amount of code to be shared by providing functionality to create a cross-platform GUI using XAML language. And every user interface control that is written using Xamarin.Forms is mapped to platform-specific native controls automatically. Such a way of creating cross-platform GUI applications was exceedingly attractive, especially for WPF and Silverlight developers who already had experience with XAML, C#, and .NET:

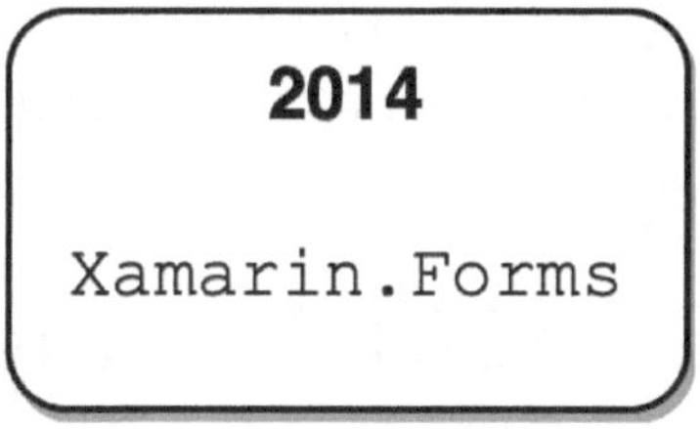

2014

Xamarin.Forms

Figure 3.6: Year 2014

The interest in Xamarin was growing. Despite Xamarin being constantly in development, adding new features, and experiencing technical problems, more and more developers wished to try it. There was a constraint there though: Xamarin was not free. That is why when Microsoft acquired Xamarin in 2016 and made it free, its popularity boomed. So, Xamarin became a member of the Microsoft family.

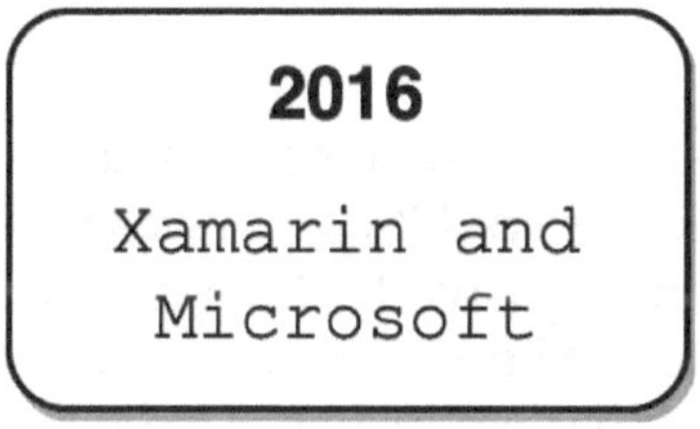

2016

Xamarin and
Microsoft

Figure 3.7: Year 2016

To support developers and popularize Xamarin, the Xamarin University online learning platform was created. It offered documentation, courses, lectures, guides, and a certification program. Since mobile development using Xamarin became the main specialization for many developers around the world, such a Xamarin Mobile Professional Certificate had value. Unfortunately, Xamarin University was swallowed up by the Microsoft Learn platform that does not offer dedicated Microsoft Mobile Developer certification. A significant number of Xamarin/MAUI developers aren't happy about it because being a mobile developer is still a separate specialty in the market. Talking about support and popularity, it is worth giving credit to both the Xamarin team and the community for the amazingly well-written documentation and lots of Xamarin/MAUI-related blogs:

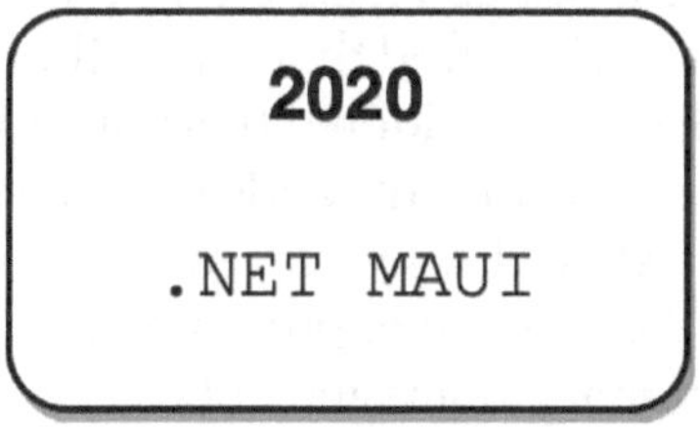

2020

.NET MAUI

Figure 3.8: Year 2020

Everything must move forward, so at the 2020 Microsoft Build Conference, .NET MAUI was announced as an evolution of Xamarin and an integral part of the new cross-platform .NET platform.

What does .NET MAUI change and why?

As mentioned before, MAUI was born as a step on a way of transforming .NET to a consistent ecosystem that allows the creation wide range of cross-platform applications. So, MAUI is part of the .NET platform. It means MAUI uses .NET CLI, class library, and other staff of .NET, while Xamarin was a separate framework with its own implementation of .NET and dependencies to the .NET Framework. Being a part of the .NET ecosystem means full support from all the teams working on the .NET platform. It also means the .NET team now considers MAUI when planning upcoming releases of the .NET platform, and new features of .NET and C# now will be available from day one.

It is not a secret that Xamarin had some congenital issues and irritating features. One of the topics of discussion around Xamarin was performance. Some people said Xamarin apps were not fast-enough, while others answered it was not about Xamarin but about developers who do not know how to build good-performing applications. However, both camps agreed that performance must have a high priority to provide as good quality as possible. So, the MAUI team applied significant efforts to optimize visual elements and make architectural changes for the sake of better application startup time and overall performance.

While MAUI has a single multi-target project, Xamarin had a project for a shared code and separate platform-specific projects, which meant additional development and maintenance efforts. For example, a simple thing like replacing an application icon required numerous image files in different resolutions specific to a platform and playing around with platform-specific settings. Pretty much the same time-consuming drudgery waited on developers in the case of splash screens, fonts, and other resources that looked the same on both platforms but could not be shared between platforms because of Xamarin constraints. Of course, experienced Xamarin developers know the right ways and external libraries that are allowed to solve some part of the issues, like sharing image resources or SVG icons support. However, a workaround is always just a workaround that solves the initial issue but creates other issues or threats. The MAUI team considered this pain and now, MAUI does all dirty work for us, allowing us to add different kinds of assets, including application icon and splash screen, once as a shared resource. And of course, now we have built-in support for SVG images. Having a single project also reduces efforts when it comes to `*.csproj` files and dependency management.

While desktop Mac and Windows platforms were presented, Xamarin focused its resources on mobile platforms, keeping desktop platforms support somewhere between preview and release. So Xamarin did not inspire enough confidence to become a solution for enterprise-level desktop apps. MAUI changes this, making Mac and Windows first-class citizens. It relies on WinUI 3 for Windows and Mac Catalyst for macOS, providing full support for cross-platform XAML-based UI. Indeed, sharing UI between mobile and desktop platforms is a topic to discuss, but the fact that you can create cross-platform desktop applications in the same way mobile apps are created using XAML and C# is what the community waited for.

Every real-world application requires to be configured and initialized somehow. In Xamarin, third-party libraries had to be initialized in one place and platform-specific customizations (renderers) of UI controls in another, while registering dependencies in the dependency injection container was not foreseen at all. All of that was just inconvenient and confusing for new Xamarin developers. .NET MAUI resolves those problems by adopting the .NET Generic Host Builder. This brings consistency with the rest of modern .NET and provides dependency injection and a way to make a setup in a single place out of the box.

While Xamarin developers had to deal with platform-native APIs to be able to use drawing, MAUI fulfills this gap by providing advanced cross-platform graphics functionality with canvas for drawing and painting shapes.

Accessibility is another area that required attention in Xamarin. Considering the number of changes planned for MAUI and the world's trend to make applications accessible, the MAUI team paid special attention to accessibility. After the MAUI team had investigated and made a series of consultations with developers and companies, the cross-platform accessibility API was modified and extended to make it more efficient and easier to use.

Where are Renderers?

Renderers have undergone significant changes. It is important to understand the mechanism of Renderers to understand how cross-platform magic works and consider why it was replaced with a new concept, which is Handlers, in MAUI.

Renderers play a crucial role in cross-platform applications. Every Xamarin developer working on real-world commercial applications sooner or later finds themselves dealing with Renderers and creating custom renderers. *Figure 3.9* shows renderer-based architecture of Xamarin.Forms:

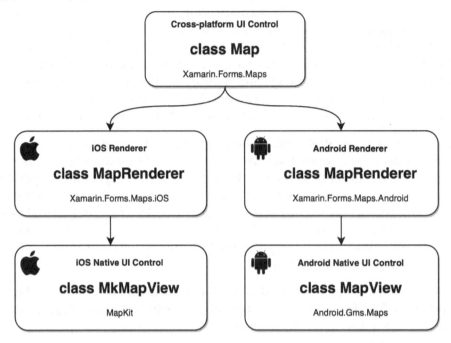

Figure 3.9: Renderer-based architecture of Xamarin.Forms

The user interface of an application is a set of interconnected UI elements called **controls** that form a visual tree. It will be described in detail in the next chapter. To build cross-platform applications (Xamarin.Forms applications), Xamarin provides a collection of UI control classes (Entry, Button, ListView, Map, and so on) that are mapped to native controls. Renderers are needed to turn a Xamarin.Forms UI control into a native UI control (*Figure 3.9*). The platform-specific renderer object gets Xamarin.Forms control object, creates a corresponding platform-native control, configures it, and then adds this native control to the native visual tree. Sounds good, right? Yes, however, everything has a price to pay.

As you might remember, Xamarin.Forms supports not only iOS and Android, as shown in *Figure 3.9*, but also Mac and Windows. Considering that Xamarin.Forms UI control must provide the same functionalities across all supported platforms, it naturally brings a constraint into the picture. Xamarin.Forms UI control exposes only the features that are presented in native UI controls of all platforms and are implemented similarly. It means sometimes you need to create a custom renderer (that derives the existing one) to reach an API of a platform-native control and extend the capabilities of built-in Xamarin.Forms control. It's the same when you need to extend the capabilities of platform native controls.

Another reason to create a custom renderer is to unify the look and feel of control across platforms. The experience says that in most cases, the cross-platform way of development is selected when an application should look the same across the platforms it is presented on. However, since Xamarin relies on native controls, sometimes controls look different depending on the platform, and that difference cannot be eliminated without dealing with the platform's native API. A canonic example is Entry UI control, which has an underline. Probably one of the most popular questions of new Xamarin.Forms developers is "How to remove the underline from Entry on Android".

Although renderers were serving its purpose for years, time has shown that this mechanism has a few architectural issues:

- Since a renderer class and UI control class are tightly coupled, it makes the codebase less maintainable.

- Creating a custom renderer is not intuitive enough and requires changes in different parts of a solution.

- The performance of renderers is not always good enough.

- Working with renderers requires some additional knowledge about the specifics of renderers. It increases the level of entry for new developers and brings with it the risk of getting unexpected performance issues.

- A custom renderer is needed even to make simple changes in native controls. It leads to redundant code. The Xamarin team built additional mechanisms that provide access to platform-specific APIs from the level of Xamarin. Forms, but their usage is usually not obvious enough for users.

Handlers

Reshaping the whole framework, .NET MAUI gave a chance to rethink the architecture of such a fundamental concept as renderers. Therefore, the **Renderer** concept was replaced with **Handlers**. It is worth noting that despite the fact that the Renderers concept is obsolete, .NET MAUI allows using Renderers and Handlers, providing backward compatibility to make it easier to convert the existing Xamarin applications to MAUI.

Let us consider what Handlers are and how they solve the issues Renderers had.

Figure 3.10 highlights a handler-based architecture. As you can see, there are no dependencies between a cross-platform UI control and a handler. The **Entry** class and its platform-specific handlers now depend on the **IEntry** interface, which, in turn, is derived from other interfaces like **IView**, **ITextInput**, and **ITextAlignment**, which are essential for the **Entry** control. Refer to the following figure showing the handler-based architecture of .NET MAUI:

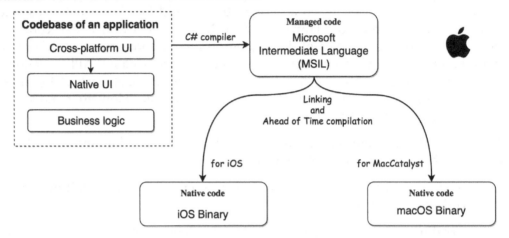

Figure 3.10: Handler-based architecture of .NET MAUI

Such a granulation of interfaces not only decouples a codebase but also makes it more flexible. So, handler knows what properties of a cross-platform control need to be mapped to a native control without having direct access to the whole **Entry** class.

The **IView** interface derives the **IElement** interface that declares the **Handler property** of type **IElementHandler**, which provides access to a platform-specific view without creating a custom handler. Since every element of the Visual Tree of an application inherits the **Element** class, the **Handler** of each element (for example, **Entry**) can be accessed easily.

In the case of Entry, the chain of inheritance looks like this:

Entry → InputView → View → VisualElement → NavigableElement → Element → BindableObject

Since the **ElementHandler** (implements **IElementHandler**) passes itself to the **Element** class (implements **IElement**), the **Element** class has an opportunity to inform possible subscribers about Handler's changes. So, the **Element** class exposes two events that represent the life cycle of a Handler:

- The **HandlerChanging** event is raised when a new handler is about to be created or removed for a cross-platform control. The event's parameter of the **HandlerChangingEventArgs** type contains the **NewHandler** and **OldHandler** properties of the **IElementHandler** type. For example, subscribing to this event might be useful to subscribe and unsubscribe events of platform-specific control (**UITextField** in the case of Entry control and iOS platform).

- The **HandlerChanged** event is raised after the handler for a cross-platform control has been created. The raised **HandlerChanged** event also means that platform-native control is available and all property values of cross-platform control (for example, Entry) have been applied to the platform-native control (**UITextField** in the case of Entry control and iOS platform).

In addition to those events, the **Element** class has virtual methods called **OnHandlerChanged** and **OnHandlerChanging**. Overriding these methods is a recommended way to get notified about changes around Handler when you need to handle changes inside your cross-platform control.

Working with handlers from the perspective of practice will be explained in detail in *Chapter 6, Deep Dive Into UI Design*. Now let us enumerate key features of Handlers:

- Unlike Renderers, Handlers are registered at the start of an application explicitly, without using the slow mechanism of reflection.

- Handler gets access to cross-platform control through an interface abstraction layer that makes the codebase more maintainable and reliable.

- Creating custom handlers is not needed in most cases, thanks to the new mechanism of mappers easily available from the cross-platform code layer.

- Thanks to new architecture, implementing a custom renderer is clear, consistent across platforms, and leaner.

Building an app from a shared code to a native application

Now that you know how cross-platform UI is turned into a native one, it is time to highlight the process of building an application to complete the bigger picture of transforming cross-platform code into a native application.

From the perspective of targeting different platforms, your MAUI application is .NET for iOS, .NET for Mac, .NET for Android, or .NET for Windows application. The process of building an application targeting Windows is straightforward because Windows is a platform supported by .NET since the beginning, and an application is run under the control of the Common Language Runtime of the .NET environment. In the case of other platforms, the application is run in a platform-specific environment, so it must be built in accordance with the specifics of each platform.

As you remember, in .NET C#, the code of an application is compiled into Intermediate Language (MSIL). This code is also called **managed code** because its execution is managed by the **.NET Common Language Runtime (CLR)**. Then, managed code is compiled by a Just-in-time (JIT) compiler during the runtime. Besides managed code, there is **native code**. Native code is code that is run natively on a specific platform without using the JIT compilation of .NET CLR.

This is where the **Ahead of Time (AOT)** compilation comes into the picture. As you already know, Apple restricts the execution of dynamically generated code on their ARM-based processors because of security reasons. So, MSIL must be compiled into a platform-specific native binary. The AOT compilator is used to compile managed code into a native binary that can be deployed on Apple's ARM-based processor. In addition, a set of optimizing tools like Linker and LLVM compiler might be turned on to make the final binary smaller and more efficient. *Figure 3.11* shows the build process for iOS and MacCatalyst platforms.

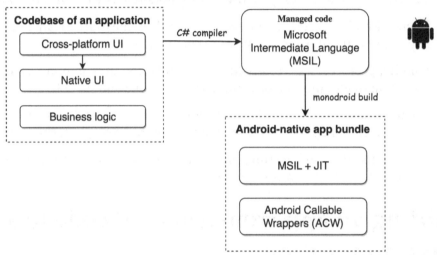

Figure 3.11: Building process for iOS and macOS

There are a few side notes to mention here. The fact is that Apple allows the use of JIT compilation on devices powered by x86 and x64 processors. However, *Figure 3.11* and the whole explanation was simplified since all iOS and iPadOS devices are ARM-based. Moreover, Apple fully switched to ARM-based architecture, releasing desktop devices powered by ARM-based Apple Silicon processors. JIT compilation is also allowed for simulators because a simulator is an isolated environment and JIT compilation speeds up the building process, which is important for debugging when a developer needs to recompile an application frequently.

Looking at *Figure 3.11*, you might be wondering what Mac Catalyst is. Mac Catalyst is a technology created by Apple that enables developers to take the code of an iOS-targeting application and build a macOS-native application. This differs from the ability of M-series-based Mac devices to run iOS applications because an application targeting Mac Catalyst is an actual Mac bundle. It means it enables you to use macOS desktop features like the menu bar. So, when you see "MacCatalyst" in your MAUI solution, it means macOS.

The situation with Android is different. Android applies so-called hybrid compilation, allowing some parts of the application to be compiled using AOT compilation and others to be compiled with JIT. So, the MSIL code is included in the final application bundle (*Figure 3.12*):

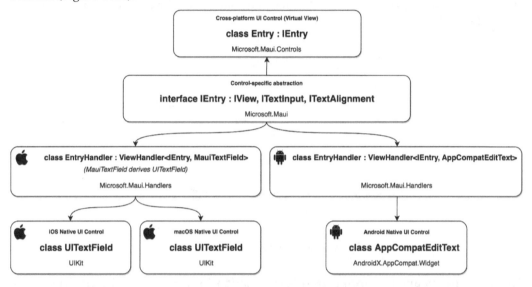

Figure 3.12: Building process for Android

.NET for Android application is executed under the control of two runtimes at the same time. .NET for Android runtime and **Android Runtime (ART)** work together, managing the code belonging to them. The ART takes the leading role though, being the runtime native for Android. So, the code coming from the Android native APIs is managed by ART, while the MAUI codebase (including your custom business logic) is managed by the runtime of .NET for Android.

The interesting thing here is that those two runtimes, despite being different technologies, must communicate with each other somehow. This was resolved by **Managed Callable Wrappers (MCW)** and **Android Callable Wrappers (ACW)**, as explained here:

- **Android Callable Wrappers (ACW)** are **Java Native Interface (JNI)** bridges used any time the ART needs to invoke MSIL code. Since it is impossible to know in advance what classes of a MAUI app will need ACWs, they are generated during the build process.

- **Managed Callable Wrappers (MCW)** are JNI bridges that lead in the opposite direction. They are used when MSIL code needs to invoke Android code. Since Android API is known, MCWs are delivered as part of .NET for Android.

Application life cycle

Every cross-platform MAUI application could be found in one of four execution states: not running, running, deactivated, and stopped. *Figure 3.13* shows how the life cycle works:

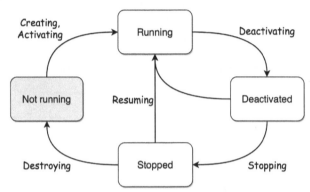

Figure 3.13: MAUI application life cycle

Not running means the application is not loaded into memory. The **running state** means an application is running. While the running state is straightforward, the difference between the **Deactivated** and **Stopped** states might not be obvious. While the **deactivated state** means different apps gain focus, the application is switched to the **stopped state** when the user switches to a different app or returns to the device's home screen, so the app is no longer visible.

.NET MAUI provides the ability to create multi-window applications for iOS (iPad only), Android, MacCatalyst, and Windows. Multi-window support does not work for iPhone. By default, every application contains a single window represented by the **Window class**. However, additional windows can be created by the application during runtime.

Exploring App.xaml.cs

Now is a good moment to get back to a code. The empty MAUI solution contains a few files with classes, and one of them is the **App** class. This class consists of two files: **App.xaml** and **App.xaml.cs**. The first one is a XAML file, while the second one is a so-called code-behind file associated with the XAML file. Both **App.xaml** and **App.xaml.cs** contribute to a class **App** that derives from the **Application** class. Technically, it is possible, thanks to a C# feature called partial classes. That is why you can see the partial keyword before the class name in the **App.xaml.cs** file. The anatomy of the XAML-based class will be detailed in *Chapter 4*, In and Out of UI Development. At this stage, you can think about the **App** class as the usual class.

The **App** class is the heart of a cross-platform MAUI application. Create a new blank application and let us explore the most important members of the **Application** class together.

Properties and methods

The following are the key properties and methods of the Application Class in MAUI:

- The Windows read-only property returns a collection of type **IReadOnlyList<IWindow>** that contains windows of an application.

- The **MainPage** property keeps the reference to the root page of the initial window. The initial Window is created when the **MainPage** is set in the constructor of the **App** class.

- The virtual **CreateWindow** method is used to create an initial window. It can be overridden in case you have to subscribe to life cycle events of the window or use your custom Window class derived from the **Window** class.

- The **OpenWindow** method is used to display the selected window. In the case of opening a new window, it will be added to the Windows collection. A new window will be ignored in the case of the iPhone since multi-window support does not work on iOS for iPhone. The new window will be also ignored in the case of iOS or MacCatalyst when the platform-specific configuration is not made.

- The **CloseWindow** method closes the selected window. The window is removed from the Windows collection. The initial window (the window of **MainPage**) cannot be removed from the Windows collection.

- The static **Current property** is a static property that keeps a reference to the Application class, so the **Application** object is accessible from any place of a MAUI application.

- The **AppLinks** property provides an access to the app links manager. Special deep links can be registered using it. Thanks to this mechanism, an application can be launched by clicking on a link (example sent by email).

- The **OnAppLinkRequestReceived** virtual method allows catching a link an application has opened with. Since the link can contain additional information in text format, it might be handled in a way business logic requires.

- The **Resources** property contains different kinds of resources, such as colors, texts, and styles, , which are used in XAML code mainly. Working with resources will be covered later.

- The **UserAppTheme** property of the **AppTheme** type is used to set the *Light* or *Dark* theme, regardless of which system theme is currently used by the operational system. Set the **AppTheme.Unspecified** value to make the application follow operational system theme settings.

- The **PlatformAppTheme** read-only property returns the team that is used by the operational system.

- The **RequestedTheme** read-only property returns **UserAppTheme** value in the case it has **Light** or **Dark** value. If **UserAppTheme** is **Unspecified**, **PlatformAppTheme** is returned.

- The static **AccentColor** property returns platform-specific accent color. Another color value can also be assigned to this property.

- The **OnStart** virtual method is called once right after the application had started and the initial window is created.

- The **OnSleep** virtual method is called each time the application goes into the background.

- The **OnResume** virtual method is called when the application is resumed, after being sent to the background.

The **OnResume**, **OnSleep**, and **OnStart** methods will not be called on iOS and MacCatalyst when an application is configured as multi-window. In such cases, life cycle events and methods of windows must be used instead.

Remember, there is no way to get notified about application termination. For example, an application sent to the background might be terminated by the operating system to free up the memory for another application that is in the foreground now.

Events

- The **RequestedThemeChanged** event is fired when the system theme of a device changes.

- The **ModalPushing** event is fired when a page is about to be modally open.

- The **ModalPushed** event is fired when a page has been popped modally.

- The **ModalPopping** event is fired when a modal page is about to be closed.

- The **ModalPopped** event is fired when a modal page has been closed.

- The **PageAppearing** event is fired when a page is about to appear.

- The **PageDisappearing** event is fired when a page is about to disappear.

Do not worry if you do not understand what modal pages are and what the difference between a page and a modal page is. It will be covered in the next chapter on learning UI-specific things. At this stage, it is important to understand that the **App.xaml.cs** class is responsible for lots of things important to a whole application.

It is important to remember that page-related events described above are raised, regardless of a source of the window navigation. Another thing is that the Window class also contains such events. So, if you work on a multi-window application, it is much better to subscribe to window-specific events.

HostBuilder pattern

Before talking about how a .NET MAUI application is configured, it is necessary to understand what the configuring mechanism is based on.

.NET Generic Host is a feature of the modern .NET, which provides a clean standardized way to configure and start any kind of .NET application. So, a .NET MAUI application utilizes the same approach, providing a single place where the application is configured.

This mechanism is based on extension methods. A C# extension method is a powerful and widely used feature that allows extending the functionality of a type without creating a derived type. An extension method is a special kind of static method where the **this** modifier is applied to the first parameter. The following code snippet shows the way the extension method is declared and consumed:

```
public static class StringExtensions
{
    public static string AddToEnd(this string initialText, string
textToAdd)
    {
        Return $"{initialText}{textToAdd}";
    }
}


//Extension method consumption
var myText = "Hello";
var finalText = myText.AddToEnd(" ").AddToEnd("World!");


Console.WriteLine(finalText);
```

Console output:

Hello World!

As you can see, from the perspective of consumption, the custom **AddToEnd** extension method is utilized as it was a member of the string type. Moreover, since the **AddToEnd** method returns the same type it extends, extension methods can be used to "chain" multiple method calls. In the example, such a chain builds the final text, which is "Hello World!".

The **HostBuilder** pattern uses the same chaining approach to configure a builder class using extension methods.

MauiProgram.cs

MauiProgram.cs is a key class of MAUI application. This is a place where an application is configured.

As you can see in the following code snippet, the default **MauiProgram.cs** class contains one static method called **CreateMauiApp**. This method returns a **MauiApp** object that contains the configuration of an application. For example, if you go to **Platforms → iOS → AppDelegate.cs**, you will find that the application delegate object calls the **CreateMauiApp** method to create a host of a MAUI application.

```
public static class MauiProgram
{
    public static MauiApp CreateMauiApp()
    {
        var builder = MauiApp.CreateBuilder();
        builder.UseMauiApp<App>()
            .ConfigureFonts(fonts =>
            {
                fonts.AddFont("OpenSans-Regular.ttf", "OpenSansRegular");
                fonts.AddFont("OpenSans-Semibold.ttf", "OpenSansSemibold");
            });


        return builder.Build();


    }
}
```

The **MauiApp.CreateBuilder** method returns a builder that is used along with its extension methods to configure a MAUI application. The **Build** method initializes some internal MAUI modules and returns the **MauiApp** host object. After that, the **MauiApp** object is used to get an **App** object from the **dependency injection** (DI) container and create a cross-platform window tied up with a native window by a handler.

Dependency injection will be covered in *Chapter 5, Layering With MVVM*. At this point, envision it as a service that maintains a configuration of interface-class pairs. This service can instantiate an object of a specific class when the object is requested by its interface name.

Figure 3.14 demonstrates the process of MAUI application startup taking a regular single-window MAUI application and an iOS platform as an example:

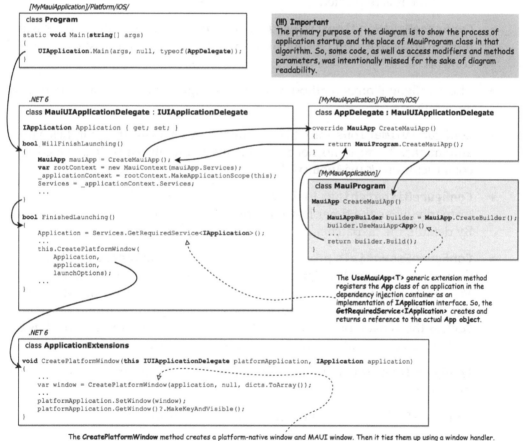

Figure 3.14: MAUI application startup process on iOS

Here, you can see what place the **MauiProgram** class takes in the process of application initialization. The UI becomes visible after a native view has been set by the **SetWindow** method called from the **CreatePlatfomWindow** extension method.

Now, let us explore the **MauiAppBuilder** properties and extension methods available out of the box:

- **UseMauiApp<T>** is probably the most important method because its main responsibility is to register the type T (the **App** class by default) as an implementation of the interface **IApplication**. In other words, it means from the moment of registration, DI container returns a reference to the **App** object every time the **IApplication** object is requested. Moreover, the **App** class is registered as singleton, meaning the DI container will create the instance of the **App** class once and return a reference to the same **App** object every time it is requested.

- **ConfigureMauiHandlers** is used to register custom handlers for existing built-in cross-platform UI controls or handlers for custom cross-platform UI controls.

- The **ConfigureFonts** method is used to configure custom fonts added to an application.

- **ConfigureAnimations** initializes a built-in mechanism that handles MAUI animations. There is no need to call this manually since it is called in a constructor of a **MauiAppBuilder** class.

- **ConfigureDispatching** initializes dispatcher provider, which is used primarily when the timer is needed or some delayed action needs to be run. By default, the dispatcher provider is also initialized automatically.

- **ConfigureEssentials** provides a way to configure **AppActions** (3D Touch/ Context menu items), assign map service token, or turn on version tracking. Version tracking is a very helpful feature represented by the static class **VersionTracking** that provides information regarding application build, such as the version of the first installation, whether the current launch is the first launch ever, and the current and previous version numbers.

- **ConfigureImageSources** allows the configuration of additional image source providers.

- **ConfigureEffects** is used to register custom reusable UI effects.

- **ConfigureLifecycleEvents** provides access to platform-specific life cycle events, so even platform-unique events can be handled, such as Android's **OnApplicationLowMemory**.

- The **Configuration** property provides access to the **ConfigurationManager**. This feature is helpful when you need to change the behavior of the application depending on the config stored in the ***.json** or ***.xml** file.

- The **Services** property provides access to the DI container to register your custom services. Besides, it enables adjusting the configuration of a logger.

- The **Logging** property returns the **ILoggingBuilder** object, which helps add new logging providers.

MAUI application life cycle events

Since .NET MAUI is window-based, the **Windows** class defines the cross-platform events and virtual methods to notify users about life cycle state changes. Virtual methods are called when events are raised. They are used to handle life cycle state changes inside a custom window class derived from the **Window** class.

To subscribe to life cycle events of the default window, override the **CreateWindow** method in the **App** class, as shown in the following code:

```
public partial class App : Application
{
    public App()
    {
        ...
    }


    protected override Window CreateWindow(IActivationState activationState)
    {
        Window window = base.CreateWindow(activationState);

        window.Created += OnWindowCreated;
        //subscribe to other lifecycle events here

        return window;
    }

    private void OnWindowCreated(object sender, EventArgs e)
    {
        Console.WriteLine("Window has been created");
    }
}
```

Open the blank MAUI application, override the **CreateWindow** method, and subscribe the following events to event handlers to get first hands-on experience with life cycle events:

- The **Created** event is raised after the native window has been created. Despite both the native window and handler having been created at this point, the window might not be visible yet. The event is accompanied by **OnCreated** virtual method.

- The **Activated** event is raised when the window has been activated. An active window can be said to have focus. The event is accompanied by **OnActivated** virtual method.

- The **Deactivated** event is raised when the window is no longer the focused window. However, the window might still be visible. The event is accompanied by **OnDeactivated** virtual method.

- The **Stopped** event is raised when the window is no longer focused and visible. It is important to stop all long-running processes to not consume device resources. Besides, save all the data that is unlikely to be lost because the application might be terminated by the operating system. The event is accompanied by **OnStopped** virtual method.

- The **Resumed** event is raised when an app resumes after being stopped. The event is raised only if the **Stopped** event has been raised earlier. It is a good point to refresh content that is on a visible page. The event is accompanied by **OnResumed** virtual method.

- The **Destroying** event is raised when the native window is being destroyed and deallocated. It does not mean the cross-platform window is destroyed. The same cross-platform window might be tied up to a new native window. Do not forget to unsubscribe native window events if you have subscribed to any, to avoid memory leaks. The event is accompanied by **OnDestroying.** virtual method.

- The **Backgrounding** event is raised on iOS and MacCatalyst when a window is going to the background and an application is configured as multi-window. The event is accompanied by **OnBackgrounding** virtual method.

Platform-specific life cycle events

.NET MAUI wraps original platform life cycle events defining delegates that are invoked when platform life cycle events are raised. Cross-platform life cycle events are mapped to platform-specific events, thanks to the built-in **LifecycleEventService**. This service implements the **ILifecycleBuilder** interface and provides a way to add handlers for each platform life cycle event.

This is what the **ConfigureLifecycleEvents** extension method of **MauiAppBuilder** is about. **ConfigureLifecycleEvents** accepts an **Action<ILifecycleBuilder>** delegate where you can declare your own handlers for any platform-specific life cycle event.

The following code demonstrates how a custom platform life cycle event handler can be declared in the **MauiProgram** class:

```
public static class MauiProgram
{
    public static MauiApp CreateMauiApp()
    {
        var builder = MauiApp.CreateBuilder();
        builder.UseMauiApp<App>()
            .ConfigureLifecycleEvents(lifecycleBuilder =>
            {
                lifecycleBuilder.AddAndroid(androidLifecycleBuilder =>
                {
                    androidLifecycleBuilder
.OnApplicationLowMemory(OnAndroidApplicationLowMemory);
                });
            });

        return builder.Build();

    }

    private static void OnAndroidApplicationLowMemory(Android.App.
Application app)
    {
        Console.WriteLine("Android is running low on memory");
    }
}
```

Here, the **OnApplicationLowMemory** extension method is called to register the life cycle event handler method **OnAndroidApplicationLowMemory**. Each platform life cycle delegate has a corresponding identically named extension method.

The coolest thing about this mechanism is that you can handle life cycle events you wish right from the cross-platform part of a solution, without diving deep into platform-specific API. .NET MAUI does all the dirty work for you. Despite that, some additional platform-specific knowledge might be needed to handle events properly.

The lists of .NET MAUI delegates that are invoked in response to each platform life cycle event are available in the official .NET MAUI documentation in the *Fundamentals* section.

MessagingCenter

Traditionally, events are used to make classes communicate. An event implements a publish-subscribe pattern and is the most straightforward approach. However, there are a few issues with events. The publisher and subscriber are coupled by object references to each other. It means there is no way to subscribe to an event to receive a message from another class without having a reference to a publisher class. Besides, the publisher's event will be kept as a reference to the subscriber until the subscriber is unsubscribed.

This may cause memory management issues, especially if someone forgets to unsubscribe an event of a long-lived object. It might seem to a developer that a subscriber object must be released by the garbage collector because of no variable that holds a reference. However, it is not, because an event of a publisher object still holds a reference to an object. Moreover, the publisher will normally call the event handler of the subscriber because the event was not unsubscribed explicitly, causing unexpected application behavior. Events might also be used for class internal communication. In that case, when a class subscribes to its own event inside the class, there is no need for unsubscribing explicitly.

Coupling is a second issue that might not seem harmful at the beginning. However, when an application grows, the need of having components/modules isolated from each other is almost inevitable. Without taking care of decoupling, maintenance costs grow fast and a codebase becomes less reusable. So, the need to have access to the whole publisher class just to subscribe to an event does not help reduce coupling and restrict access to class members that the subscriber does not need to have access to.

The **MessagingCenter** class provided by .NET MAUI is one of the ways to solve those issues. This mechanism allows publishers and subscribers to communicate without having reference to each other. In this approach, both the subscriber and publisher work with **MessagingCenter** (*Figure 3.15*):

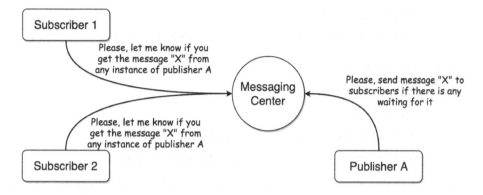

Figure 3.15: MessagingCenter flow

A subscriber asks **MessagingCenter** to let it know when a specific message arrives, giving the **MessagingCenter** an **Action** delegate to call. And subscriber does not care if any publisher object that can send such a message exists. A publisher also does not know if any object in memory is waiting for a message. It just asks **MessagingCenter** to forward a message if it knows any subscriber waiting for the message. This way, the **MessagingCenter** helps reduce code coupling.

The **MessagingCenter** provides two overloads of the static **Send** method with the following signatures declared in the **IMessagingCenter** interface:

- **TSender** is a type of publisher that must be a class. So, only classes are allowed to use **MessagingCenter**.

- **TArgs** is a type of argument. The second overload of the method enables the publisher to send a payload of any type:

  ```
  void Send<TSender>(TSender sender, string message) where TSender
  : class;
  ```

  ```
  void Send<TSender, TArgs>(TSender sender, string message, TArgs
  args)
      where TSender : class;
  ```

There are also two overloads of the static **Subscribe** method:

- **TSender** is a type of publisher a subscriber expects to receive a message from.

- **TArgs** is a type of argument a subscriber expects to receive from a publisher as a payload:

  ```
  void Subscribe<TSender>(
      object subscriber,
      string message,
  ```

```
        Action<TSender> callback,

        TSender source = null) where TSender : class;

    void Subscribe<TSender, TArgs>(

        object subscriber,

        string message,

        Action<TSender, TArgs> callback,

        TSender source = null) where TSender : class;
```

The important thing here is the composition of sender type, message argument value, and type of **args** (in the case of the second overload), which is used by the **MessagingCenter** to find appropriate subscribers in the list of subscriptions. For example, a subscriber will not receive a message when a publisher tries to send the message without a payload while the subscriber expects to receive the payload, even though the type of sender and message string value match.

Now, let us explore how to use **MessagingCenter**. In *"Chapter 3/1_MessagingCenter"* of the repository that accompanies this book, you will find an application that demonstrates how **MessagingCenter** works and some of the good practices applied to it.

Launch the application and follow the instructions shown in *Figure 3.16*. The application contains two pages: **HomePage** and **LoginPage**. This application simulates a login-like flow where the entered name and surname of the user are applied to the welcome page by tapping the **Login** button of the **LoginPage**. Here, the **HomePage** subscribes the message and **LoginPage** publishes it with a payload that contains the name and the surname of the user:

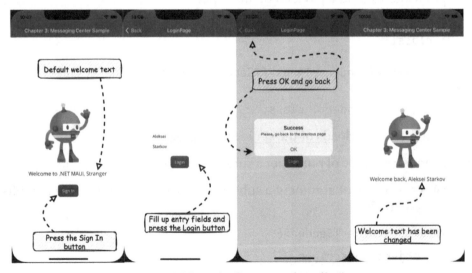

Figure 3.16: MessagingCenter sample application

In **LoginPage.xaml.cs**, you will find the button click handler that displays an alert and call of the **MessagingCenter.Send** method (see the following code):

```
private void OnLoginButtonClicked(object sender, EventArgs e)
    {
        var user = new User(FirstNameEntry.Text, LastNameEntry.Text);
        DisplayAlert("Success", "Please, go back to the previous page",
"OK");

        MessagingCenter.Send<LoginPage, User>(
            this,
            MessagingCenterMessages.LoginSuccess,
            user);
    }
```

HomePage.xaml.cs subscribes the message passing handler method delegate as a parameter to the **MessagingCenter** (see the following code):

```
public HomePage()
{
    InitializeComponent();

    MessagingCenter.Subscribe<LoginPage, User>(
        this,
        MessagingCenterMessages.LoginSuccess,
        OnLoginSuccessMessageRecieved);
}

private void OnLoginSuccessMessageRecieved(LoginPage sender, User user)
{
    MessagingCenter.Unsubscribe<LoginPage, User>(
        this,
        MessagingCenterMessages.LoginSuccess);

    WelcomeLabel.Text = $"Welcome back, {user.FirstName} {user.
LastName}";
    SignInButton.IsVisible = false;
}
```

There are a few things that need to be clarified here. The **this** keyword refers to the current instance of the class. As you remember, the **Send** and **Subscribe** methods require references to sender and subscriber objects, respectively. That is why **this** is passed to the **Send** and **Subscribe** methods as a first parameter.

As you learned from the signatures of methods, the second parameter must be a string value of the message. However, the value of the **MessagingCenterMessages. LoginSuccess** property is passed instead.

MessagingCenterMessages is a static class you can find in the **MessagingCenter Messages.cs** file and the following code snippet:

```
public static class MessagingCenterMessages
{
    public static string LoginSuccess => nameof(LoginSuccess);
}
```

Thanks to the **nameof** expression, the **LoginSuccess** property returns a string that contains the name of the property. This is a good practice to use as few hand-written string values (also called magic strings) in a codebase as possible. **MessagingCenter** uses message value while searching for the right subscription to send a message to. It means the developer must be extremely careful with a hand-written message string value because a simple typo easily breaks the behavior of the application. Moreover, with a magic string, the compiler cannot catch a problem. Sometimes the source of a problem might be identified quickly. Other times, such reliance on magic strings leads to issues in production, unsatisfied end user, and hours spent by a tester and a developer trying to figure out where the problem is. So, the simple class that holds message strings reduces the risk of issues and increases code maintainability.

The **User** class shown in the following code is used by the application as a payload of the message. This class serves a few purposes here. Obviously, it holds values that must be sent to a subscriber:

```
public class User
{
    public string FirstName { get; }
    public string LastName { get; }

    public User(string firstName, string lastName)
    {
        FirstName = firstName;
```

```
        LastName = lastName;

    }

}
```

However, along with fixed message values stored in a separate place, it represents another good practice: use the **message** parameter only as an identifier of a message but use the **args** parameter for any data that needs to be sent. Besides, create a separate class or struct for that data even when you need to send a simple piece of data, like a single number. It might not seem obvious, but on the one hand, creating a separate data transfer class costs nothing to a developer, while on the other hand, such an approach significantly increases code readability, maintainability, and scalability when an application grows.

When you do not want to receive messages anymore, the **Unsubscribe** method comes in. There are two overloads of this method, i.e., for the message with and without payload (args):

void Unsubscribe<**TSender**>(

    object subscriber,

    string message) where **TSender** : **class**;

void Unsubscribe<**TSender**, **TArgs**>(

    object subscriber,

    string message) where **TSender** : **class**;

In the sample application, the **Unsubscribe** method is called inside the **OnLoginSuccessMessageRecieved** handler method.

There is a significant difference here in comparison to C# events related to coupling and memory management issues mentioned earlier. Unlike the event that must be unsubscribed explicitly to avoid memory leaks caused by longer-lived publisher object, **MessagingCenter** takes cares of it for you. With **MessagingCenter**, you must unsubscribe messages only when an application's business logic requires it.

This is possible thanks to weak references represented by the **WeakReference** class. The **MessagingCenter** uses weak references to hold references of subscriber and message handler delegate. A weak reference provides access to the object while allowing the GC to collect the object at the same time. So, before calling the callback delegate of a subscriber, the **MessagingCenter** checks whether the subscriber object was not collected by the GC.

The task for you: launch the application again, set breakpoints in different places, and observe how it executes.

There are a few things worth keeping in mind about the **MessagingCenter**. It does not guarantee that the message will be received. There is a chance a message will be sent before any subscription is registered.

The next thing is coupling: while subscriber and publisher objects do not have access to each other, the subscriber still must know the type of publisher class. This is not a big problem, but it makes full decoupling impossible.

The **MessagingCenter** is a helpful tool, especially when some information or notification should be sent by the fire-and-forget principle. However, it is better to consider if **MessagingCenter** is the best solution for a particular case. If so, following good practices is highly recommended.

Dealing with image resources

It is hard to imagine an application, especially a mobile one, without images. Images lend a sophisticated look and feel to an application. However, each platform has different image requirements, different naming conventions, and so on. Moreover, numerous devices with different screens leads to the requirement for adding each image at different resolutions for better rendering performance.

In a .NET MAUI application, you do not need to specify multiple copies of an image. In. .NET MAUI, an image is added once, and then it is prepared and added to the app package automatically in a build time to meet the requirements of every platform.

With this section, we start working on the application that we will improve in each subsequent chapter by applying new knowledge. As a first step, we must create an initial clean project. Follow the given instructions and use the project in the **Chapter_3/2_LearningMauiBankingApp_CleanProject** folder of the repository accompanying the book as an inspiration:

1. Create a new project using the **.NET MAUI App** template of Visual Studio and call it **LearningMauiBankingApp**.

2. Remove the **AppShell** and **MainPage** pages (both ***.xaml** and ***.xaml.cs** files).

3. Remove all existing images from the **Resources/Images** folder.

4. Remove all files from the **Resources/Fonts** folder.

5. Remove the call of the **ConfigureFonts** method from the **MauiProgram. CreateMauiApp** method.

6. Remove all files from the **Resources/Styles** folder.

7. Remove all Resources from the **App.xaml** file. Here's a result you should get:

```
<Application xmlns="http://schemas.microsoft.com/dotnet/2021/maui"
             xmlns:x="http://schemas.microsoft.com/winfx/2009/xaml"
             x:Class="LearningMauiBankingApp.App"/>
```

8. Add a new folder to the project called **Pages**.

9. Add a new page to the **Pages** folder called **HomePage**. Use .NET MAUI **ContentPage** (XAML).

10. Assign **HomePage** to the **MainPage** property of the **App** class instead of the AppShell we had removed recently. Do not forget to add **using LearningMauiBankingApp.Pages;** at the top of the **App.xaml.cs** file.

Now, let us add a background image for the **HomePage**. Right-click on the **Resource/Image** folder and select **Add → ExistingFiles**. Then, choose the **light_background.png** image from the **LearningMauiBankingApp_Assets/Images** folder of the repository. After the image has been added to the project, set the build action for the image file to **MauiImage** (*Figure 3.17*):

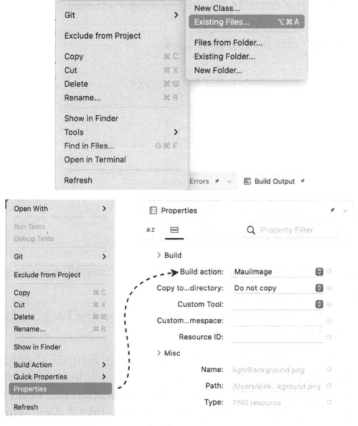

Figure 3.17: *Configuring image resource*

Next, go to the **HomePage.xaml** and **HomePage.xaml.cs** files and modify them as shown in the following code snippet:

```
//HomePage.xaml
<ContentPage xmlns="http://schemas.microsoft.com/dotnet/2021/maui"
             xmlns:x="http://schemas.microsoft.com/winfx/2009/xaml"
             x:Class="LearningMauiBankingApp.Pages.HomePage"
             Title="HomePage">
    <Grid>
        <Image Source="light_background.png" Aspect="AspectFill"/>
    </Grid>
</ContentPage>


//HomePage.xaml.cs
using Microsoft.Maui.Controls.PlatformConfiguration;
using Microsoft.Maui.Controls.PlatformConfiguration.iOSSpecific;

namespace LearningMauiBankingApp.Pages;

public partial class HomePage : ContentPage
{
    public HomePage()
    {
        InitializeComponent();
        On<iOS>().SetUseSafeArea(false);
    }
}
```

Use the **Chapter_3/3_LearningMauiBankingApp_ImageResources** project from the repository in case of any doubts.

Congratulations! Now your application has a nice-looking background. Let us take a closer look at image resources.

.NET MAUI supports all standard platform image formats, including **Scalable Vector Graphics (SVG)**. However, it is important to know that SVG images are converted to PNGs and are added to the actual application in a build time. Because of that, the ***.png** extension must be used in XAML and C# code while consuming SVG images.

When you check the code of the ***.csproj** file, you will find that each image resource has its own entry specifying the resource. Look at the following code; the **MauiImage** here is actually the build action of the resource:

```
<ItemGroup>

    <MauiImage Include="Resources\Images\light_background.png" />

</ItemGroup>
```

Looking at the filename of the image, you might notice that it has only lowercase letters and an underscore. Since resources are cross-platform, they should comply with the naming rules of each platform. In the case of image filenames, Android rules require image filenames to be in lowercase, to start and end with a letter character, and to contain only alphanumeric characters and underscores. Breaking those rules causes a compilation error.

Besides the **Include** attribute, the following attributes might be added to the image resource:

- The **BaseSize** attribute value represents the baseline density of the image and is effectively the 1.0 scale factor for the image. In fact, this is a size you would use in your code. The .NET MAUI uses this size to generate copies of the image with appropriate resolutions. Next, the runtime decides which resolution option to choose according to the screen characteristics of a given device. For example, there are five scale factor options on Android: 1.0 (mdpi), 1.5 (hdpi), 2.0 (xhdpi), 3.0 (xxhdpi), and 4.0 (xxxhdpi). iOS has three options: 1.0 (@1x), 2.0 (@2x), and 3.0 (@3x). Example: BaseSize="300,200", where 300 is the width and 200 is the height. If you do not specify a **BaseSize** (as we did with **light_background.png**), the image is not resized. If you do not specify a **BaseSize** value for an SVG image, the dimensions specified in the SVG are assumed to be the base size.

- Setting the Resize attribute to false stops vector SVG images from being resized, for example: Resize="false".

- The **TintColor** attribute is used when you want to render an icon or simple image in a different color than the original image. Hex value or a .NET MAUI color value can be used, for example: TintColor="#FF0000" or TintColor="Red".

- The **Color** attribute is used to specify the background color for an image. Hex value or a .NET MAUI color value can be used, for example: TintColor="#FF0000" or TintColor="Red".

The general recommendation regarding images is to use vector images as much as possible. Here are a few crucial advantages of vector images:

- Thanks to the XML-based format, SVG vector images are lightweight and easy to modify.

- It is hard to make a mistake dealing with resource resolution and sizes. Bringing bitmap resources without big enough resolution leads to blurring when upscaled, while vector images always look sharp.

- The SVG format is extremely popular. There are tons of free and paid ready-to-use SVG icons and images on the internet.

Application icon

The icon of the application is the first thing that an end user interacts with. The application icon appears in multiple places across the ecosystem of whatever operating system a user prefers. For example, on iOS, the app icon appears in the App Store, on the home screen, in Settings, notifications, and so on.

Similar to image resources, .NET MAUI takes care of generating appropriate copies of the application icon for each platform, and in each specific place of an ecosystem, the icon is displayed. At build time, the icon is automatically resized and added to the package of an application.

If you take a look at the source code of the **LearningMauiBankingApp.csproj** file, you will find the entry specifying the application icon:

```
<!-- App Icon -->

<MauiIcon Include="Resources\AppIcon\appicon.svg"

        ForegroundFile="Resources\AppIcon\appiconfg.svg"

        Color="#512BD4" />
```

Besides, the **AppIcon** folder of the **Resources** directory contains two vector images: **appicon.svg** and **appiconfg.svg**. Let's try to figure out what is it all about.

- The **MauiIcon** entry of the ***.csproj** file specifies the icon of the application. Since the .NET MAUI generates numerous images of different sizes for each platform using that specification, it is highly recommended to use vector images. As in the case of the **MauiImage**, the **MauiIcon** is a build action for the **appicon.svg** file, letting the builder know what image must be used as the application icon.

- The **Include** attribute specifies a file that must be used as an application icon.

- Instead of adding a single image containing both background and icon, a so-called **Composed** icon can be applied. In such a case, the **ForegroundFile** optional attribute is used for the actual icon, and the **Include** attribute is used for the background.

- If you wish to specify a composite icon but with a solid-colored background, you can use the **Color** attribute instead of the image for the background. In such a case, add an image with transparent background to the **Include** attribute value and specify the **Color** attribute value for the solid background. Hex value or a .NET MAUI color value can be used in the same manner as with a **MauiImage**.

- The image used as **ForegroundFile** can be tinted using the **TintColor** attribute.

- The **ForegroundScale** attribute value is used to apply the scale factor to the **ForegroundFile** image.

Let's now replace the icon of our **LearningMauiBankingApp**. We will use the composite icon with transparent background and solid background color.

1. Replace the existing **appicon.svg** and **appiconfg.svg** files with the ones in the **LearningMauiBankingApp_Assets** folder of the repository.

2. Modify the **MauiIcon** entry of the ***.csproj** file, as shown in the following code snippet:

```
<!-- App Icon -->

<MauiIcon Include="Resources\AppIcon\appicon.svg"

          ForegroundFile="Resources\AppIcon\appiconfg.svg"

          ForegroundScale="0.65" />
```

The important thing here is that you must uninstall the application from the device or the simulator/emulator you use before deploying the application with an updated icon. It is also recommended to perform the **Build → Clean All** action in Visual Studio before deploying.

Congratulations! Now you have your custom icon for the application. Again, in the case of any doubts, look at the **Chapter_3/4_LearningMauiBankingApp_AppIcon** project in the repository.

The .NET MAUI enables you to specify different application icons per platform if needed. To do so, add files to the **Resources/AppIcon** folder and add another **MauiIcon** entry with the **Condition** attribute to the **.*csproj** file, as follows:

```
<!-- App icon for Android -->

<MauiIcon Condition="$([MSBuild]::GetTargetPlatformIdentifier('$(Target-
Framework)')) == 'android'"
```

```
    Include="Resources\AppIcon\anothericon.svg"

    ForegroundFile="Resources\AppIcon\anothericonfg.svg"

    TintColor="#40FF00FF" />


<!-- App Icon -->

<MauiIcon Include="Resources\AppIcon\appicon.svg"

    ForegroundFile="Resources\AppIcon\appiconfg.svg"

    ForegroundScale="0.65" />
```

You can set the target platform by changing the value compared in the condition to one of the following values:

- ios
- maccatalyst
- android
- windows

Using the icons with a different filename than the default means you must remember to update the platform-specific configuration.

For Android

1. Go to **Platforms/Android/AndroidManifest.xml**.

2. Modify the values of the **android:icon** and **android:roundIcon** attributes. For the icon with the **anothericon.svg** filename, it should be **android:icon="@mipmap/anothericon" android:roundIcon="@mipmap/anothericon_round"** consequently.

For iOS and macOS (MacCatalyst)

1. Go to **Platforms/iOS(or MacCatalyst)/info.plist**. To edit the source code of the ***.plist** files, right-click on the file and select **Open With → XML (Text) Editor**, or use an external editor, e.g., Visual Studio Code.

2. Find the **XSAppIconAssets** entry with a corresponding string node defined after it.

3. Modify the string value. For the icon with the **anothericon.svg** filename, it should be **Assets.xcassets/anothericon.appiconset**.

Splash screen

A splash screen is a special view on Android and iOS that is displayed during application initialization. The splash screen is displayed immediately when an app is launched to let the user know that an application is initialized.

In .NET MAUI, a splash screen is initialized in a single place, automatically resized, and added to an app package. The splash screen icon is placed in the **Resources/Splash** folder and has its own build action, that is **MauiSplashScreen**. Knowing the name of a build action, you can easily find the corresponding entry in the ***.csproj** file.

The process of specifying your custom splash screen is similar to the application icon. Let's change the splash screen on **LearningMauiBankingApp**. Use the **Chapter_3/5_LearningMauiBankingApp_SplashScreen** and **Chapter_3/ 5_ LearningMauiBankingApp_SplashScreen_AndroidAnimated** applications in case there are any doubts related to this section.

1. Replace the existing **splash.svg** file with the one from the **LearningMauiBankingApp_Assets** folder of the repository.

2. Modify the **MauiSplashScreen** entry of the ***.csproj** file, as shown in the following code snippet:

```
<!-- Splash Screen -->

<MauiSplashScreen Include="Resources\Splash\splash.svg"

                  Color="#171717"

                  BaseSize="200,200" />
```

In addition, you can also define different **MauiSplashScreen** items for different platforms by specifying the **Condition** property (look at the **SupportedOSPlatform Version** entries of ***.csproj** for the example).

Starting from v12, Android supports animation to be played on the splash screen. Since other platforms do not currently support splash screen animations, the splash screen animation file cannot be unified or assigned from the cross-platform level for Android only. However, the splash screen can be overridden on a platform level with Android **Animated Vector Drawable** in three simple steps.

First, create the **drawable** folder in **Platforms/Android/Resources** and add your Animated Vector Drawable image (suppose it is called **splash_screen_icon.xml**). Do not forget to apply the **AndroidResource** build action to it.

Then, create **styles.xml** file in the **Platforms/Android/Resources/values** folder and add the following content to it:

```xml
<resources>
    <style name="MainTheme" parent="Maui.SplashTheme">
        <item name="android:windowSplashScreenBackground">#171717</item>
        <item name="android:windowSplashScreenAnimatedIcon">@drawable/
splash_screen_icon</item>
        <item name="android:windowSplashScreenAnimationDuration">1000</
item>
        <item
name="android:windowSplashScreenIconBackgroundColor">#171717</item>
        <item name="android:windowSplashScreenBehavior">icon_preferred</
item>
    </style>
</resources>
```

Next, apply the **MainTheme** in the **MainActivity.cs**, as follows:

```
[Activity(Theme = "@style/MainTheme", MainLauncher = true ...
```

A task for you:

Try to specify a different splash screen for Android using any image you wish. Use additional entry with the Condition attribute.

Fonts

It is hard to imagine a modern application with advanced UI without custom fonts. .NET MAUI enables you to add **TTF** and **OTF** fonts and use them in the code of an application.

As with many other resources, fonts are added and registered once. They are typically stored in the **Resources/Fonts** folder. Every custom font must have **MauiFont** build action and must be registered using MauiAppBuilder.

Before adding resources, let us add some text to the **HomePage** of our banking app. Modify **HomePage.xaml** as shown in the following code snippet:

```xml
<ContentPage xmlns="http://schemas.microsoft.com/dotnet/2021/maui"
             xmlns:x="http://schemas.microsoft.com/winfx/2009/xaml"
             x:Class="LearningMauiBankingApp.Pages.HomePage"
             Title="HomePage">
    <Grid>
        <Image Source="light_background.png" Aspect="AspectFill"/>
```

```
    <Label Text="Learning MAUI Banking App"
           VerticalOptions="Center"
           HorizontalOptions="Center"
           FontSize="22"/>
  </Grid>
</ContentPage>
```

As a next step, add font files from **LearningMauiBankingApp_Assets/Fonts** to the **Resources/Fonts** directory of the project. Do not forget to set the **MauiFont** build action for each file.

Then, register fonts as follows:

```
public static class MauiProgram
{
    public static MauiApp CreateMauiApp()
    {
        var builder = MauiApp.CreateBuilder();
        builder
            .UseMauiApp<App>()
            .ConfigureFonts(fontCollection =>
            {
                fontCollection.AddFont("Poppins-Bold.ttf", "Poppins-Bold");
                fontCollection.AddFont("Poppins-Regular.ttf", "Poppins-Regular");
                fontCollection.AddFont("Poppins-SemiBold.ttf", "Poppins-SemiBold");
            });

        return builder.Build();
    }
}
```

Here, the first parameter accepts the name of a file, but the second parameter is your custom alias that can be used in XAML and C# code as a string value. There are no limitations regarding the alias name. When fonts are ready to be consumed, it is time to apply one of them to the recently added label. So, assign Poppins-Bold font to the label control, as shown in the following code:

```
<Label Text="Learning MAUI Banking App"

        VerticalOptions="Center"

        HorizontalOptions="Center"

        FontSize="22"

        FontFamily="Poppins-Bold"/>
```

Use the project named **6_LearningMauiBankingApp_Fonts** from the repository in case of any doubts.

> **A task for you: Try to apply different fonts to the text and check whether it changes.**

Conclusion

Congratulations! You did an impressive job learning the fundamentals of .NET MAUI. While Xamarin was amazing technology for the time, everything is going forward. Including cross-platform GUI application development into a single .NET platform became a perfect opportunity to reshape the good old Xamarin into a modern .NET MAUI framework, making changes in basics and improving the whole platform.

Meanwhile, the main idea remains the same: to turn cross-platform code into platform-native code while adding new features to maximize the performance of development teams.

You probably were confused about touching *.xaml and *.xaml.cs files. So, in the next chapter, we will start answering your questions about UI-related code and continuing work on our banking app.

Points to remember

- In the .NET MAUI platform, native APIs are bound to the .NET, for example, .NET for iOS, .NET for Android.

- Xamarin.Forms renderers were replaced with Handlers. However, .NET MAUI allows the use of renderers to make the transition from Xamarin to MAUI easier for existing applications.

- The cross-platform UI control and handler both depend on an abstraction of the interface instead of a dependency on concrete classes.

- Handler has its own life cycle and life cycle events.

- Reflection is not used to register Handlers since Handlers are registered manually at the start of an application.

- .NET Runtime and Android Runtime work together on Android.

- .NET MAUI supports multi-window cross-platform applications (except iOS).

- After an application is turned to the Stopped state, the operating system might terminate the application without any notification.

Questions

1. What are the advantages and disadvantages of cross-platform development?

2. When is cross-platform development with MAUI most beneficial?

3. What are mappers?

4. What is a managed code?

5. Why is JIT compilation restricted on iOS?

6. What is a MacCatalyst?

7. What is an extension method in C#?

8. What is MauiAppBuilder needed for?

9. What are the best practices while working with MessagingCenter?

Join our book's Discord space

Join the book's Discord Workspace for Latest updates, Offers, Tech happenings around the world, New Release and Sessions with the Authors:

https://discord.bpbonline.com

CHAPTER 4
In and Out of UI Development

Introduction

The look and feel of an application plays a crucial role when it comes to making a user fall in love with the application and keeping this feeling consistent in the long run. UI/UX professionals do awesome jobs these days, researching and creating beautiful and interactable user interfaces. So, we as developers should be ready to make designers' fantasies come alive and provide our technical opinion about constraints and implementation complicity. Besides, it's equally important to know how to create extendable and maintainable cross-platform UI code.

Structure

In this chapter, we will cover the following topics:

- Challenge of screens and sizes: pixels, points, and units
- What is XAML about?
- Markup extensions
- UI: Looking through the developer's eyes
- Base types of UI elements

- Content page

- Image

- Label

- Text input controls

- Button and ImageButton

- Layouts Overview

- StackLayout

- Bindings Mechanism

- Attached properties

- NavigationPage

- Grid

- BindableLayout and DataTemplate

- Showing modal pages

- Picker

- Pop-ups

- View-to-view binding

- Resources

- Styles

Objectives

This chapter is all about creating a user interface. You will learn essential fundamentals such as XAML language, layering, bindings, pages, and how different platforms handle various device screens.

Continuing the development of the banking app, we will add many new UI elements by applying newly learned theory to practice.

By the end of the chapter, you should be able to create custom-designed user interfaces and optimize your codebase using XAML resources and styles.

During practical parts, feel free to experiment with settings of UI controls and look at the previous sections or the previous chapter, if needed. Such a self-driven exploration can double the effect of learning. Access to the book's repository is strongly recommended.

Challenge of screens and sizes: pixels, points, and units

There are several different devices with different screens. Each screen has a set of characteristics that play a crucial role when it comes to the look and feel of a device and the applications it runs.

Physical **display size** and **display resolution** are the basic characteristics. While the display size is the length of its screen measured diagonally in inches (e.g., the display size of the iPhone 13 is 6.1 inches), the display resolution is quoted as *width x height*, in *pixels* (the display resolution of the iPhone 13 is 1170 x 2532 pixels, as shown in *Figure 4.1*). Thus, it can be said that the display with a resolution of 1170 x 2532 pixels holds 2,962,440 pixels:

iPhone 13

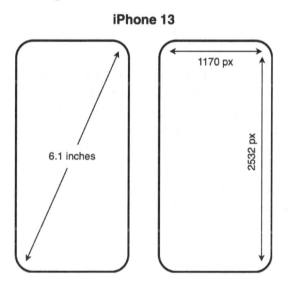

Figure 4.1: *The screen size and resolution of the iPhone 13*

The pixel is the smallest piece of viewable information displayed by a screen. It's a tiny colored dot where the required color is achieved by mixing red, green, and blue. Thanks to the huge number of pixels, a meaningful image can be shown. Moreover, the display of the same size, but with a bigger resolution, ensures an better quality images (refer to *Figure 4.2*):

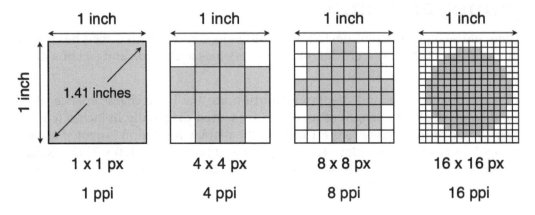

Figure 4.2: *Dependency between resolution, pixel density, and image quality*

As you can see, a single pixel can't display any meaningful image; a circle becomes more and more accurate as the resolution increases. Since same-sized screens may differ by resolution, as shown in *Figure 4.2*, that must be represented by another characteristic: **Pixel Per Inch (PPI)** often called **Pixel Density**. Pixel Density or PPI is a calculated characteristic of a display that mentions how many pixels are contained in one inch of a display's length.

Reading articles or even some documentation, you may encounter another anagram used instead of PPI: **Dots Per Inch (DPI)**. Despite the seeming similarity and the fact that DPI and PPI are commonly used interchangeably, there are differences between them:

- **DPI** refers to the number of printed dots contained within one inch of an image **printed by a printer**. DPI is a method to determine the print size of an image on paper.

- **PPI** refers to the number of pixels contained within one inch of an image **displayed on a display**. It represents the quality of a digital image displayed on-screen.

Before the era of smartphones, there was no variety of screen sizes and PPIs. Moreover, very few people in the world dealt with touchscreens, and almost no one interacted with them directly; touch pens were used instead. So, there was no demand to build applications that look and feel equally good on an infinite number of devices with unpredictable display characteristics. Thus, pixels stayed the main sizing units while programming the user interface.

The first generations of the iPhone had a 3.5" display of 320x480 px resolution and 163 PPI of pixel density. Then, iPhone 4 came with the same 3.5" size of display but doubled pixel density for better image quality. It had a resolution of 640x960 px with 326 PPI of density. Then came other iPhones with bigger screens and higher PPI, providing better image quality. The market of Android-based devices was developing more or less in the same way. The only significant difference was a wider variety of screen sizes and resolutions, apart from the new type of portable device, called tablets, which became available for the mass market. Desktop and laptop computer vendors also actively experimented with new types of screens. The only thing that stayed the same was a human user with the same hands, fingers, and eyes.

Now, suppose you need to add a button to your application. The application might be launched on any smartphone, from budget ones with low-resolution screens to high-end devices with full-HD or 4K resolution and high pixel density. Next requirement, since users' fingers are not becoming smaller as pixel density rises, the physical size of the button cannot be smaller than 0.4x0.4 inches, regardless of the screen resolution and pixel density. A display with a higher resolution should make UI look better, but elements' physical sizes should not be changed.

As you might have already guessed, the user interface that uses pixels as a sizing unit will be displayed properly only on one screen. Attempting to display the same elements sized with pixels on any other display leads to UI issues or even the inability to use an application (*Figure 4.3*):

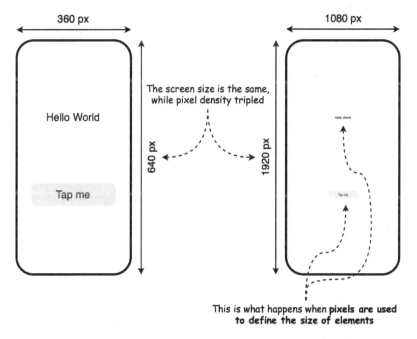

Figure 4.3: The issue with using pixels for UI elements

To resolve this problem, all major vendors introduced abstract units to work with the sizes and coordinates of user interface elements. Apple called it *Point*, Android developers used *Density-Independent Pixels (dp)*, and Windows introduced *Density-Independent Unit (DIU)*. Despite different names, the underlying idea is the same: the 1 abstract point equals 1 pixel for the screen with a baseline density (for example, 163 ppi). In the case of higher-density screens, the scaling factor is applied, recalculating points into an appropriate number of pixels. So, the 20 points of the height of a button defined by a developer are recalculated by a system into 40 pixels for a screen of 326 PPI.

In .NET MAUI, device-independent units used for sizes and coordinates of UI elements are recognized independently by each platform. In other words, the .NET MAUI unit is considered *density-independent pixels* on Android and points on Apple's systems.

What is XAML about?

XAML, which stands for **eXtensible Application Markup Language**, is an XML-based declarative language created by Microsoft. It was introduced in the late 2000s as a part of **Windows Presentation Framework** (**WPF**), changing the way the user interface is written. In *Windows Forms* (predecessor of WPF), a user interface was created using the same language that is used for business logic code, for example, C# or VB.NET. But with WPF, Microsoft offered a different, much like HTML, way to describe the hierarchy of the user interface. Many developers fell in love with XAML because the UI code became much more readable and maintainable. Later, Microsoft and third-party developers used XAML for other frameworks, mostly as a user interface markup language, to define UI hierarchy, UI elements, data bindings, and events. Xamarin was one of them. When the Xamarin team designed Xamarin. Forms, the WPF's approach, along with XAML, was adopted for cross-platform UI development as something natural.

This section is not a complete guide to XAML. It covers the basic XAML features and approaches. Lots of different XAML features and MAUI features related to XAML will be revealed in the upcoming sections and chapters.

A XAML-based user interface unit, whether a page, view, or control, consists of two files: ***.xaml**, and ***.xaml.cs**. The following code snippet shows a user interface code of a page called "**HomePage**".

```
<ContentPage xmlns="http://schemas.microsoft.com/dotnet/2021/maui"
             xmlns:x="http://schemas.microsoft.com/winfx/2009/xaml"
             x:Class="LearningMauiBankingApp.Pages.HomePage"
             Title="Home">
```

```
<ContentPage.Content>

    <VerticalStackLayout>

        <Label Text="Welcome to .NET MAUI!"

               VerticalOptions="Center"

               HorizontalOptions="Center" />

    </VerticalStackLayout>

</ContentPage.Content>

</ContentPage>
```

The syntax rules for XAML are similar to those of XML. However, unlike XML, where the value of attributes must be a string, the value of the attributes (also called Properties) can be any type in XAML.

An object element can be defined in two ways using brackets:

- **`<Label />`**: The simple object element that has no child elements is defined using the left-angle bracket (**`<`**), followed by the name of an object's class, for example, Label. The combination of slash and right-angle bracket (**`/>`**) closes the definition of the object.

- **`<VerticalStackLayout>Child     elements</VerticalStackLayout>`**: Both open and closing tags, along with object class name, are usually used when elements serve as containers for other elements (VerticalStackLayout contains Label) or to assign an object to some property of an element.

The next thing every root element (**ContentPage** in the case of **HomePage**, as shown earlier) contains is the declaration of namespaces. An XAML namespace is really an extension of the concept of an XML namespace. The primary concept that is added to the XAML is that the XAML namespace implies both a scope of uniqueness for the markup usage and influences how markup entities are potentially backed by specific CLR namespaces and referenced assemblies.

There are three types of XAML namespace declarations. The first declaration maps the default namespace for the MAUI framework.

`Xmlns="http://schemas.microsoft.com/dotnet/2021/maui"`

This namespace contains **ContentPage**, **VerticalStackLayout**, **Label**, and many other MAUI classes.

The second type of declaration maps a separate XAML namespace to the **x:** prefix.

`xmlns:x="http://schemas.microsoft.com/winfx/2009/xaml"`

`x:Class="LearningMauiBankingApp.Pages.HomePage"`

The relationship between the first and second types of declarations is that the **x:** prefix mapping supports the intrinsics that are part of the XAML language definition, and MAUI is an implementation that uses XAML as a language and defines a vocabulary of its objects for XAML. The MAUI vocabulary is mapped as the default because its usages will be far more common than the XAML ones, so it's optimal to use MAUI namespace members without any prefix. It's highly recommended to use the default **x:** prefix for mapping the XAML language intrisics to ensure consistency with project templates, documentation, and code samples.

The XAML namespace defines many commonly used features and datatypes that are essential, even for basic MAUI applications. For example, the **x:Class** attribute in the root element is necessary to join ***.xaml** and ***.xaml.cs** (also known as code-behind). The preceding code shows the **x:Class** attribute value containing the full path to the code-behind partial class, including its namespace (**LearningMauiBankingApp. Pages**).

Finally, any CLR namespace that contains public types can be mapped within an **xmlns** declaration, similar to how XAML namespaces are mapped to prefixes:

```
<ContentPage xmlns="http://schemas.microsoft.com/dotnet/2021/maui"

             xmlns:x="http://schemas.microsoft.com/winfx/2009/xaml"

             xmlns:customControls="clr-namespace:LearningMauiBankingApp.
Controls;assembly=LearningMauiBankingApp"

             x:Class="LearningMauiBankingApp.Pages.HomePage"

             Title="Home">

    <ContentPage.Content>

        <VerticalStackLayout>

            <customControls:MyCustomButton Text="Click Me" />

        </VerticalStackLayout>

    </ContentPage.Content>

</ContentPage>
```

The preceding example shows how to map the **LearningMauiBankingApp. Controls** namespace to the **customControls** prefix to consume your custom-made **MyCustomButton** in XAML code. The controls from third-party NuGet plugins can be utilized in XAML code in the same way by mapping the appropriate namespace to a prefix.

The code-behind ***.xaml.cs** file is used to describe the code that is joined with markup-defined objects. The following code is a code-behind of the preceding **HomePage**:

```
namespace LearningMauiBankingApp.Pages
{
    public partial class HomePage : ContentPage
    {
        public HomePage()
        {
            InitializeComponent();
        }
    }
}
```

As you can see, the namespace and the class name match the one assigned to the **x:Class** attribute, while the **HomePage** class derives **ContentPage**, a root element of XAML markup. Another important thing here is a call of the **InitializeComponent** method. This method loads the **HomePage.xaml** file and instantiates the whole UI tree described in it. It's highly recommended to put only necessary logic into the constructor to affect the constructor execution time to the minimum.

Elements described in XAML can be accessed from the code-behind class, as follows:

HomePage.xaml:

```
<Label x:Name="WelcomeLabel"
       VerticalOptions="Center"
       HorizontalOptions="Center" />
```

HomePage.xaml.cs:

```
public partial class HomePage : ContentPage
{
    public HomePage()
    {
        InitializeComponent();
        WelcomeLabel.Text = "Welcome to .NET MAUI!";
    }
}
```

To access an element from a code-behind class, the element must have the **x:Name** attribute specified. Then, the given name can be used in C# code to access the object of an element described in XAML and instantiated by the **InitializeComponent** method.

As was mentioned in the property, values of elements can be specified inline or between starting and closing tags. Look at the following code snippets:

```
<Label FontSize="32" Text="Hello World" />
```

```
<Label FontSize="32">

    <Label.Text>Hello World</Label.Text>

</Label>
```

These two elements are identical. The only difference is the way the **Text** property value is specified.

Exploring the XAML code of the **HomePage** provided, you might also notice that the content of **ContentPage** is described by putting **VerticalStackLayout** between starting and closing tags (**ContentPage.Content**), just like we specified the **Text** property of the **Label** element recently. However, the **VerticalStackLayout** element doesn't use the **Children** tag explicitly to describe child elements. The **Children** tag was skipped intentionally to show that some elements (so-called containers mostly) whose main purpose is to keep other elements inside, don't require **Content** or **Children** properties to be written explicitly. This is possible because those properties are marked as **ContentProperty** inside container classes. So, the following page markups are equivalent:

```
<ContentPage xmlns="http://schemas.microsoft.com/dotnet/2021/maui"

            xmlns:x="http://schemas.microsoft.com/winfx/2009/xaml"

            x:Class="LearningMauiBankingApp.Pages.HomePage">

    <VerticalStackLayout>

        <Label Text="Welcome to .NET MAUI!"

            VerticalOptions="Center"

            HorizontalOptions="Center" />

    </VerticalStackLayout>

</ContentPage>
```

```
<ContentPage xmlns="http://schemas.microsoft.com/dotnet/2021/maui"

            xmlns:x="http://schemas.microsoft.com/winfx/2009/xaml"
```

```
                x:Class="LearningMauiBankingApp.Pages.HomePage">
    <ContentPage.Content>
        <VerticalStackLayout>
            <VerticalStackLayout.Children>
                <Label Text="Welcome to .NET MAUI!"
                    VerticalOptions="Center"
                    HorizontalOptions="Center" />
            </VerticalStackLayout.Children>
        </VerticalStackLayout>
    </ContentPage.Content>
</ContentPage>
```

In XAML, all the controls expose not only properties but also events. The following code of a page and its code-behind show how to subscribe **Clicked event** of a **Button** control and handle it using a method declared in the code-behind class:

```
<ContentPage xmlns="http://schemas.microsoft.com/dotnet/2021/maui"
            xmlns:x="http://schemas.microsoft.com/winfx/2009/xaml"
            x:Class="LearningMauiBankingApp.Pages.HomePage">
    <VerticalStackLayout>
        <Button Text="Click me" Clicked="OnClickMeButtonClicked" />
    </VerticalStackLayout>
</ContentPage>


public partial class HomePage : ContentPage
{
    public HomePage()
    {
        InitializeComponent();
    }

    private void OnClickMeButtonClicked(object sender, EventArgs e)
    {
    }
}
```

As you can see, the **Clicked attribute** represents the **Clicked** event of a **Button** class. To subscribe to this event in XAML, the name of the event handler method must be used as a value of the **Clicked attribute**. Besides, you can subscribe to the event of an element from the code-behind class, just like an event of any other class. The only additional action needed here is to specify the **x:Name** attribute of the element to get access to its object. The **x:Name** attribute is not required when subscribing in XAML. Moreover, Visual Studio simplifies subscribing in XAML. Simply start writing event subscription markup, and Visual Studio will offer to finish markup for you. The event handler will be generated automatically in the code-behind file in this case.

Despite XAML being used as a primary tool for creating a user interface in MAUI, XAML is not required. The same result can be achieved by creating a user interface with C#. For example, the following page markup and C# class produce the same UI:

```xaml
<ContentPage xmlns="http://schemas.microsoft.com/dotnet/2021/maui"
             xmlns:x="http://schemas.microsoft.com/winfx/2009/xaml"
             x:Class="UIBasicsHelloWorld.XamlPage">
    <VerticalStackLayout VerticalOptions="Center">
        <Label Text="Welcome to .NET Multi-platform App UI"
               HorizontalOptions="Center" />
    </VerticalStackLayout>
</ContentPage>
```

```csharp
public class NoXamlPage : ContentPage
{
    public NoXamlPage()
    {
        var welcomLabel = new Label()
        {
            Text = "Welcome to .NET Multi-platform App UI",
            HorizontalOptions = LayoutOptions.Center
        };

        var stackLayout = new VerticalStackLayout()
        {
```

```
            VerticalOptions = LayoutOptions.Center
        };
        stackLayout.Children.Add(welcomLabel);


        Content = stackLayout;
    }

}
```

Markup extensions

XAML markup extensions allow element attributes to be set from sources other than literal text strings. On the programmatic level, a XAML markup extension is a class that implements the **IMarkupExtension** or **IMarkupExtension<T>** interface. The **IMarkupExtension** interface contains the **ProvideValue** method that returns a value of the **object** type. The **IMarkupExtension<T>** interface derives from **IMarkupExtension** and overloads the **ProvideValue** method, specifying the return value type using the generic parameter **T**.

The following markup extension allows you to construct a translucent color value using two parameters, i.e., source color and opacity parameter, to specify the value of the alpha channel:

```
[ContentProperty(nameof(SourceColor))]
public class TraslucentColorExtension : IMarkupExtension<Color>
{
    public Color SourceColor { get; set; }
    public double Opacity { get; set; } = 1;


    public Color ProvideValue(IServiceProvider serviceProvider)
    {
        return Color.FromRgba(
            SourceColor.R,
            SourceColor.G,
            SourceColor.B,
            Opacity);
    }


    object IMarkupExtension.ProvideValue(IServiceProvider
serviceProvider)
```

```
    {
        return ProvideValue(serviceProvider);
    }
}
```

Since the **IMarkupExtension<T>** interface derives from **IMarkupExtension**, it contains both versions of the **ProvideValue** methods. The new color here is created by the static **FromRgba** method, taking Red, Green, and Blue channel values from **SourceColor** and the Alpha channel value from the **Opacity** property.

The following code snippet shows how this markup extension can be consumed in XAML:

```
<ContentPage xmlns="http://schemas.microsoft.com/dotnet/2021/maui"
             xmlns:x="http://schemas.microsoft.com/winfx/2009/xaml"
             xmlns:mex="[specify the namespace here]"
             x:Class="UIBasicsHelloWorld.XamlPage">
    <VerticalStackLayout VerticalOptions="Center">
        <Label Text="First"
               TextColor="{mex:TranslucentColorExtension
SourceColor=LightCoral, Opacity=0.65}" />


        <Label Text="Second"
               TextColor="{mex:TranslucentColorExtension LightCoral,
Opacity=0.65}" />


        <Label Text="Third"
            <Label.Color>
                <mex:TranslucentColorExtension SourceColor="LightCoral",
Opacity="0.65" />
            </Label.Color>
    </VerticalStackLayout>
</ContentPage>
```

Any XAML attribute setting in curly braces is always a XAML markup extension (**First** and **Second** labels). However, the third label shows how markup extension can also be referenced without using curly braces. Another interesting thing is the difference between the markup of the first and the second labels. As you can see, the markup of the second label passes the source color value without specifying the property of the **TranslucentColorExtension** that the value is assigned. This is possible because the **SourceColor** property is marked as a **ContentProperty** (refer to the code snippet of the **TranslucentColorExtension** class).

XAML and .NET MAUI provide several ready-to-use built-in markup extensions. Here are some of them:

- The **x:Static** markup extension has a single property named **Member** of type string and marked as a **ContentProperty** that accepts a public constant, static property, static field, or enumeration. The extension retrieves the value of the **Member** and passes it to the XAML attribute.

- The **x:Reference** markup allows passing the reference of some XAML element to an attribute. The extension contains a single property named **Name** of type string where the value of the **x:Name** parameter of the referenced element must be assigned.

- The **x:Array** markup extension enables you to define an array in an XAML markup. The extension contains two properties: **Type** of type **Type** and **Items** of type **IList**.

- The **OnPlatform** markup extension enables you to set different values to the property of a UI element on a per-platform basis. For example, you can apply different fonts to text for iOS and Android.

- The **OnIdiom** markup extension is similar to the **OnPlatform** one. This extension enables you to apply different values per idiom. For example, you can apply different widths to a button for a phone, tablet, or desktop.

Of course, this is not a comprehensive list of built-in markup extensions. We will learn and use other markup extensions and those mentioned in the subsequent sections and chapters.

UI - looking through the developer's eyes

While a user sees UI as a flat set of elements, from the developer's perspective, UI is a structure organized in terms of UI elements hierarchy and Z-order.

The following XAML code describes a page that contains a scrollable list of colored rectangles and the **Add** button placed in the right-bottom corner of the screen:

```
<ContentPage xmlns="http://schemas.microsoft.com/dotnet/2021/maui"
             xmlns:x="http://schemas.microsoft.com/winfx/2009/xaml"
             BackgroundColor="LightSalmon"
             x:Class="BlankApp.MainPage">
  <Grid BackgroundColor="Gold">
```

```
    <ScrollView BackgroundColor="Violet" >
        <VerticalStackLayout Spacing="20"
BackgroundColor="DarkGray">
            <Rectangle BackgroundColor="Blue" HeightRequest="200"/>
            <Rectangle BackgroundColor="Red" HeightRequest="200"/>
            <Rectangle BackgroundColor="GreenYellow"
HeightRequest="200"/>
            <Rectangle BackgroundColor="Brown" HeightRequest="200"/>
            <Rectangle BackgroundColor="Green" HeightRequest="200"/>
            <Rectangle BackgroundColor="Pink" HeightRequest="200"/>
        </VerticalStackLayout>
    </ScrollView>

    <Button HeightRequest="100"
            WidthRequest="100"
            CornerRadius="50"
            FontSize="40"
            Text="+"
            VerticalOptions="End"
            HorizontalOptions="End"
            Margin="0,0,25,25"
            BackgroundColor="LightBlue"/>
    </Grid>
</ContentPage>
```

The Grid container here occupies the whole space of its parent, **MainPage**. Next, Grid contains two elements: the **VerticalStackLayout** container and the **Button**. They are on the same level of the visual tree hierarchy, but while stack layout occupies the whole space of the **Grid**, the **Button** is pinned to the right-bottom corner by applying the **End** value to **Vertical-** and **HorizontalOptions** settings. But how does MAUI know that the button must overlap **ScrollView**? When two elements are on the same level of the visual tree hierarchy, an element described lower is rendered in front.

Let's consider **ScrollView**. The **ScrollView** element is responsible for making an element it contains scrollable. Since no settings related to layout were changed, the **VerticalStackLayout** element occupies the whole space of the **ScrollView**. However, thanks to the **Spacing** setting, the child elements are rendered with a gap, so the background of **VerticalStackLayout** is visible. The difference between what is seen on a screen and the real structure of the visual tree is shown in *Figure 4.4*:

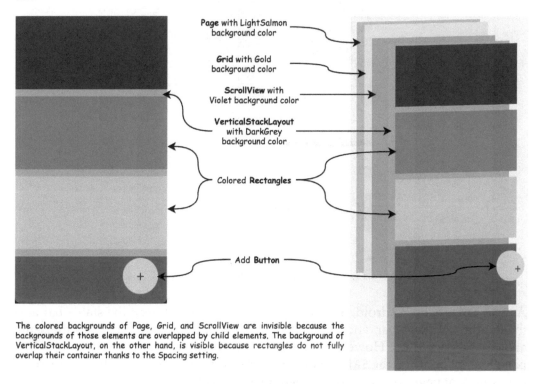

The colored backgrounds of Page, Grid, and ScrollView are invisible because the backgrounds of those elements are overlapped by child elements. The background of VerticalStackLayout, on the other hand, is visible because rectangles do not fully overlap their container thanks to the Spacing setting.

Figure 4.4: *The structure of UI elements*

By default, elements have a transparent background. As you might notice, all elements, including **Page**, have the color of a background specified. But the deeper an element is in the hierarchy, the closer it is to the front relative to its parent. That is why the colors of elements behind the **VerticalStackLayout** are invisible. However, try to add **Margin="20,0,20,0"** to the **VerticalStackLayout**, and you will see the Violet color of the **ScrollView** because **VerticalStackLayout** doesn't occupy the whole space of its parent anymore.

There is one more topic that must be covered in this section. There is a difference on mobile devices between the screen size, the space occupied by a page, and the space of a page available for its content. *Figure 4.5* demonstrates this difference:

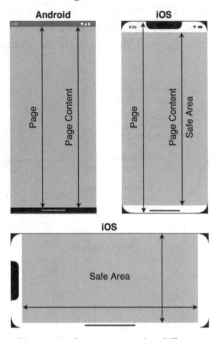

Figure 4.5: Screen occupation difference

As you can see, on Android, a page occupies the space between the status bar and the bottom soft keys bar, and the content of a page, by default, occupies the same area as the page does. However, on iOS, a page occupies the whole screen, while page content occupies the **Safe Area**. The **Safe Area** is an iOS-specific feature used to ensure that page content is positioned on an area of the screen that is fully visible and free from system elements. Fortunately, it's possible to ignore the Safe Area, which is good for applications with fully custom UI where you need full control under UI elements positioning.

Base types of UI elements

The UI of an application is made up of multiple elements like pages, labels, buttons, containers, and so on. However, there are characteristics and behaviors that are common for a few or even all elements. Moreover, it's sometimes necessary to create a custom UI control that must be compatible with the other elements. That is why .NET MAUI has a hierarchy of classes describing such common characteristics and behaviors of specific groups of UI elements. *Figure 4.6* shows the hierarchy of those base classes with lists of specific UI controls derived from each of them. Besides, it shows each base class's most important events, properties, and methods. Before detailing particular UI controls and features that base classes introduce, let's look at this hierarchy of base classes and describe their responsibilities:

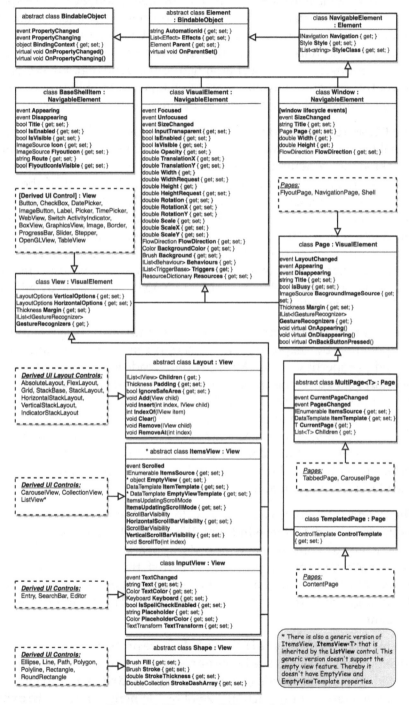

Figure 4.6: *Hierarchy of UI control classes*

Here are explanations of fundamental UI-related classes:

- The very base class in the hierarchy is the **BindableObject**. The responsibility of this class is to make UI controls support one of the most remarkable and fundamental features of MAUI related to UI: bindings. In short, binding enables you to make a connection between the property of the UI control and the property of an object assigned to the **BindingContext** property, so UI control can automatically react to changes in the binding context object. The mechanism of bindings will be detailed further in this chapter.

- The **Element** class introduces the **Parent** property that helps configure the visual tree of UI. For example, the **Parent** property of a button put into the **StackLayout** container contains the reference of that **StackLayout** object. Besides, thanks to the **Element** class, the child element of the visual tree inherits a binding context object of a parent. The **AutomationId** property is helpful when you need to test a UI by automated UI tests. An **Effect** allows the creation of a reusable set of platform-specific instructions to modify a native control the cross-platform control based on. So, the **Effects** property of the **Element** class makes reusability possible because effects can be attached to particular elements of UI in XAML or C# code by adding effects to the **Effects** collection.

- The **NavigableElement** class adds another two basic features to UI components by exposing the **Navigation** property and stylization-related properties. The **Navigation** read-only property contains a **NavigationProxy** object that enables you to perform navigations like we did while exploring **MessagingCenter**. Besides, **NavigationProxy** enables you to manage the navigation stack of a whole application. Handling styles is another responsibility of **NavigableElement**. The **Style** and **StyleClass** properties are used to store **Styles** applied to a UI component. Styles help reduce repetitive markups by grouping a collection of property values into one object to apply them to multiple UI elements.

- The **Window** class is already familiar to you. It contains a set of events and methods related to the window's life cycle, the root page, and different parameters to control the window's appearance. Besides, here we meet the **FlowDirection** property for the first time. It takes the eponymous **FlowDirection** enum that specifies whether the way of writing is Left-to-Right, Right-to-Left, or match parent element. The default direction is Left-to-Right.

- The members of the **VisualElement** class are probably met most often during development since **VisualElement** exposes the most basic appearance-related events, properties, and methods. **Width** and **Height** read-only properties represent the actual size of an element, while the **WidthRequest** and **HeightRequest** properties are used to enforce the fixed size of the element. The **Translation**, **Rotation**, and **Scale** properties are responsible for transformations. Those parameters are quite independent of the size or location of an element. For example, the element that is put into a container can be visually moved out of the border of the container using **Translation** properties. In a practice, such transformations are helpful when you need to implement a temporary visual effect. For example, you can make elements fly out of the screen edge while a user is scrolling the content by animating an element's position with the **TranslationX** property or draw a user's attention to some element by making the element pulsating using a scale factor animation. There are two properties to specify the background of an element: **BackgroundColor** and Background. **BackgroundColor** is used to set a solid color, while Background is used to apply a gradient brush. The **Opacity** property allows controlling the transparency of an element and accepts values from 0.0 to 1.0. It's important to remember that 0.0 opacity is not the same as a **False** value that might be set to the **IsVisible** property. While the **IsVisible** parameter set to false prevents an element from being rendered, **Opacity** set to 0 just makes an element transparent. In practice, it means that although an element with 0 opacity is invisible to the human eye, computing power is used to render it. Therefore an element with 0 opacity takes place on a screen and keeps being responsive to eventual touches while the element with False **IsVisible** is not. The **InputTransparent** flag controls the ability of an element to be responsive to user interactions like touch, swipe, and so on. Besides, the **InputTransparent** value is propagated to all child elements in a cascade way. The **IsEnabled** property controls not only the ability of an element to be interactable but may also affect the visual state of an element using **VisualStateManager**. For example, setting **IsEnabled** of the **Button** control to false greys the button out. The value of the **IsEnabled** property is not propagated to child elements.

- The **View** class is a base class for most UI controls. **VerticalOptions** and **HorizontalOptions** are responsible for the alignment of an element relative to its parent. For example, setting **Start** to **HorizontalOptions** positions an element on the left of the parent layout, and for **VerticalOptions**, it positions the element at the top of the parent layout. The **Margin** property represents the distance between an element and its adjacent elements. The value of the **Margin** property affects the element's rendering position and the rendering position of its neighbors. The collection of **GestureRecognizers** enables you to make any UI element interactable by adding a gesture recognizer object of a proper type to the element.

- **Pages** are derived from **VisualElement**. A page usually occupies the whole screen or window, and each page typically contains at least one layout (sometimes called container) derived from the **Layout** class. The **Page** class extends the **VisualElement** by adding page life cycle events and virtual methods. The **OnBackButtonPressed** virtual method can be overridden when you need to add some specific logic or disable the back button for a particular page.

- The generic **MultiPage** class is a base class for **TabbedPage** and **CarouselPage**, which provide alternative ways of navigating between pages. The generic parameter here is constrained by the **Page** class type. The common trait of **TabbedPage** and **CarouselPage** is that they keep several other pages as child elements and provide a mechanism to change a currently shown page.

- The main purpose of the **TemplatedPage** class is to add support for the **ControlTemplates**. **ControlTemplates** separate the UI for a custom page from the logic that the page implements. For example, a **ControlTemplate** can be created to define any common UI that will be used by multiple pages in an app. The **ControlTemplate** can then be consumed by multiple pages, with each page still displaying its unique content thanks to a place in a template reserved for the unique content of an actual page.

- The **Layout** class is a base class for the group of UI controls called **layouts**. The main idea of layouts is that they work as containers, storing and organizing other UI elements (including layouts) in a specific way. So, the most important class members of a base **Layout** class ensure child elements' management (for example, **Children** property, and the **Add, Insert, Clear, Remove** methods). The **Padding** property is similar to **Margin**; however, the **Padding** represents the distance between the edges of the layout and its children. The **IgnoreSafeArea** setting is helpful in situations when the Safe Area of iPhone and iPad must be ignored for some UI/UX-related reason.

- The **ItemsView** base class contains a common logic of controls that display a scrollable collection of elements. The **ItemsSource** property takes a collection of data objects, which are then used as binding contexts for the visual unit shown on a screen. The **ItemTemplate** property takes the UI template defined by a developer (usually in XAML) that says how a single visual unit must be presented on a screen. The view template assigned to **EmptyViewTemplate** is shown when the **ItemsSource** collection is empty.

- The **InputView** base class is responsible for handling features common to controls that support text input.

- The **Shape** class is a base class that handles common parameters of controls used to draw simple shapes.

Don't be scared by the amount of new information because most of the described features will be considered and practiced further.

Content page

When you create a page, your custom page (for example, **HomePage** in our **LearningMauiBankingApp**) is derived from some built-in page type. As you learned from the previous section, **ContentPage** is one of them. As you might have seen in the previous examples, pages derived from the **ContentPage** display a single child assigned to the **Content** property. The **ContentPage** is the simplest and the most commonly used type of page.

Image

You already know, from the previous chapter, how to add an image to the application. Now's the time to take a closer look at the **Image** control that displays an image.

The **Image** UI control derives the **View** class. The image displayed by the control can be loaded from a local file, a URI, an embedded resource, or a stream. It supports all popular image formats, including GIF animations and vector SVG files.

Let's consider the most important properties of the Image UI control:

- The **Source** property of type **ImageSource** specifies the source of the image.

- The **IsLoading** flag indicates the loading status of the image. For example, it can be useful when an image is loaded from the internet and you want to show some notification to the user while the download is in progress.

- The **IsAnimationPlaying**, of type **bool**, determines whether an animated GIF is playing or stopped.

- The **Aspect**, of enum type **Aspect**, defines the scaling mode of the image. We already used this property while adding the background image to our banking app in the previous chapter. The **AspectFill** value ensures that the image fills the parent container, preserving the aspect ratio.

- The abstract **ImageSource** class defines several static methods that can be used in C# code to load images from different sources. Each method returns an object of a source-specific type that derives the **ImageSource**.

- The **ImageSource.FromFile** method accepts the path of the local image file and returns a **FileImageSource**.

- The **ImageSource.FromUri** method returns an **UriImageSource** that downloads and reads an image from a specified URI.

- **ImageSource.FromResource** returns a **StreamImageSource** that reads an image file embedded in an assembly of an application.

- **ImageResource.FromStream** returns a **StreamImageSource** that reads an image from a stream that supplies image data.

When it comes to XAML, images can be loaded from files and URIs by specifying the filename of the URI as a string value for the **Source** property, as shown in the following code snippet:

```
<Image Source="background.png"/>
```

```
<Image Source="https://mywebsite.com/background.png"/>
```

In addition, you can create custom markup extensions to load images from resources or streams.

UriImageSource images are cached by default, with cached images being stored for 1 day. The caching strategy can be changed by setting the desired **TimeSpan** to the **CacheValidity** property and setting the **CachingEnabled** flag of **UriImageSource** as shown in the following code snippet:

```
<Image>
    <Image.Source>
        <UriImageSource Uri="https://mywebsite.com/background.png"
                        CacheValidity="15:00:00.0"
                        CachingEnabled="true"/>
    </Image.Source>
</Image
```

Label

The UI of every application contains at least a few lines of text. This makes the **Label** one of the most popular UI controls. The **Label** control displays single-line or multi-line text and exposes several properties to configure the appearance and behavior of a text.

To explore and describe the capabilities of the **Label** control, let's open the solution of the banking app we started creating, and modify the content of the **HomePage** XAML code as shown in the following code snippet. You can also use the **Chapter_4/1_ LearningMauiBankingApp_Label** solution from the book repository:

```
<Grid IgnoreSafeArea="True">
    <Image Source="light_background.png" Aspect="AspectFill"/>

    <VerticalStackLayout VerticalOptions="Center" Padding="16,16" >
        <Label Text="Main card"
```

```
                HorizontalOptions="Start"
                FontSize="20"
                FontFamily="Poppins-SemiBold"/>

        <Label Text="1882 8245 0010 0505"
                Margin="0,10"
                HorizontalOptions="Start"
                FontSize="16"
                FontFamily="Poppins-Regular"/>

        <Label HorizontalOptions="Start"
                FontSize="16"
                FontFamily="Poppins-Regular">
            <Label.FormattedText>
                <FormattedString>
                    <Span Text="05"/>
                    <Span Text=" / "/>
                    <Span Text="29"/>
                </FormattedString>
            </Label.FormattedText>
        </Label>

        <Label HorizontalOptions="Start"
                FontSize="32"
                FontFamily="Poppins-Light"
                Margin="0,64,0,0">
            <Label.FormattedText>
                <FormattedString>
                    <Span Text="$" FontFamily="Poppins-Bold" />
                    <Span Text="5253" FontFamily="Poppins-Bold" />
                    <Span Text="."/>
                    <Span Text="45"/>
                </FormattedString>
            </Label.FormattedText>
        </Label>

    </VerticalStackLayout>
</Grid>
```

This page's content markup describes a background image and a basic view of a user's bank card in the center of a root Grid layout. Let's move through the code.

The **IgnoreSafeArea** of the Grid layout is used to allow the Grid to occupy the whole screen on iOS devices.

Since **HorizontalOptions** and **VerticalOptions** are not specified explicitly for **Image** control, the default **FillAndExpand** value is used to occupy the whole Grid layout. The **AspectFill** value of the **Aspect** property ensures that the image fills the whole space available to the **Image** control without changing the proportions of the picture.

As you might notice, some elements have the **Margin** and **Padding** properties defined. As it was told recently, the **Margin** and **Padding** properties describe an element's outer and inner free spaces. Those properties accept the value of type **Thickness** that can be described in XAML using a few formats of string values where numbers are divided by commas. The "L,T,R,B" format specifies Left, Top, Right, and Bottom values. The "LR,TB" format specifies values to be applied to **Left&Right** and **Top&Bottom**, respectively. The "LTRB" format applies the value to each side. Try to add some **BackroundColor** to the **VerticalStackLayout** element and experiment with the **Padding** values.

A text might be set in two ways. The most common one is to just specify the **Text** property. The second way is to use the **FormattedText** property that accepts an object of the **FormattedString** type. With **FormattedString**, you can specify separate pieces of text (Spans) that are assembled into a single text later. The main thing here is that each Span not only exposes the text property but also other properties, allowing you to configure a unique appearance to a particular piece of text. In the preceding XAML code, the **FormattedText** is used to split the label text into pieces of text and apply a specific font to the dollar sign and the integer part of the bank card balance. The Span derives values of properties that are not specified explicitly from the parental **Label**.

A text declared in XAML can also contain unicode characters. For example, **
** adds the new line.

The **Label** control offers many possibilities for customization, thanks to its advanced properties. You are already familiar with the **Text** and **FormattedText** properties. Now let's explore and describe others to be ready to use them in the following sections:

- **VerticalTextAlignment** and **HorizontalTextAlignment** of type **TextAlignment** define the alignment of the displayed text. Don't confuse it with **HorizontalOptions** and **VerticalOptions** of an entire UI control.

- **TextType** of type **TextType** determines whether the **Label** should display plain text or HTML text.

- **TextTransform** enables you to specify the casting of the displayed text.

- The **TextDecorations** property provides an ability to apply underline and/ or strikethrough to the text. Apply the "Underline, Strikethrough" value to the property to set both.

- **TextColor** defines the color of the displayed text.

- **MaxLines** of type int specifies the maximum number of lines allowed in the **Label**.

- **LineBreakMode** determines how text should be handled when it can't fit in one line. Possible values: **NoWrap**, **WordWrap**, **CharacterWrap**, **HeadTruncion**, **TailTruncion**, **MiddleTruncion**.

- **FontSize** of type double defines the font size.

- **FontFamily** of type string defines the font family according to an alias set in the **MauiProgram.CreateMauiApp** method.

- The **FontAutoScaled** property defines whether the text will reflect the scaling preferences of the operating system. The default value is true.

- **FontAttributes** determines whether Bold or Italic styles need to be applied. Not every custom font supports font attributes.

- The **CharacterSpacing** property of type double sets the spacing between characters in the displayed text.

- **LineHeight** of type double specifies the multiplier to be applied to the line height.

The task for you: Try to experiment and explore the customization capabilities of the **Label** UI control by using the preceding properties.

Text input controls

There are three built-in UI controls derived from the **InputView** class: **Entry**, **Editor**, and **SearchBar**. Each serves its own purpose, but the text input is a feature common for them and propagated by the base **InputView** class. Let's look at the most important members they got from the **InputView**:

- The **Text** property contains the value entered by a user, or it can be pre-set from XAML or C# code.

- **TextColor** of type Color specifies the color of the text.

- The **TextChanged** event is raised right after the **Text** property has been changed. The arguments object contains old and new text values.

- The **IsSpellCheckEnabled** property controls whether spell-checking is enabled. It's enabled by default, but setting might be ignored for some types of keyboards.

- The **Placeholder** and **PlaceholderColor** properties define the placeholder text and color, respectively.

- **TextTransform** property is similar to one available in **Label** and specifies the casting of the entered text.

- **IsReadOnly** helps prevent an entry from being modified by a user.

- **MaxLength** of type int defines the maximum input length.

- The **CharacterSpacing** property of type double specifies the space between characters of **Text** and **Placeholder** values measured in device-independent units.

- The **Keyboard** property of type **Keyboard** specifies a type of keyboard presented when a user edits entry text. There are the following types of keyboards: **Default**, **Chat**, **Email**, **Numeric**, **Plain**, **Telephone**, **Text**, and **Url**.

The **Keyboard** class also has the **Create** factory method allowing a keyboard's behavior to be customized as shown in the following code snippet:

```
<Entry TextColor="Red">
    <Entry.Keyboard>
        <Keyboard x:FactoryMethod="Create">
            <x:Arguments>
                <KeyboardFlags>CopitalizeWord,Suggestions</KeyboardFlags>
            </x:Arguments>
        </Keyboard>
    </Entry.Keyboard>
</Entry>
```

x:FactoryMethod and **x:Arguments** are used to instantiate objects in XAML markup. A factory method is a public static method of a class that returns an object or value of the class or structure that defines that method. The **x.Arguments** markup specifies the arguments of a constructor or a factory method. For example, the following markup declares the **Color** object using the **FromRgba** factory method of the **Color** class:

```
<Label>
    <Label.TextColor>
        <Color>
            <x:Arguments>
                <x:Int32>92</x:Int32>
                <x:Int32>112</x:Int32>
                <x:Int32>32</x:Int32>
                <x:Int32>255</x:Int32>
            </x:Arguments>
        </Color>
    </Label.TextColor>
</Label>
```

In the case of the **Keyboard** class, the factory method accepts enum flags of the **KeyboardFlags** enum.

The **Entry** control is used to enter and edit a single line of text. It's worth saying that the **Entry** and **Editor** controls are very similar. The key difference between them is that the **Editor** control is used to enter and edit multiple lines of text, and the size of the **Editor** control can change its size automatically to accommodate the user's input, thanks to the **AutoSize** property. The **Entry** editor, in turn, can serve as a password entry field.

Now, let's add the simple login page to our banking app. Create a new page called **LoginPage** in the **Pages** folder and add the following content to it. Don't forget to assign a **LoginPage** object to the **MainPage** property in the **App.xaml.cs**. Use the **Chapter_4/ 2_LearningMauiBankingApp_Entry** application sample if needed:

```
<Grid IgnoreSafeArea="True">
    <Image Source="light_background.png" Aspect="AspectFill"/>

    <VerticalStackLayout VerticalOptions="Center" Margin="50,0">
        <Label HorizontalOptions="Center"
                HorizontalTextAlignment="Center"
                TextColor="#000000"
                FontFamily="Poppins-Regular"
                FontSize="24">
            <Label.FormattedText>
                <FormattedString>
```

```
                <Span Text="Welcome to the&#10;"/>
                <Span Text="Learning MAUI Banking"
FontFamily="Poppins-SemiBold"/>
            </FormattedString>
        </Label.FormattedText>
    </Label>


    <Entry Margin="0,40, 0, 10"
            BackgroundColor="#FFFFFF"
            PlaceholderColor="#8E8E93"
            TextColor="#000000"
            Placeholder="E-mail"
            FontFamily="Poppins-Regular"
            Keyboard="Email"
            ReturnType="Next"
            Completed="OnClientIdEntryCompleted"
            ClearButtonVisibility="WhileEditing"/>


    <Entry x:Name="PasswordEntry"
            BackgroundColor="#FFFFFF"
            PlaceholderColor="#8E8E93"
            TextColor="#000000"
            FontFamily="Poppins-Regular"
            Placeholder="Password"
            IsPassword="True"/>

 </VerticalStackLayout>
</Grid>
```

This page contains two **Entry** controls: for email and password. As you might notice, the first entry uses the **Next** appearance option for the return button of the keyboard. This is because we want to switch focus to the password entry by pressing the **Next** button. One of the members of the **Entry** control is the **Completed** event. The preceding code shows how the event handler (**OnClientIdEntryCompleted**) can be assigned to the event in XAML. This event handler must be placed in a code-behind file. So, add the following event handler method to the **LoginPage.xaml. cs** file:

```
private void OnClientIdEntryCompleted(object sender, EventArgs e)
{
    PasswordEntry.Focus();
}
```

Since the **x:Name** was specified for the second entry, the focus can be switched to the **PasswordEntry** control from the code-behind. Here are other class members the **Entry** exposes:

- **ClearButtonVisibility** controls whether a clear button is displayed.

- **CursorPosition** of type int represents the current position of the cursor. It can be also used to change the cursor position programmatically.

- **HorizontalTextAlignment** and **VerticalTextAlignment** define text alignment within the **Entry** control.

- The **SelectionLength** property of type int represents the length of selected text within the entry starting from the cursor position. Selection can also be made programmatically using the **SelectionLength** and **CursorPosition** properties.

- The **FontAutoScalingEnabled** flag defines whether the text will reflect the scaling preferences of the operating system.

- The **ReturnType** property defines the look of the return button of the keyboard.

- The **Completed** event is raised when the user finalizes the text with the return key.

The **SearchBar** control is similar to the **Entry** control and looks like Entry with extra features, such as the following:

- The **SearchBar** adds the **Cancel** button and the **CancelButtonColor** to define the color of the **Cancel** button.

- The **SearchButtonPressed** event is raised when the return button is pressed.

Button and ImageButton

Every login page must have a button that initiates the sign-in process and navigates a user further into an application. So, let's add a fancy-looking **Login** button below the password entry control. The markup of the button is shown as follows. Use the **Chapter_4/3_LearningMauiBankingApp_Button** application from the book repository if needed.

```
<Button Text="Login"
        Margin="0, 25, 0, 0"
        HorizontalOptions="Center"
        BackgroundColor="#FFFFFF"
        HeightRequest="44"
        WidthRequest="107"
        CornerRadius="12"
        TextColor="#000000"
        FontFamily="Poppins-Regular"
        FontSize="16"
        Clicked="OnLoginButtonClicked" />
```

Next, add the following event handler method for the **Clicked** event to the code-behind of the page. Let's allow this event handler to clear the text of the **PasswordEntry** so far.

```
private void OnLoginButtonClicked(object sender, EventArgs e)
{
    PasswordEntry.Text = string.Empty;
}
```

As you might notice while writing the button's markup, most of the **Button** class members, such as **TextColor** or **LineBreakMode**, are already familiar. However, here are a few new and old ones that require separate explanations:

- The **BorderColor** property of type Color describes the border color of the button.

- The **BorderWidth** property of type double defines the width of the button's border.

- The **CornerRadius** of type int enables you to specify the radius of every corner of the button's border.

- The **ImageSource** of type **ImageSource** specifies an image to be displayed next to the text. Just like in other controls, **ImagesSource** handles different image types (png, svg, and so on).

- The **ContentLayout** defines the **ButtonContentLayout** object that controls the position of the button image and the spacing between the image and text.

- The **Padding** property determines the button's padding.

Button also defines the **Clicked**, **Pressed**, and **Released** events. The **Pressed** event is raised when the button is pressed by a finger or a mouse button. The **Released** event is raised when the finger or mouse button is released. The **Clicked** event is raised when the finger or mouse pointer is released from the button's surface. The difference between the **Clicked** and **Released** events is that the **Clicked** event might not be raised if the finger or mouse pointer slides away from the surface of the button before being released.

The **ImageButton** control is a view that combines two controls: the **Button** and the **Image**. However, unlike the **Button**, **ImageButton** doesn't contain any text, and the image occupies all available surface of the button.

Layouts overview

As you already know, each visible UI element takes its place in the hierarchy of the visual tree. However, when multiple elements are on the same level of the hierarchy, there is a need to arrange and group them in a specific manner. This is where layouts come into the picture, allowing users to arrange and group UI elements put into them. As layouts are invisible in most cases but contain visible controls like labels or buttons, they are also called containers.

There are four layouts, as shown in the following figure:

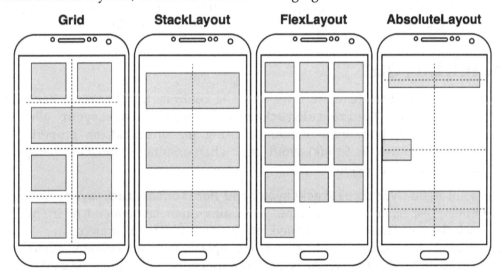

Figure 4.7: .NET MAUI Layouts

Grid and **StackLayout** are the most used layouts. Grid is used for displaying elements in rows and columns. **StackLayout**, along with its kinds **HorizontalStackLayout** and **VerticalStackLayout**, organizes elements in a one-dimensional stack. You already had a chance to observe the **VerticalStackLayout** in multiple previous application examples. The **FlexLayout** can arrange its children in a stack and can also wrap its children if there are too many to fit in a single row or column. **FlexLayout** accepts the set of rules to align and size multiple children with potentially unknown sizes. The gallery of anything is a common example of **FlexLayout** usage.

AbsoluteLayout is used to position and size elements using explicit values, or values relative to the size of the layout. **AbsoluteLayout** should be treated as a layout for special purposes when the element's size doesn't affect the positioning of other children. There are very few real-world examples of **AbsoluteLayout** use because almost every case can be covered much more easily using other layouts. For example, **AbsoluteLayout** can be used to implement the tutorial overlay UI pattern where the application highlights different elements of UI one by one, explaining the purpose of each element. However, the general advice is to avoid the **AbsoluteLayout** if possible.

Each layout has an accompanying **LayoutManager** responsible for measuring and positioning views. The **Measure** method measures all the layout's children by taking height and width constraints. The **ArrangeChildren** method then sets each view's size and position according to the layout's rules. That is why you must be careful with nesting. The more levels in the visual tree hierarchy, the more calculations are needed that might affect the performance of the application. The general advice is to think twice when adding another level of UI hierarchy and check whether the required look and feel can be achieved without additional nesting.

StackLayout

As mentioned earlier, there are three separate controls: **StackLayout**, **Vertical StackLayout**, and **HorizontalStackLayout**. Despite **StackLayout** allowing setting vertical or horizontal orientation using the **Orientation** property, it's recommended to use the **StackLayout** only when orientation must be changed in the runtime for some reason.

The point is that **VerticalStackLayout** and **HorizontalStackLayout** are more performant, especially when it comes to nesting other layouts and their children in stack layout. Those pre-oriented stack layouts avoid unnecessary layout calculations and enable nesting, for example, **HorizontalStackLayouts** in **VerticalStackLayouts**, which is not recommended for regular **StackLayout**. However, it's recommended in such cases to consider if the Grid layout can help reach the same look and feel without nesting.

The size of the stack layout depends on its children. Stack layouts wrap their children and can be compared to a stretchable bag whose size is defined by the things it contains.

Those are class members that can be used to configure stack layouts:

- The **Spacing** property of type double specifies the empty space between children; this is applicable to any kind of stack layout.

- The **Orientation** property of the **StackLayout** control controls the direction in which child views are positioned. The default value is **Vertical**.

Stack layouts don't provide scrolling. So, the stack layout must be wrapped in **ScrollView** when the size of the stack layout is expected to be bigger than the size of a stack layout parent element.

Bindings Mechanism

Every page of an application usually contains data that can be changed behind the scenes or by a user interacting with the UI elements. Tracking all those changes and updating every single property of every single UI element manually in the code behind can turn the codebase into an unreadable unmaintainable mess very soon. The mechanism of bindings automates this task by replacing the traditional procedural approach with declarative code or markup of bindings.

Binding links a pair of properties between two objects, at least one of which is an object of a class derived from the **BindableObject** class. This is because the **BindableObject** class business logic handles the bindings for a particular object we wish to be bound to some source object. As you already know, the **BindableObject** class is a basic class for every single UI element. So, we can claim that the properties of every UI control (called binding target) can be bound to some other class (called binding source).

Another key element of the binding mechanism is the **BindableProperty** class. Bindable properties play a crucial role in shaping the entire mechanism of bindings. Bindable properties extend regular CLR property's functionality by backing a property with a static field of a **BindableProperty** type. Almost all properties UI controls expose, including ones we have learned about, are bindable because they are backed by static **BindableProperty** fields. For example, the following code is a declaration of the **Text** property of the **Label** control class:

```
Public static readonly BindableProperty TextProperty = BindableProperty.
Create(
    nameof(Text),    //name of CLR property
    typeof(string),  //return type
    typeof(Label),   //declaring type
    default(string), //default return value
    propertyChanged: OnTextPropertyChanged);
```

```
public string Text

{

    get => (string) GetValue(TextProperty);

    set => SetValue(TextProperty, value);

}
```

As you can see, the value of the **Text** property is retrieved and set using **GetValue** and **SetValue** methods. Those methods are actually part of the binding infrastructure coming from the **BindableObject** class.

Being a base class for the **Label** class, the **BindableObject** class holds a dictionary of type **Dictionary<BindableProperty, BindablePropertyContext>**, where the **BindablePropertyContext** object contains the information specific to this concrete instance of the UI control, such as current value and binding object. The binding object, in turn, holds a subscription to the **PropertyChanged** event of the binding source object, tracking the changes of source property (that is passed to binding via the **Path** property) and applying changed value to the target property. When the property value is set without binding (that is, hardcoded in XAML), the **GetValue** and **SetValue** methods get and set the **Value** property of **BindablePropertyContext** by finding the right one in the dictionary using a **BindableProperty** argument as a dictionary key.

Now, let's get back to our banking app and bind **Entry** controls of the **LoginPage** to some model class preparing the user's credentials to be sent to some authentication service. See the **Chapter_4/4_LearningMauiBankingApp_Binding** application.

First of all, we have to ensure that our binding source object can notify bindings about changes. As mentioned earlier, a binding object expects that a source object has the **PropertyChanged** event. It's the responsibility of the **INotifyPropertyChanged** interface. Since we expect not only the credentials model but many other classes to be sources for bindings, it's worth adding an abstract class that implements **INotifyPropertyChanged**. So, add a new **Tools** folder to the solution and the **NotifyPropertyChangedBase** abstract class to it, as follows:

```
public abstract class NotifyPropertyChangedBase : INotifyPropertyChanged

{

    public event PropertyChangedEventHandler PropertyChanged;


    protected void OnPropertyChanged(string propertyName)

    {
```

```
        if (string.IsNullOrEmpty(propertyName))
            return;


    PropertyChanged?.Invoke(this,newPropertyChangedEventArgs(propertyName));
    }
}
```

Now, every class deriving **NotifyPropertyChangedBase** can call the **OnPropertyChanged** method to let subscribers (that is, bindings) know about changes. By the way, the **BindableObject** class also implements the **INotifyPropertyChanged** interface, so all UI elements including pages and layouts can also serve as sources for bindings.

As the next step, add a new **Models** folder and the **LoginCredentials** model class to it, as follows:

```
public class LoginCredentials : NotifyPropertyChangedBase
{
    private string _username;
    public string Username
    {
        get => _username;
        set
        {
            _username = value;
            OnPropertyChanged(nameof(Username));
        }
    }


    private string _password;
    public string Password
    {
        get => _password;
        set
        {
            _password = value;
```

```
            OnPropertyChanged(nameof(Password));
        }
    }
}
```

Here, backing private fields are used to enable the property setter to perform an additional job calling the **OnPropertyChanged** method of the base class every time a new value is assigned.

Let's now add the credentials model field to the login page and modify the page's constructor as shown below.

```
private readonly LoginCredentials _credentials;


public LoginPage()
{
    InitializeComponent();

    _credentials = new LoginCredentials();

    ContentStackLayout.BindingContext = _credentials;

}
```

Note that we have set the **LoginCredentials** object as **BindingContext**; then, modify the XAML markup of the **LoginPage**, as follows:

```
<ContentPage xmlns="http://schemas.microsoft.com/dotnet/2021/maui"
             xmlns:x="http://schemas.microsoft.com/winfx/2009/xaml"
             xmlns:models="clr-namespace:LearningMauiBankingApp.Models"
             x:Class="LearningMauiBankingApp.Pages.LoginPage">
    <Grid IgnoreSafeArea="True">
        <Image Source="light_background.png" Aspect="AspectFill"/>

        <VerticalStackLayout x:Name="ContentStackLayout"
                             VerticalOptions="Center"
                             Margin="50,0"
                             x:DataType="models:LoginCredentials">
            <Label HorizontalOptions="Center"
                   HorizontalTextAlignment="Center"
```

```
                    FontFamily="Poppins-Regular"

                    FontSize="24">
                <Label.FormattedText>
                    <FormattedString>
                        <Span Text="Welcome&#10;"/>
                                    <Span Text="{Binding Path=Username}"
FontFamily="Poppins-SemiBold"/>
                    </FormattedString>
                </Label.FormattedText>
            </Label>

            <Entry Margin="0,40, 0, 10"

                . . .

                Text="{Binding Username, Mode=OneWayToSource}"/>


            <Entry x:Name="PasswordEntry"

                . . .

                Text="{Binding Password, Mode=OneWayToSource}"/>
        </VerticalStackLayout>
    </Grid>
</ContentPage>
```

Although some things have been changed besides bindings, the most important changes are highlighted in bold.

Probably, the most important thing here is the **x:DataType** assignment. Data bindings have two problems caused by the way the binding mechanism was designed. The first is that bindings are not cost-efficient; they are resolved during runtime using reflection that adds some overhead related to it. And second, there is no compile-time validation of binding expressions, so invalid bindings are not detected until an application is run. To resolve those problems, compiled bindings were introduced. Compiled bindings resolve binding expressions at compile-time rather than runtime, improving performance. In addition, compile-time validation identifies invalid bindings and reports them as build errors. To enable compiled bindings, two things must be done:

- Add the **[assembly: XamlCompilation(XamlCompilationOptions. Compile)]** assembly attribute to the project. It's recommended to add it to the **MauiProgram.cs** file.

- Set the **x:DataType** attribute on a UI element to the type of the object that the element and its children will bind to (usually an object referenced by the **BindingContext** property).

The **BindingContext** property of the **VerticalStackLayout** container we have set in the constructor comes from the **BindableObject** class. It has two main treats to remember:

- The object referenced by **BindingContext** is used as a **default binding source** until the source object is defined explicitly using the **Source** property of the **Binding** markup extension.

- The default binding context of a child element is the binding context of its parent. So, since the **LoginCredentials** object was assigned to **BindingContext** of **VerticalStackLayout**, the **BindingContext** properties of the welcome label, username entry, and password entry reference the same **LoginCredentials** object.

As you can see, the binding is created by the **Binding** markup extension. There are the following properties to be used:

- The **Path** property is used to specify the name of the source property. The **Path** property is marked as a **ContentProperty**, so the source property name can be passed without specifying the **Path** property.

- The optional **Source** property is used when the binding context of the control can't be used and the binding source object must be referenced explicitly.

- The optional **Mode** property of enum type **BindingMode** overrides the default binding mode of a **BindableProperty**. The binding mode specifies the direction of a binding. The default mode in most cases is **OneWay**. **OneWay** means data goes from source to target only. **TwoWay** means data goes both ways, the changed source value is applied to the target, and the changed target value is set to the source property. Bindable properties don't signal a property change unless the property value actually changes, preventing an infinite loop. **OneWayToSource** is where data goes from target to source only. **OneTime** is where data goes from source to target, but only when the **BindingContext** changes.

- The optional **Converter** property of type **IValueConverter** enables you to perform any custom conversion of data during the data transfer between source and target. For example, thanks to the converter, you can bind a **BindableProperty** of type bool to a source property of type int by adding your custom conversion business logic. The **IValueConverter** interface defines two methods, i.e., **Convert** and **ConvertBack**, for source-to-target and target-to-source conversion directions, respectively.

- The optional **ConverterParameter** property allows passing some value to the **Convert** and **ConvertBack** methods of a converter as the **parameter** argument.

- The optional **StringFormat** property allows including other text along with the values being formatted similar to well-known **String.Format** method of .NET used in C# code.

- The optional **FallbackValue** property is used when the binding source can't be resolved or returns a null.

- The optional **TargetNullValue** property works the same as **FallbackValue** but for target-to-source direction.

There are three main types of bindings:

- The **Binding** type is the most commonly used. Its responsibility is to link a pair of properties between two objects. The naming might be confusing, so it's worth saying that the **Binding markup extension** returns the object of a **Binding** class.

- **MultiBinding** provides the ability to attach a collection of Binding objects to a single binding target property. **MultiBinding** is usually used along with a converter implementing the **IMultiValueConverter**.

- **AppThemeBinding** helps respond to system theme changes. The most common use case is applying different colors for light and dark themes to align the look of an application to the settings of a device.

Attached properties

.NET MAUI attached property is a variant of bindable property that enables an object to assign a value for a property that its own class doesn't define. For example, child UI elements can use attached properties to inform their parent of how the parent element must present them in the user interface.

NavigationPage

Since our **LearningMauiBankingApp** already has two pages, it's time to add navigation between them. The **NavigationPage** provides the classic hierarchical navigation experience where a user can navigate through pages forward and backward. The navigation page has its own visual representation, so the root page must be passed as a constructor parameter of the **NavigationPage** class.

Let's make the **Login** button of the **LoginPage** perform navigation to the **HomePage**. Assign a **NavigationPage** object in the **App.xaml.cs** file. By the end of this section, you should get an application similar to the **Chapter_4/ 5_ LearningMauiBankingApp_NavigationPage** application, so use it as inspiration if needed:

```
MainPage = new NavigationPage(new LoginPage());
```

Then, change the click event handler of the **Login** button, as follows:

```
private void OnLoginButtonClicked(object sender, EventArgs e)
{
    Navigation.PushAsync(new HomePage());
}
```

At this stage, you might notice significant changes in the look of the application. First of all, **NavigationPages** adds a customizable navigation bar that has a platform-specific look and feel. Besides, the navigation bar reduces the height of the displayed page, so the content page is placed below the navigation bar.

NavigationBar contains a few bindable properties to adjust colors. So, the background of the navigation bar can be customized using the **BarBackground** and **BarBackgroundColor** properties. The text color can be changed thanks to the **BarTextColor** property. Since the **NavigationPage**, like any other page, derives the **Page** class, the whole set of bindable properties like **BackgroundColor** or **Padding** are also available.

NavigationBar can also be customized per page using the set of attached properties of the **NavigationPage** class. Modify the markup of the **LoginPage**, shown as follows, to disable the navigation bar for the **LoginPage**:

```
<ContentPage xmlns="http://schemas.microsoft.com/dotnet/2021/maui"
             xmlns:x="http://schemas.microsoft.com/winfx/2009/xaml"
             xmlns:models="clr-namespace:LearningMauiBankingApp.Models"
             x:Class="LearningMauiBankingApp.Pages.LoginPage"
             NavigationPage.HasNavigationBar="False">
```

By default, the navigation bar displays the title of the page described by the **Title** property of a **Page**. However, the title can be replaced with the custom view using the **NavigationPage.TitleView** property, as shown in the following code snippet:

```
<ContentPage xmlns="http://schemas.microsoft.com/dotnet/2021/maui"
    ...
```

```
      x:Class="LearningMauiBankingApp.Pages.LoginPage">
  <NavigationPage.TitleView>
    <Grid>
        <HorizontalStackLayout HorizontalOptions="Center"
Spacing="10">
            <Label Text="Don't press it!" VerticalOptions="Center"/>
            <Button Text="Press me" BackgroundColor="DarkGrey"/>
        </HorizontalStackLayout>
    </Grid>
  </NavigationPage.TitleView>
```

...

Although **TitleView** can contain pretty much everything, specifying size with **WidthRequest** and **HeightRequest** might be required to make some views appear in the navigation bar. Some other useful navigation page attached properties:

- The **BackButtonTitle** property value enables you to change the default text of the back button.

- The **HasBackButton** flag represents whether the navigation bar includes the back button. Remember that on Android, navigation to the previous page can be performed by pressing the device's back button. Disabling that button can be accomplished by overriding the **OnBackButtonPressed** method and returning the **true** value. It will also disable the back button of the navigation bar.

- **TitleIconImageSource** defines the icon representing the title on the navigation bar.

- **IconColor** defines the background color of the navigation bar icon.

The **Navigation** property of type **INavigation** we have used to navigate from the **LoginPage** to the **HomePage** comes from the **NavigableElement** class (refer to the *Base types of UI Elements* section). **NavigationPage** provides the type of navigation where pages are stacked one on another so that the user can go through the navigation stack forward and backward. This navigation stack can be reached via the read-only **Navigation.NavigationStack** property. The actual navigation actions can be performed using the following set of methods exposed by the **INavigation** (**Navigation** property):

- The **Navigation.PushAsync** method adds a new page to the navigation stack and initiates the navigation to that page.

- The **Navigation.PopAsync** method does the same as the back button: it initiates the navigation to the previous page and pops the active page from the navigation stack.

- The **Navigation.PopToRootAsync** method initiates the navigation back to the very first page of the navigation stack and pops all other pages.

Make note that methods responsible for navigation have overloads defining whether navigation must be animated.

You can also perform manipulations with the navigation stack using the following methods:

- The **Navigation.InsertPageBefore** method inserts a specified page in the navigation stack before an existing page.

- The **Navigation.RemovePage** method removes the specified page from the navigation stack.

Once a user has successfully passed through the sign-in procedure and has been navigated to the **HomePage**, the **LoginPage** is not needed anymore. So, there is no reason to keep it in the navigation stack and provide navigation to it. Let's use the things we have learned and modify the **HomePage**. Override the **OnNavigatedTo** method:

```
protected override void OnNavigatedTo(NavigatedToEventArgs args)
{
    Navigation.RemovePage(Navigation.NavigationStack[0]);
    base.OnNavigatedTo(args);
}
```

As you can see, we got the first page of the **NavigationStack**, which is **LoginPage**, and then passed it to the **RemovePage** method. Since there was no page before the **LoginPage**, the **HomePage** automatically became the root page of the **NavigationPage**. As a result, the back button disappeared from the navigation bar of the **HomePage**. Now, we can even disable the navigation bar since it's not needed anymore.

The **OnNavigatedTo** method is another new thing that must be covered since it's tightly bound to navigation. The navigation process is accompanied by life cycle events. Let's explore what events are invoked step by step. The **A** page will be the one a user is navigating from, and the **B** page will be the one the user is navigating to.

1. **Before the navigation procedure is started**, the following life cycle methods along with events are called: **OnDisappearing**, **OnNavigatingFrom** of page A and **OnAppearing** of page B.

2. **When navigation has been finished** by a handler, the following methods and corresponding events are called: **OnNavigatedTo** of page A and **OnNavigatedFrom** of page B.

The following events of the **NavigationPage** are called **once the navigation process has been finished**: **Pushed**, **Popped**, and **PoppedToRoot**.

Grid

Probably the most spectacular example of attached properties use is how relationships between **Grid** layout and its children are set. As mentioned earlier, the **Grid** layout enables you to arrange children using rows and columns.

By default, a **Grid** contains one row and one column. However, the number and sizes of rows and columns can be defined using the **RowDefinitions** and **ColumnDefinitions** properties.

Let's make our **HomePage** look like an actual home page of the banking app by populating it with placeholders of the top and bottom bars, and by populating the page with nine buttons put into cells of three rows and three columns. By the end of this section, you should be able to get an application like the one placed in the **Chapter_4/6_LearningMauiBankingApp_Grid** folder of the book repository.

But before adding buttons, we need to organize the screen space by splitting it into zones configured to support smartphones with different screen sizes. Modify the content of **HomePage.xaml** as shown here:

```
<Grid IgnoreSafeArea="True">

    <Image Source="light_background.png"
           Aspect="AspectFill"/>


    <Grid RowDefinitions="64, 0.47*, 0.53*, 94">
        <!--Top bar placeholder-->
        <Grid Grid.Row="0" BackgroundColor="Red"/>


        <!--Bank Card Info-->
        <VerticalStackLayout Grid.Row="1" ...>


        <!--Buttons Grid to be added-->


        <!--Bottom bar placeholder-->
```

```
        <Grid Grid.Row="3" BackgroundColor="Blue"/>
    </Grid>
</Grid>
```

Let's explore what we have here. First of all, we have added the new Grid layout that takes all space of the root Grid and overlays the background image. That new Grid has four rows declared. Here, it is important to explain how the sizes of rows and columns are declared. The two ways of declaring sizes shown in the following code snippet are equivalent:

XAML Markup:

RowDefinitions="64, 0.47*, 0.53*, 94"

C#:

```
var firstRow = new RowDefinition(new GridLength(64, GridUnitType.
Absolute));

var secondRow = new RowDefinition(new GridLength(0.47, GridUnitType.
Star));

var thirdRow = new RowDefinition(new GridLength(0.53, GridUnitType.
Star));

var fourthRow = new RowDefinition(new GridLength(94, GridUnitType.
Absolute));


SomeGrid.RowDefinitions.Add(firstRow);

SomeGrid.RowDefinitions.Add(secondRow);

SomeGrid.RowDefinitions.Add(thirdRow);

SomeGrid.RowDefinitions.Add(fourthRow);
```

The behavior of a Grid is defined with the **RowDefinitions** and **ColumnDefinitions** properties of the **RowDefinition** and **ColumnDefinition** types, respectively. The **GridLength** class defines a row's height or a column's width. However, the most important is a second parameter of the **GridLength** constructor of a **GridUnitType** enumeration type. The **GridUnitType** has three members:

- **Absolute**: The row height or column width is a value in device-independent units (represented by a regular numeric value in XAML). Unlike other grid unit types, Absolute can be considered better for performance since fewer calculations must be performed to render a view.

- **Star**: Leftover row or column dimension is allocated proportionally (in XAML, a number must be followed by the * sign). For example, if we have two rows to proportional allocation and the first must take 25% of available space while the second must take the rest 75% of the space, the XAML markup might look like this: „**1*, 4***", „**0.25*, 0.75***", and so on.

- **Auto**: The row height or column width is autosized, based on the measured dimensions of the cell contents (**Auto** in XAML).

So, the new Grid has four rows. The first and fourth rows have fixed heights, while the second and third allocate the rest of the space proportionally. The new Grid contains three children at this moment: two **Grids** that are used as placeholders for the elements to be added in the future, and the **VerticalStackLayout** of the bank card information that we moved here from the root Grid. Please pay attention to the **Grid.Row** attached properties of the child elements of the Grid. The Grid class defines the following properties that can be attached to the child elements to specify the alignment of each child of a Grid:

- **Grid.Row** and **Grid.Column** indicate the row and column alignment of a child element within a parent Grid. The default value is 0, but it's recommended to declare it explicitly to enhance the readability of the entire markup.

- **Grid.RowSpan** and **Grid.ColumnSpan** indicate the total number of rows and columns that a view spans within the parent Grid, starting from the row or column specified by the **Grid.Row** or **Grid.Column** property.

Now, we need a container for the buttons, so put the following grid between the bank card info stack layout and the bottom bar's placeholder:

```
<!--Buttons Grid-->
<Grid Grid.Row="2"
    ColumnDefinitions="1*, 1*, 1*"
    RowDefinitions="1*, 1*, 1*"
    ColumnSpacing="10"
    Margin="16,0">
</Grid>
```

This Grid markup declares three rows and three columns that take equal amounts of available space of the third row of the parent Grid. This grid also has side margins defined. The **ColumnSpacing** and **RowSpacing** properties define the specified amount of space between columns and rows, respectively.

ImageButton and the corresponding description text will be used to give buttons a modern look, so add all images from the **LearningMauiBankingApp_Assets/Light** folder of the repository to the application and add the first button to the buttons grid, as shown in the following code. Don't forget to set the **MauiImage** build action to each image resource:

```
<Grid Grid.Row="2"
    ColumnDefinitions="1*, 1*, 1*"
    RowDefinitions="1*, 1*, 1*"
    ColumnSpacing="10"
    Margin="16,0">

    <!—Transfer Button-->
    <VerticalStackLayout Grid.Column="0" Grid.Row="0"
                    Spacing="10"
                    VerticalOptions="Center">
        <ImageButton Padding="10"
                HeightRequest="44"
                CornerRadius="12"
                BackgroundColor="#FFFFFF"
                Source="light_transfer_icon.png"
                Aspect="AspectFit"/>
        <Label HorizontalOptions="Center"
            Text="Transfer"
            TextColor="#8E8E93"
            FontSize="16"
            FontFamily="Poppins-Regular"/>
    </VerticalStackLayout>
...
```

As you can see, we put the stack layout that contains a button and description label to the cell of the first row and first column. The task for you: add the rest of the buttons using the image files and descriptions from the table that follows:

		Columns		
		0	**1**	**2**
Rows	0	light_transfer_ icon.png Transfer	light_exchange_icon. png Exchange	light_payments_icon. png Payments
	1	light_credits_ icon.png Credits	light_deposits_icon. png Deposits	light_cashback_icon. png Cashback
	2	light_atm_icon.png ATM	light_security_icon. png Security	light_more_icon.png More

Table 4.1: Stack layout

BindableLayout and DataTemplate

The **BindableLayout** class with its attached properties enables any class that derives from the **Layout** class to generate child UI elements by binding a collection of items containing the data required for those children. Imagine the user of a **BankingApp** with more than one bank card. The set of data to be displayed is the same for each card, and the visual representation is also the same. So, it would be nice to bind a collection of bank card model objects to a stack layout and ask the stack layout to generate child elements using this collection and some blueprint of the bank card view.

While the **BindableLayout** class makes such a binding possible, the **DataTemplate** class provides the ability to define the presentation of data and is widely used by different UI controls.

Let's turn our single bank card into a collection of cards presented on a screen as a horizontal scrollable stack of cards. It will help us learn how **BindableLayout** and a few more things are used. This can be done in multiple ways, and a combination of stack layout and bindable layout is one of them. The resulting application of this section is placed in the **Chapter_4/7_LearningMauiBankingApp_BindableLayout** folder.

First of all, add the **BankCard** model class to the **Models** folder, and the **BankCards** property to the **HomePage**, as shown here:

BankCard.cs

```
public class BankCard
{
    public string Alias { get; }
```

```csharp
    public long CardNumber { get; }

    public DateTime ExpirationDate { get; }

    public decimal Balance { get; }


    public BankCard(string alias, long cardNumber, DateTime expirationDate,
decimal balance)
    {
        Alias = alias;

        CardNumber = cardNumber;

        ExpirationDate = expirationDate;

        Balance = balance;

    }

}
```

HomePage.xaml.cs

```csharp
public IEnumerable<BankCard> BankCards { get; }


public HomePage()
{
    InitializeComponent();

    BankCards = new List<BankCard>
    {
        new BankCard("Main card", 1882824500100505, new DateTime(2029, 5,
1), 3253.45m),

        new BankCard("Emergency card", 4004799964524057, new DateTime(2028,
2, 1), 8500m),

        new BankCard("Savings card", 4576241367871031, new DateTime(2025,
10, 1), 4300m),
    };

    BankCardsStackLayout.BindingContext = this;

}
```

As you can see, the **BankCards** property doesn't have a setter at all because we don't want to change this collection in runtime, so binding will transfer data to a target once when the **BindingContext** of **BankCardsStackLayout** control changes.

To present the collection of cards, we need to put the existing **VerticalStackLayout** into a **DataTemplate** used by a **HorizontalStackLayout** that is wrapped into a **ScrollView**. **ScrollView** is needed to ensure that each card is reachable despite the card width and screen size. So, modify the content of row 1 of the **ValueableContentGrid** as follows:

```
<ContentPage xmlns:pages="clr-namespace:LearningMauiBankingApp.Pages"
            xmlns:models="clr-namespace:LearningMauiBankingApp.Models"
            xmlns:converters="clr-namespace:LearningMauiBankingApp.
Converters"
...
<!--Bank Card Info-->
<ScrollView Grid.Row="1"
            Orientation="Horizontal"
            HorizontalScrollBarVisibility="Never"
            VerticalOptions="Center">
    <HorizontalStackLayout x:Name="BankCardsStackLayout"
                            Padding="16,0"
                            Spacing="10"
                            x:DataType="pages:HomePage"
                            BindableLayout.ItemsSource="{Binding
BankCards}">
        <BindableLayout.ItemTemplate>
            <DataTemplate x:DataType="models:BankCard">
                <Grid WidthRequest="311" HeightRequest="214"
                    RowDefinitions="1*, 1*">
                    <Image Source="{Binding Balance,
Converter={converters:AccountBalanceToCardBackgroundImage}}"
                            Aspect="AspectFit"
                            Grid.RowSpan="2"/>
                    <VerticalStackLayout Grid.Row="0"
Margin="16,16,16,0">
                        <Label Text="{Binding Alias}"
```

```
                    ...
                    FontFamily="Poppins-SemiBold"/>


            <Label Text="{Binding CardNumber,
StringFormat='{0:0000 0000 0000 0000}'}"
                    ...
                    FontFamily="Poppins-Regular"/>


            <Label Text="{Binding ExpirationDate,
Converter={converters:DateOnlyToBankCardExpirationDate}}"
                    ...
                    FontFamily="Poppins-Regular"/>
        </VerticalStackLayout>


        <Label Grid.Row="1"
               Margin="16,0,0,16"
               ...
               FormattedText="{Binding Balance,
Converter={converters:AccountBalanceToBankCardFormattedString}}"/>
        </Grid>
      </DataTemplate>
    </BindableLayout.ItemTemplate>
  </HorizontalStackLayout>
</ScrollView>
```

Note that the initial **VerticalStackLayout** has been put into two rows of Grid, and the account balance label has been moved out from the stack layout to the second row of that grid. This is needed to ensure that the label is pinned to the bottom edge of a card. Another new thing is a card background image and converters that correspond to a few bindings.

Add the new **Converters** folder to the solution and add three new converters, as follows:

```
public class DateOnlyToBankCardExpirationDate : IValueConverter
{
    public object Convert(object value, Type targetType, object
parameter, CultureInfo culture)
```

```
    {
        if (value is not DateTime date)
            return string.Empty;


        return $"{date:MM} / {date:yy}";
    }


public object ConvertBack(object value, Type targetType, object
parameter, CultureInfo culture)
    {
        throw new NotImplementedException("One way converter");
    }
}
```

The preceding converter turns a **DateTime** struct into a string presenting the expiration date of the bank card. Remember what we learned in the previous sections: formatting operations can also be done in XAML using the **StringFormat** property of **Binding** markup extension. Moreover, in most cases, it's preferable to put string formatting in XAML until the same format needs to be reused in multiple places in an application.

Here are some tasks for you. Implement the two remaining converters on your own and explore the code added during this section. Specify the background colors of elements to see how every element is rendered. Change margins and sizes, and see how the application behaves on devices/simulators of different screens. Use the application from the repository if needed. Here are the descriptions of converters:

- **AccountBalanceToBankCardFormattedString** must turn the decimal value of the **BankCard.Balance** property into the formatted string of the same look we had before.

- **AccountBalanceToCardBackgroundImage** must return "bank_card_background1.png" when the balance is less than 5000 and "bank_card_background2.png" otherwise. In general, it's considered a bad practice to put business logic into a converter. However, it's fine for the sake of this chapter and until the proper approach is learned.

Let's explore the entire list of **BindableLayout** properties:

- **ItemsSource** attached property specifies the collection of data items to be presented.

- **ItemTemplate** attached property specifies the **DataTemplate** to apply to each item displayed by the layout.

- **ItemTemplateSelector** attached property specifies the **DataTemplate Selector** object that allows choosing a specific **DataTemplate** for an item at runtime. For example, a classic VISA card and platinum American Express cards look completely different. So, you can create different data templates for VISA and AE cards, and thanks to **DataTemplateSelector**, you can choose the proper one in runtime by checking the **Provider** enum property of the **BankCard** model during runtime.

- The **EmptyView** bindable property specifies the view that will be displayed when the ItemsSource is null or when the collection bind to **ItemsSource** is null or empty.

- **EmptyViewTemplate** specifies the **DateTemplate** that behaves just like **EmptyView**. However, when both **EmptyView** and **EmptyViewTemplare** are set, **EmptyViewTemplate** takes precedence.

It's recommended to use **BindableLayout** in cases when source collections have a predictable relatively small number of objects and source collection doesn't change frequently. In cases where the size of the source collection might be big and/or the source collection might change often, there are other UI controls that are more performant when handling big collections and provide additional functionalities.

Showing modal pages

Sometimes it's necessary to show a temporary modal page sliding in from the bottom of the screen that overlaps a normal page without changing the navigation stack. It's called modal page navigation in .NET MAUI. A modal page usually encourages users to complete a self-contained task that cannot be navigated away from until the task is completed or canceled. Additionally, regular navigation methods and modal navigation methods are accessible via the **Navigation** property on any page-derived types. Besides, you might notice that the **INavigation** interface provides access to **ModalStack**. The modal page navigation doesn't require the **NavigationPage** to be set as a root page of an application. So, modal page navigation can be performed from any page by calling the following methods:

- **Navigation.PushModalAsync** adds a specified page object to the modal stack and displays that page over other pages.

- **Navigation.PopModalAsync** allows programmatically closing the currently active modal page. If **ModalStack** contains other pages, it automatically becomes an active modal page. The modal page can also be popped from the modal stack by pressing the physical or on-screen **Back** button on a device.

Let's add a simple modal page acting as a bottom sheet. Add a new folder called **ModalPages** to the **Pages** folder and add a new content page called **TransferModalPage**. Then, modify the newly added page as shown in the following code. Use the application placed in the **Chapter_4/ 8_LearningMauiBankingApp_ ModalPage** folder of the repository if needed:

TransferModalPage.xaml content:

```
<Grid IgnoreSafeArea="True">
    <Grid RowDefinitions="59, *"
          VerticalOptions="End"
          HeightRequest="600">
        <BoxView Grid.RowSpan="2"
                 CornerRadius="30, 30, 0, 0"
                 Color="#FFFFFF">
            <BoxView.Shadow>
                <Shadow Brush="Black" Radius="10" Offset="0,-10"
Opacity="0.15"/>
            </BoxView.Shadow>
        </BoxView>

        <ImageButton Grid.Row="0" HeightRequest="44" WidthRequest="44"
                     HorizontalOptions="End" VerticalOptions="End"
                     Margin="0, 0, 15, 0"
                     Padding="8"
                     BackgroundColor="Transparent"
                     Source="light_close_icon.png"
                     Clicked="OnCloseButtonClicked"/>
    </Grid>
</Grid>
```

TransferModalPage.xaml.cs members:

```
protected override void OnAppearing()
{
    BackgroundColor = new Color(0, 0, 0, 0.0001f);
    base.OnAppearing();
```

```
}


private void OnCloseButtonClicked(object sender, EventArgs e)
{
    Navigation.PopModalAsync();
}
```

Next, add the following button click handler for the **Transfer** button of the **HomePage**:

```
private void OnTransferButtonClicked(object sender, EventArgs e)
{
    Navigation.PushModalAsync(new TransferModalPage());
}
```

Modal pages occupy the whole screen/window. It's possible to change this behaviour by using platform-specific settings to change the modal page presentation style. However, since every platform does not have such a functionality, it's beneficial to use the way shown earlier in the case of cross-platform applications, especially when an application has a fully custom UI design. Here, **TransferModalPage** still occupies the whole screen, but the markup describes the nested **Grid** container of height 600 units aligned to the bottom of the page. This **Grid** contains the **BoxView** acting as a background and the actual meaningful content (**Close** button).

The background of the modal page can't be truly transparent. Setting a truly transparent background color doesn't make the background transparent. So, we have applied a color with so small an alpha channel value that the human eyes consider the background transparent but MAUI considers it an actual color.

Picker

The Picker UI control is used to enable a user to select an item from a list of items. Picker receives the list of source objects and returns selection via the **SelectedIndex** and **SelectedItem** properties. The **ItemsSource** collection might be specified in markup, assigned programmatically or received via binding.

Since the **Picker** control represents a selected item using text, it contains all necessary text-related properties, such as **FontFamily** and **FontSize**. Besides, it contains the following control-specific members:

- **ItemsSource** of type **IList** defines the list of selectable object items.

- **SelectedItem** returns the selected item object. It can be also used to set the selected item programmatically.

- **SelectedIndex** represents the collection index of the selected item. It can also be used to set the selected item programmatically. The default value of **SelectedIndex** is -1, indicating that the selection wasn't made yet.

- **ItemDisplayBinding** accepts binding to some property of a source item that will be used to represent the source item on a list of selectable options.

- **Title** defines the placeholder and the title that is applied to the picker selector provided by the operating system.

- The **SelectedIndexChanged** event is raised when the user had selected an item and the **SelectedIndex** property value was changed.

The following code snippet shows a simple picker that enables a user to select a bank card from the collection of **BankCard** objects:

```
<Picker Title="From card"
        ItemsSource="{Binding Cards}"
        ItemDisplayBinding="{Binding Alias}"/>
```

It's time to implement the entire feature on your own. Using the knowledge from the current and previous sections, money transfer functionality to the **TransferModalPage**. Here are the requirements and hints:

- The modal page must contain two pickers populated by a collection of the user's **BankCards**. The first picker is to select the transfer source card, while the second picker is for the transfer target card.

- Add an entry for a transfer value.

- Add the **Transfer** button with a click event handler that transfers the specified amount of money from the source card to the target card.

- The setter of the **BankCard.Balance** property and the **TransferModalPage. Cards** collection of type **IEnumerable<BankCard>** must call **OnPropertyChanged**.

The application containing the solution is in the **Chapter_4/ 9_LearningMaui BankingApp_Picker** folder of the book repository.

Sometimes it's necessary to pick a date or time. The .NET MAUI has dedicated UI controls for tasks called **DatePicker** and **TimePicker**. They are similar to regular picker but use different picker selectors and have their own sets of members.

DatePicker

- The **Date** property of type **DateTime** represents the selected date and defaults to the value **DateTime.Today**. The default binding mode of the backing bindable property is **TwoWay**.

- The **Format** property of type string, a .NET formatting string, defaults to the "**D**" date pattern.

- The **MinimumDate** property of type **DateTime** defines the minimum allowed date.

- The **MaximumDate** property of type **DateTime** defines the maximum allowed date. **MaximumDate** value must always be greater or equal to the **MinimumDate** value. Otherwise, **DatePicker** will raise an exception.

TimePicker

- The **Time** property of type **TimeSpan** represents the selected time. The default binding mode of the backing bindable property is **TwoWay**.

- The **Format** property defines a .NET formatting string and defaults to the "**t**" time pattern.

Pop-ups

Sometimes it's needed to show a simple pop-up similar to the one displayed by an operating system, asking for some permission. Such pop-ups are also called alerts. There are three kinds of pop-ups that can be shown by calling the following methods exposed by the **Page** class:

- The **DisplayAlert** method is used to show a simple modal notification or capture a user's response by presenting two buttons and returning a boolean value. The title, message, and button texts are customizable.

- The **DisplayActionSheet** method displays a modal pop-up with a set of alternatives to choose from. After the user taps one of the buttons, the button text will be returned as a string.

- The **DisplayPromtAsync** method displays a modal pop-up to ask a user to provide an answer to a question by filling up the entry field.

Go back to our **TransferModalPage** and display a short notification using the **DisplayAlert** method if a user tries to transfer from the source card that doesn't have enough money to make a transfer.

View-to-view binding

As you already know, UI controls can not only act as a binding target but also as a binding source. It means we can bind two properties of UI controls without an intermediate model class. So, we can bind a **LoginPage** title directly to the username entry control. Let's modify the **Text** property binding of the second span of the welcome title label, as shown in the following code. Don't forget to set

"**UsernameEntry**" as the **x:Name** property to the username entry. Use **Chapter_4/ 10_LearningMauiBankingApp_ViewBinding** if needed.

```
Text="{Binding Text, Source={x:Reference UsernameEntry}}"
```

The **Source** property of the **Binding** markup extension here overrides **BindingContext** with the reference provided by the **x:Reference** markup extension. The important thing here is to specify the **x:Name** property value for a UI control that acts as a binding source.

Resources

You probably noticed that the XAML code of our application is full of repetitive values, although the application is simple and small. Sometimes the entire controls are configured in the exact same way. Color values are probably the most prominent example of this. Now, consider a common situation: designers decide to make the color used by every button a little bit darker because research showed users like the new color more. It means you need to go through every page, every view, and every custom control, carefully making changes in dozens of files. Therefore, there is a big chance of making a mistake or typo, so the QA must also go through the whole application, testing every modified page. Besides, such a major modification increases the chance of getting merge conflicts.

Wouldn't be better to define color or any other resource once, give it some alias and apply the resource using that alias when needed? This is possible, thanks to the **Resources** property of type **ResourceDictionary** exposed by the **VisualElement** class. XAML resources that are stored in a **ResourceDictionary** can be referenced and applied to elements by using the **StaticResource** or **DynamicResource** markup extension. A **ResourceDictionary** can also be defined in C# and applied to elements by using a string-based indexer. A **ResourceDictionary** can be defined on every level of the visual tree. The following code defines **ResourceDictionary** with the color resource accessible across the application since it's defined in **App. xaml** file:

```
<Application xmlns="http://schemas.microsoft.com/dotnet/2021/maui"
             xmlns:x="http://schemas.microsoft.com/winfx/2009/xaml"
             x:Class="LearningMauiBankingApp.App">
    <Application.Resources>
        <ResourceDictionary>
            <Color x:Key="LightPrimaryTextColor">#000000</Color>
        </ResourceDictionary>
    </Application.Resources>
</Application>
```

This is how the **LightPrimaryTextColor** resource can be utilized in XAML:

```
TextColor="{StaticResource LightPrimaryTextColor}"
```

The **StaticResource** markup extension searches the visual tree upward using the **Parent** property of each element and checking whether the element has a defined resource dictionary that contains a resource with a specified key. The **App** class is the last place where the resource is looked for. So, if a resource is used on a level of a particular page, it's better to not define the resource as global in **App.xaml** to reduce overhead and to not make upper visual tree elements responsible for storing resources they don't need. A **DynamicResource** is similar to **StaticResource**. However, if the resource dictionary associated with the resource key is replaced in runtime, the changed dynamic resource value is applied to the UI element.

Go through our banking application and replace all colors with static resources using the following color resource names. Use the **Chapter_4/ 11_ LearningMauiBankingApp_Resources** application if needed:

- **#000000 – LightPrimaryTextColor**
- **#8E8E93 – LightSecondaryTextColor**
- **#FFFFFF – LightPrimaryBackgroundColor**
- **#F5F5F5 – LightSecondaryBackgroundColor**

Styles

You probably noticed that we often copied the same XAML code multiple times to make some controls have an identical appearance. The buttons on the **HomePage** are a great example of this. Such an approach makes code less readable. Besides, it makes the XAML code less maintainable because as you remember, it might be needed to change, let's say **CornerRadius** at any time. This is where the **Style** class comes into the picture.

The **Style** class groups a collection of property values into one object that can then be applied to multiple visual elements. Styles objects are typically defined in XAML **ResourceDictionary** markup as a XAML resource. So, the **Style** objects defined at the control level can only be applied to the UI element and to its children, just like the color resource from the previous section. Styles defined at the **App.xaml** level are available globally. Let's add a **Style** at the **HomePage** level and apply it to the transfer button, as shown in the following code. The resulting application of this section is in the **Chapter_4/12_LearningMauiBankingApp_Styles** folder.

```
<ContentPage xmlns="http://schemas.microsoft.com/dotnet/2021/maui"
        ...>
    <ContentPage.Resources>
        <ResourceDictionary>
```

```
            <Style x:Key="BankingServiceImageButtonStyle"
TargetType="ImageButton">
                    <Setter Property="Padding" Value="10"/>
                    <Setter Property="HeightRequest" Value="44"/>
                    <Setter Property="CornerRadius" Value="12"/>
                    <Setter Property="BackgroundColor"
Value="{StaticResource LightPrimaryBackgroundColor}"/>
                    <Setter Property="Aspect" Value="AspectFit"/>
            </Style>
        </ResourceDictionary>
    </ContentPage.Resources>


...

<ImageButton Style="{StaticResource BankingServiceImageButtonStyle}"
            Source="light_transfer_icon.png"
            Clicked="OnTransferButtonClicked"/>
```

The **Style** class contains the collection of **Setter** objects. Each **Setter** object, in turn, defines what value must be applied to what property of an object of the type specified for the **TargetType** property of a style.

The **Style** resource shown earlier is explicit style because it has the **x:Key** property defined to be used along with **StaticResource** or **DynamicResource** markup. A **Style** resource, however, can be defined as an implicit resource by not specifying an **x:Key** property. The difference is that an implicit style will be applied to all elements of **TargetType** automatically. However, it will not be applied to the subclasses of the **TargetType**. In other words, an implicit style will not be applied to UI controls derived from the **ImageButton** (based on the preceding example). To apply the implicit style to derived UI control classes, the true value must be set to the **ApplyToDerivedTypes** property of the **Style** class.

Sometimes styles can also partially duplicate other styles while being different styles for different purposes. In such a case, a **Style** can inherit from another style to reduce duplication. **Style** inheritance is achieved by setting the **BasedOn** property of the **Style** class. Let's create a style for the descriptions of the **HomePage** by adding new styles and modifying the transfer button description label code as follows:

App.xaml resources:

```
<Style x:Key="PrimaryContentLabelStyle" TargetType="Label">
    <Setter Property="FontFamily" Value="Poppins-Regular"/>
    <Setter Property="FontSize" Value="16"/>
```

```
    <Setter Property="TextColor" Value="{StaticResource
LightPrimaryTextColor}"/>
</Style>
<Style x:Key="SecondaryContentLabelStyle" TargetType="Label">
    <Setter Property="FontFamily" Value="Poppins-Regular"/>
    <Setter Property="FontSize" Value="16"/>
    <Setter Property="TextColor" Value="{StaticResource
LightSecondaryTextColor}"/>
</Style>
```

HomePage.xaml resources:

```
<Style x:Key="BankingServiceButtonDescriptionStyle"
        TargetType="Label"
        BasedOn="{StaticResource SecondaryContentLabelStyle}">
    <Setter Property="HorizontalOptions" Value="Center"/>
</Style>
```

Button description label markup:

```
<Label Text="Transfer"
        Style="{StaticResource BankingServiceButtonDescriptionStyle}"/>
```

A style can only be inherited from styles defined at the same level, or above, in the view hierarchy.

A task for you: Go through our **BankingApp** and create styles for cases where it would help reduce code duplication. Then, check the sample application and synchronize your styles with the sample.

Conclusion

Congratulations! You are ready to create user interfaces based on platform-default elements and fully custom UIs providing a unique look and feel of an application. You might notice that although our simple BankingApp doesn't have complex business logic and has very few models and bindings, code-behind files start looking little bit messy. Imagine having all button handlers, proper validations for **Entry** controls, data access logic, and more. So, before making the UI more sophisticated, it's worth learning how to create extendable and maintainable applications readable to other developers.

The next chapter explores all about MAUI application architecture.

Points to remember

- The abstract device-independent units are used instead of pixels to make the code of a user interface less dependent on the actual device it's being executed.

- The **InitializeComponents** method loads the XAML file and instantiates the whole UI tree described in it.

- Constructors of visual elements must contain the necessary code only.

- Custom markup extensions can be created by implementing the **IMarkupExtensions<T>** interface.

- UI is a structure organized in terms of UI elements hierarchy and Z-order.

- The more the levels in the visual tree hierarchy, the more calculations must be perfumed by **LayoutManagers**.

- A binding source class must implement **INotifyPropertyChanged**.

- Every UI control can be both source and target of binding.

- Modal pages stack doesn't require a **NavigationPage** to be the root page of the application.

Questions

1. What does PPI stand for?

2. What is the default prefix for mapping the XAML language intrinsics?

3. Is it possible to utilize the UI controls from external plugins in XAML?

4. Why is it important to keep the constructors of pages and visual elements as lightweight as possible?

5. Is it possible to implement UI with C# without using XAML?

6. What is the difference between visual tree hierarchy and Z-order?

7. What is a **SafeArea**?

8. What is the **BindableObject** class responsible for?

9. What are **Layouts** used for?

10. What is the only case wherein **StackLayout** can be used over **VerticalStackLayout** and **HorizontalStackLayout**?

11. What are **CompiledBindings** needed for?

Join our book's Discord space

Join the book's Discord Workspace for Latest updates, Offers, Tech happenings around the world, New Release and Sessions with the Authors:

https://discord.bpbonline.com

CHAPTER 5
Layering with MVVM

Introduction

No one real-world application can survive the middle- and long-term run without thoughtful architecture. Often, a messy pile of unstructured code in which everything depends on everything starts to bury itself, along with a development team, under the weight of bugs and tech debt even before the release of a **Minimum Valuable Product (MVP)**. On the other hand, applying best practices and design principles might seem complex at the beginning, but they make maintenance and product development much easier, painless, cheap, and pleasant, which reflects on overall product quality and user satisfaction.

Structure

In this chapter, we will cover the following topics:

- What is MVVM?
- ViewModel as a BindingContext
- Commanding and ICommand interface
- Navigation with MVVM
- Dependency Inversion Principle

- Inversion of Control
- Dependency Injection
- Third-Party DI Container Integration (StrongInject)
- Invoke platform code from shared code
- Gesture Recognizers
- LiteDB database
- Local storage implementation

Objectives

The main purpose of this chapter is to give you essential knowledge about architectural principles, MAUI application design patterns, and best practices that are necessary for enterprise software development. We will continue applying theoretical knowledge to our **LearningMauiBankingApp** by focusing on making it solid and reliable.

This chapter provides solutions for some problems, such as the MVVM navigation problem, that can be applied as is to real-world applications. Additionally, we will get familiar with some useful third-party frameworks.

What is MVVM?

Up to this point, we have used ***.xaml.cs** files for almost everything. We've used them to store data, make navigations, handle buttons, etc. Now suppose every single feature of the banking app is implemented accordingly to the strict UI/UX guidelines and business logic requirements, including the behavior of UI elements, custom animations, data validations, network communication, working with a local database, and other advanced business logic. In the case of real commercial applications, utilizing code-behind of pages for all of this inevitably makes the codebase unreadable and unmaintainable. The ***.xaml.cs** files would count thousands of lines of code; everything would depend on everything, and no one would want to touch it because only God knows how it actually works.

To resolve those problems, Microsoft's engineers Ken Cooper and Ted Peters invented an architectural pattern called **Model-View-ViewModel (MVVM)**. MVVM was announced in 2005 and became the default architectural pattern incorporated into the WPF and Silverlight.

The basic idea of MVVM is to split an application into three layers: View, ViewModel, and Model (*Figure 5.1*). This makes the codebase less coupled, which leads to better maintainability. Besides, it makes the codebase much easier to cover by tests.

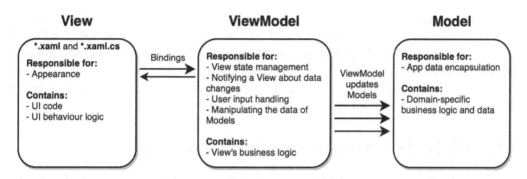

Figure 5.1: *MVVM Layers*

Let's describe MVVM layers:

- The **View** layer is a UI layer usually represented by ***.xaml** and ***.xaml. cs** files. According to MVVM, it must contain UI-related code only. The code-behind might contain logic that implements visual behavior that is difficult to express in XAML, for example, animations or switching focus between entries we have done on **LoginPage**. A View communicates with a **ViewModel** object used as a **BindingContext** via bindings. So, View keeps a reference to **ViewModel** and has access to its public members.

- The classes of the **Model** layer usually encapsulate application-specific data and business logic. The model should not depend on any client class that uses it. For example, the **BankCard** class might contain the **Balance** property and the **Decrease** method, ensuring that the Balance value isn't less than zero. Such a model encapsulates the bank card-related logic and data to be used anywhere in the app. Besides, the model can implement **INotifyPropertyChanged** for bindings if **BankCard** is about to be used as a type of ViewModel property.

- The **ViewModel** layer contains the view-specific business logic. It handles the user's input, retrieves the required models, manipulates the model's data, and exposes public properties required for bindings. **ViewModel** classes also implement **INotifyPropertyChanged** to notify bindings about property data changes. The **ViewModel** defines the functionality to be offered by the UI displayed by the **View**. The properties of **ViewModel** often provide data from models in a form that a particular view can easily consume by converting data or combining the data of a few models into a new object, sometimes called a design model or a UI model. The **ViewModel** layer can be considered a mediator between the **View** and **Models**.

Besides those layers, real-world applications usually contain classes called services. These are helper classes that encapsulate some business logic that is not dependent on a specific ViewModel and is likely to be used by multiple ViewModels and/

or other services. For example, **LoginService** might encapsulate the business logic that handles logging a user in and out, including requests to REST API and caching user data. The **LoginService**, in turn, might use **NetworkService** and **LocalStorageService**, which handle network communication and local database, respectively. Such responsibility distribution significantly increases code reusability, maintainability, and testability.

ViewModel as a BindingContext

In our banking app, we already have classes representing the **View** layer and the **Model** layer. The **View** layer is represented by **Pages**, and the **Model** layer is represented by the **BankCard** and the **LoginCredentials** classes. So, all we need to do is create **ViewModel** classes for each page and move certain logic to it. Create a new folder called **ViewModels** and add the following class to it; use the **Chapter_5/1_ LearningMauiBankingApp_ViewModel** application from the repository if needed:

```
public class TransferModalPageViewModel : NotifyPropertyChangedBase
{
    private IEnumerable<BankCard> _cards;
    public IEnumerable<BankCard> Cards
    {
        get => _cards;
        set
        {
            _cards = value;
            OnPropertyChanged(nameof(Cards));
        }
    }
}
```

As you must have probably guessed, **TransferModalPage** and **HomePage** need to be adjusted to use **TransferModalPageViewModel**.

First, remove the **Cards** property from **TrasferModalPage** and modify its constructor as follows:

```
public TransferModalPage(Ienumerable<BankCard> cards)
{
    InitializeComponent();
    BindingContext = new TransferModalPageViewModel()
    {
```

```
        Cards = cards
    };
}
```

Next, apply the **TransferModalPageViewModel** as a **DataType** for the entire **TransferModalPage**. Do not forget to remove the **x:DataType** property definition from the **VerticalStackLayout** element markup since the ViewModel object is now a **BindingContext** of the entire page.

```
<ContentPage xmlns="http://schemas.microsoft.com/dotnet/2021/maui"

            ...

                        x:Class="LearningMauiBankingApp.Pages.ModalPages.
TransferModalPage"

                xmlns:viewModels="clr-namespace:LearningMauiBankingApp.
ViewModels"

            x:DataType="viewModels:TransferModalPageViewModel">
```

Finally, go to **HomePage.xaml.cs** and modify the **OnTransferButtonClicked** method as shown here:

```
private void OnTransferButtonClicked(object sender, EventArgs e)
{
    Navigation.PushModalAsync(new TransferModalPage(BankCards));
}
```

Commanding and ICommand interface

As you remember, handling user interaction is also the responsibility of a ViewModel layer. However, it's impossible to move the **OnTransferButtonClicked** handler from **TransferModalPage.xaml.cs** to **TransferModalPageViewModel.cs** because a ViewModel layer must not contain a reference to a View layer object. According to MVVM, a View has direct access to ViewModel, and communication is performed using bindings defined by the View's layer side. This is where the **ICommand** interface comes into the picture.

The **ICommand** interface is defined in the **System.Windows.Input** namespace and consists of two methods and one event:

```
public interface ICommand
{
    public void Execute (Object parameter);
```

```
    public bool CanExecute (Object parameter);
    public event EventHandler CanExecuteChanged;
}
```

Basically, the **ICommand** interface promises a class has some method to execute and the flag indicating if it's allowed to call the **Execute** method. You might notice that UI controls often duplicate events with bindable properties of type **ICommand**. It means those controls are MVVM ready. Besides, in most cases, the **Command** property is accompanied by the **CommandParameter** bindable property of the type of object. The command parameter bindable property is used when some data must be passed to the **Execute** method of command.

The **Command** and **Command<T>** (**T** is the expected type of command parameter) classes provide a basic implementation of the **ICommand** interface. They have multiple constructors that enable you to use a command with or without a command parameter, with or without the **canExecute** validation method delegate.

Let us now move the money-transferring business logic from the **TransferModalPage** code-behind to the page's ViewModel. Modify the following files as shown, and don't forget to add the required **usings**; use **Chapter_5/ 2_LearningMauiBankingApp_ ICommand** application if needed:

TransferModalPageViewModel.cs:

```
private readonly INavigation _navigation;


private IEnumerable<BankCard> _cards;

...


public BankCard SelectedFromCard { get; set; }
public BankCard SelectedToCard { get; set; }
public ICommand TransferCommand { get; }
public ICommand CloseCommand { get; }


public TransferModalPageViewModel(INavigation navigation)
{
    _navigation = navigation;
    CloseCommand = new Command(() => _navigation.PopModalAsync());
    TransferCommand = new Command<string>(OnTransferCommandCalled,
CanTransfer);
}
```

```csharp
private void OnTransferCommandCalled(string parameter)
{
    var valueToTransfer = Math.Abs(decimal.Parse(parameter));

    SelectedFromCard.Balance -= valueToTransfer;
    SelectedToCard.Balance += valueToTransfer;
    _navigation.PopModalAsync();
}


private bool CanTransfer(string parameter)
{
    if (SelectedFromCard is null || SelectedToCard is null
        || ReferenceEquals(SelectedFromCard, SelectedToCard)
        || !decimal.TryParse(parameter, out decimal valueToTransfer)
        || SelectedFromCard.Balance < Math.Abs(valueToTransfer))
        return false;

    return true;
}
```

TransferModalPage.xaml.cs:

```csharp
public TransferModalPage(IEnumerable<BankCard> cards)
{
    InitializeComponent();
    BindingContext = new TransferModalPageViewModel(Navigation)
    {
        Cards = cards
    };
}


protected override void OnAppearing()
{
```

```
        BackgroundColor = new Color(0, 0, 0, 0.0001f);
}
```

TransferModalPage.xaml:

```
...
<ImageButton Grid.Row="0" HeightRequest="44" WidthRequest="44"
            ...
            Source="light_close_icon.png"
            Command="{Binding CloseCommand}"/>
...


<Picker Style="{StaticResource PickerStyle}"
        Title="From card"
        ItemsSource="{Binding Cards}"
        ItemDisplayBinding="{Binding Alias}"
        SelectedItem="{Binding SelectedFromCard, Mode=OneWayToSource}"/>


<Picker Style="{StaticResource PickerStyle}"
        Title="To card"
        ItemsSource="{Binding Cards}"
        ItemDisplayBinding="{Binding Alias}"
        SelectedItem="{Binding SelectedToCard, Mode=OneWayToSource}"/>
...


<Button Text="Transfer"
        Margin="0, 25, 0, 0"
        Style="{StaticResource RegularSmallButton}"
        HorizontalOptions="Center"
        Command="{Binding TransferCommand}"
        CommandParameter="{Binding Text, Source={x:Reference
TransferValueEntry}}"/>
```

As you can see, we have moved the entire business logic from the page's code-behind to the **ViewModel**. The **ViewModel** class now contains commands that handle both the **Close** and **Transfer** buttons the page contains. The anonymous method passed to the **CloseCommand** simply closes the modal page. The **TransferCommand**, in turn, expects the **CommandParameter** of the string type. The **OnTransferCommandCalled** method is called by the **Execute** method of command, and **CanTransfer** is called by the **CanExecute** method of command. The **SelectedFromCard** and **SelectedToCard** properties do not call **OnNotifyPropertyChanged** since **SelectedItem** bindings are **OneWayToSource** bindings that do not track source property changes. Such a binding just forwards the selected item to the source.

The task for you: create **ViewModel** classes for other pages and move business logic from the code-behind to ViewModels using commands and bindings. Don't forget about compiled bindings.

Navigation with MVVM

You might notice that the navigation process introduces a misconception when it comes to codebase decoupling. Although we have split the application into three layers, every page is responsible for defining and initializing its ViewModel, and pages (view layer) have direct access to the data one ViewModel passes to another. And finally, we were forced to pass the **INavigation** object, giving ViewModel excessive access to navigation capabilities. Besides, navigation of real-world enterprise applications can be much more complex, and you may face the following challenges:

- How can we make **ViewModel** responsible for navigation without providing full access to navigation capabilities, such as access to navigation stacks? Placing navigation logic in **ViewModel** classes allows that logic to be covered by **ViewModel** unit tests. Moreover, the **ViewModel** can then control navigation according to business rules.

- How can we cleanly separate the navigation logic from the **ViewModel** business logic to make navigation logic reusable and more encapsulated so that **ViewModel** is responsible for **View**-related business logic only?

- How can we free a **View** layer object from the need to define and initialize **ViewModel** so that a **Page** is responsible for UI-related things only?

- How can we handle navigation life cycle events (that is, **OnNavigatedTo**) on **ViewModel**'s side?

Those challenges are usually addressed by a service class that is responsible for creating a **Page-ViewModel** pair, assigning the **ViewModel** object to the **BindingContext** of a page, initializing the **ViewModel**, making navigation actions, and handling navigation life cycle events on **ViewModel**'s side.

To implement the mechanism described earlier, the following preparation steps must be performed:

1. Remove everything except the **InitializeComponent** method call from constrictors of pages (***.xaml.cs** files).

2. Remove all parameters from constructors of pages and **ViewModels**.

3. Remove the **_navigation** fields of type **INavigation** from **ViewModels**.

4. Add the **override** modifier to the **OnNavigatedTo** method of **HomePageViewModel**. Don't worry about IDE saying that the base class has no such method to override.

5. Remove the overridden **OnNavigatedTo** method from **HomePage.xaml.cs**.

Our views are now in the desired state: they are responsible for UI and bindings only. However, all our **ViewModels** are full of errors because **ViewModels** have no way to perform navigations.

First, we need to add a few new elements that the navigation service will rely on. Add the following **ViewModelBase** class to the **ViewModels** folder and make all **ViewModels** derive it; use the **Chapter_5/3_LearningMauiBankingApp_Navigation** application from the repository for this section if needed:

```
public abstract class ViewModelBase : NotifyPropertyChangedBase
{
    protected readonly HierarchicalNavigationService _navigationService;

    public ViewModelBase()
    {
        _navigationService = new HierarchicalNavigationService();
    }

    public virtual void OnNavigatedTo() { }
}
```

The **ViewModelBase** class provides its children access to the navigation service object and contains the virtual **OnNavigatedTo** method that will be called by our future **HierarchicalNavigationService** class.

Next, add a new folder called **Interfaces** to the solution and add the **IInitialize** interface to it:

```
public interface IInitialize<T>
{
    void Initialize(T navigationParameter);
}
```

The navigation service will check whether the **ViewModel** class implements this interface. If so, the service will call the **Initialize** method passing navigation data to it, so ViewModel will be initialized before being assigned to View. It's important to remember that all time-consuming operations must be executed in the background using **Task Parallel Library** to not block the UI of the application and to ensure that navigation is performed as quickly as possible.

The only page initialized by data we have now is **TransferModalPage**, so make **TransferModalPageViewModel** implement the **IInitialize** interface, as follows:

```
public class TransferModalPageViewModel :
    ViewModelBase, IInitialize<IEnumerable<BankCard>>
{
    ...

    public void Initialize (IEnumerable<BankCard> navigationParameter)
    {
        Cards = navigationParameter;
    }
}
```

Since our service must be responsible for creating ViewModel and assigning it to **BindingContext**, the application **MainPage** initialization must also be done by the service. So, modify the constructor of the **App** class as follows:

```
public App()
{
    InitializeComponent();
    var navigationService = new HierarchicalNavigationService();
    navigationService.Initialize<LoginPage, LoginPageViewModel>();
}
```

Now, it looks like the only element we need is **HierarchicalNavigationService**. Based on the current needs of the application, the navigation service must contain the following methods:

- The **Initialize** method should instantiate the first page of the application and set it as a **MainPage** of the application.

- The **NavigateToAsync** method should take the type of a **Page**, create an instance of the **Page** and perform navigation to it.

- The **NavigateBackAsync** method should call the **PopAsync** method, navigating to the previous page of the navigation stack.

- The **ClearBackStack** method should remove all previous pages from the navigation stack.

- **CloseCurrentModalPageAsync** should call the **PopModalPageAsync** method, closing the current visible modal page.

Add a new folder called **Services** to the solution and add the following class to it:

```
public class HierarchicalNavigationService
{
    public void Initialize<TPage, TViewModel>()
        where TPage : ContentPage
        where TViewModel : ViewModelBase
    {

        var page = CreatePage<TPage, TViewModel>();
        App.Current.MainPage = new NavigationPage(page);
        var viewModel = (ViewModelBase)page.BindingContext;
        viewModel.OnNavigatedTo();
    }

public async Task NavigateToAsync<TPage, TViewModel, TParameter>(
    TParameter navigationParameter, bool isModal = false)
    where TPage : ContentPage
    where TParameter : class
    where TViewModel : ViewModelBase
{

    if (App.Current.MainPage is not NavigationPage navigationPage)
        return;

    var page = CreatePage<TPage, TViewModel>();
    await NavigateByPageInternalAsync<TParameter>(navigationPage.
Navigation, page, isModal, navigationParameter);
}

public async Task NavigateToAsync<TPage, TViewModel>(bool isModal =
false)
    where TPage : ContentPage
    where TViewModel : ViewModelBase
{

    if (App.Current.MainPage is not NavigationPage navigationPage)
```

```
        return;

    var page = CreatePage<TPage, TViewModel>();
    await NavigateByPageInternalAsync<object>(navigationPage.Navigation,
page, isModal);
}

public async Task NavigateBackAsync()
{
    if (App.Current.MainPage is not NavigationPage navigationPage)
        return;

    await navigationPage.PopAsync();
}

public void ClearBackStack()
{
    if (App.Current.MainPage is not NavigationPage navigationPage)
        return;

    var currentPage = navigationPage.Navigation.NavigationStack.Last();
    var pagesToRemove = navigationPage.Navigation.NavigationStack.
TakeWhile(x => !ReferenceEquals(x, currentPage)).ToList();

    foreach (var pageToRemove in pagesToRemove)
    {
        navigationPage.Navigation.RemovePage(pageToRemove);
    }
}

public async Task CloseCurrentModalPageAsync()
{
    await App.Current.MainPage.Navigation.PopModalAsync();
}

private async Task NavigateByPageInternalAsync<TParameter>(
    INavigation navigation,
    ContentPage page,
    bool isModal,
    TParameter parameter = null) where TParameter : class
```

```
{
    var viewModel = (ViewModelBase) page.BindingContext;

    if (viewModel is IInitialize<TParameter> initializableViewModel)
        initializableViewModel.Initialize(parameter);

    if (isModal)
        await navigation.PushModalAsync(page);
    else
        await navigation.PushAsync(page);

    viewModel.OnNavigatedTo();
}

private ContentPage CreatePage<TPage, TViewModel>()
    where TPage : ContentPage
    where TViewModel : ViewModelBase
{
    var page = (TPage)Activator.CreateInstance(typeof(TPage));
    var viewModel = (TViewModel)Activator.
CreateInstance(typeof(TViewModel));
    page.BindingContext = viewModel;
    return page;
}
```

The basic idea of a navigation service is to concentrate common navigation logic in a single place: a third-party class. The navigation service provides simple API encapsulating navigation stacks and instances of other pages. Besides, it's easy to extend the navigation service if needed. Don't be confused by the number of generics. The core methods of the service are the **CreatePage** and **NavigateByPageInternalAsync** private methods. The **CreatePage** method creates instances of a **Page** and **ViewModel** using types provided by generic type parameters and defines the **BindingContext** of the **Page**. The **NavigateByPageInternalAsync** method takes the newly created page, initializes it, and initiates the navigation. Since our application uses hierarchical navigation, the service was based on **NavigationPage** navigation. However, other types of navigation might be handled in a similar way, following the same idea of extracting navigation logic to the external service.

Experienced developers might notice that a **ViewModel** that utilizes the service must "know" a type of **Page** and **ViewModel** of a **Page** navigating to. This doesn't eliminate the coupling issue completely. There are two reasons for that. First, depending on the specifics of concrete application, additional patterns like state machine can be applied to make the codebase even less coupled. However, the main purpose of the introduced navigation service is to provide a minimum valuable tool demonstrating the simple common way of solving MVVM navigation problems. Second, there is an alternative approach allowing to pass the type of a **ViewModel** only. However, this approach is based on reflection and the hope that developers will strongly follow the naming convention while creating **Pages** and corresponding **ViewModels**. It's up to you what approach to use, but it's hard to deny that a strongly typed approach is more reliable in the long run.

The task for you: Go through the application and use the navigation service for navigation in every **ViewModel** where navigation action is required.

Dependency Inversion Principle

The main idea of this principle is that high-level modules should not depend on low-level modules. Both modules should depend on abstractions instead. In practice, in C# strongly typed languages like C#, abstraction dependency means that a class should refer to interfaces or abstract classes instead of concrete classes. Following Dependency Inversion Principle (DIP) makes a codebase much more flexible and maintainable.

For example, we used the **ICommand** interface while declaring the **OpenTransfer ModalCommand** property of **HomePageViewModel**, but the **Command** class while defining the property. Here, the **HomePageViewModel** class is the high-level module, and the **Command** class is the low-level module. Both depend on the **ICommand** interface. Moreover, the **Button's Command** bindable property being a high-level module also depends on the **ICommand** interface. Such an inversed dependency ensures that even if an implementation of the **Command** class changes in a new version of MAUI, **ViewModel** classes and **Button** class will not need to change. Besides, a command property can be defined with another kind of command providing some extra features or changing internal logic to be safer or faster, and the **Button** class wouldn't need any change while the new command implements the **ICommand** interface.

Let's improve our banking app by applying DIP. If you look at the **HomePageViewModel** class, you might notice the **GetBankCards** method that creates a list filled with dummy cards. It's not a good idea to put such logic into the ViewModel. First, it's not the responsibility of a ViewModel to retrieve the user's bank card details since this logic has nothing to do with HomePage-specific business logic and can be easily extracted from the **ViewModel**, reducing code coupling. Second, a separate class that is responsible for the user's bank card info management is much easier to cover by unit tests and extend. Third, the separate class that depends on an interface is easy to replace with the one implementing the real mechanism of getting bank cards by sending requests to the web API, caching data, and so on.

First of all, we need to add an interface declaring signatures that are unlikely to be changed so that other classes can rely on this interface. Add the following interface to the **Interfaces** folder of the solution of our banking app; use **Chapter_5/4_ LearningMauiBankingApp_DIP** application for this section if needed:

```
public interface IBankCardManager
{
    Task<IEnumerable<BankCard>> GetBankCardsAsync();
}
```

The **GetBankCardsAsync** returns **Task** because we foresee that some method implementations may contain calls to web API, local cache database, and so on. So now, classes that consume implementations of **IBankCardManager** can "await" the execution of **GetBankCardsAsync** to not block the UI thread. Now, move the logic of the existing **GetBankCards** method to the class, as follows:

```
public class DummyBankCardManager : IBankCardManager
{
    public async Task<IEnumerable<BankCard>> GetBankCardsAsync()
    {
        var bankCards = new List<BankCard>
        {
            new BankCard("Main card", 1882824500100505, new
DateTime(2029, 5, 1), 3253.45m),
            new BankCard("Emergency card", 4004799964524057, new
DateTime(2028, 2, 1), 8500m),
            new BankCard("Savings card", 4576241367871031, new
DateTime(2025, 10, 1), 4300m),
        };

        return await Task.FromResult(bankCards);
    }
}
```

Then, remove the **GetBankCards** method and consume **DummyBankCardManager**, as follows:

```
public class HomePageViewModel : ViewModelBase
{
    private readonly IBankCardManager _bankCardManager;

    private IEnumerable<BankCard> _bankCards;
    public IEnumerable<BankCard> BankCards
    {
        get => _bankCards;
        private set
        {
            _bankCards = value;
            OnPropertyChanged(nameof(BankCards));
        }
    }

    public ICommand OpenTransferModalCommand { get; }

    public HomePageViewModel()
    {
        _bankCardManager = new DummyBankCardManager();
        OpenTransferModalCommand = new Command(OpenTransferModal);
    }

    public override void OnNavigatedTo()
    {
        _navigationService.ClearBackStack();
        Task.Run(async () => BankCards = await _bankCardManager.
GetBankCardsAsync());
    }
    ...
}
```

Since the **BankCards** property isn't defined in the constructor anymore, it returns null when binding tries to get data the first time. It happens when the **HomePageViewModel** is assigned to the **BindingContext** of the **HomePage**. Now, the constructor doesn't contain potentially time-consuming operations and ensures navigation to the **HomePage** is done without delay. The constructor is responsible for defining the command property and the **_bankCardManager** field only now. Bank cards, in turn, are gotten in the **OnNavigatedTo** method being called by the navigation service. Note that the **BankCard** property is updated from a "background task", and we can't be sure what thread is used for that operation. However, the application doesn't throw any exception claiming we try to update (via binding) UI control from a thread other than the main thread. It works fine because the binding mechanism ensures that UI control is updated on the main thread. You can also force some actions to be executed on the main thread, thanks to the static **BeginInvokeOnMainThread** method of the **MainThread** class.

You might be curious why we've given different suffixes, Service and Manager, to **NavigationService** and **BankCardManager**. It's mostly about codebase readability. The naming convention, and the naming convention around pages and **ViewModels** differ from company to company, from team to team, while the internet is full of hot discussions about it. The author's experience say that a suffix has to reflect the mission. Moreover, it's worth adding a suffix only when the class name is not descriptive enough. For example, a **NavigationService** provides services for navigating between pages. The **BankCardManager** is suggested to manage bank cards or a user, their getting, adding, removing, caching, and so on. However, naming conventions is often a tricky topic where only in-team/in-company agreement matters.

The task for you: Create **INavigationService** containing signatures of **HierarchicalNavigationService** public methods, and then replace the type of the **_navigationService** field of **ViewModelBase** with **INavigationService**.

Inversion of Control

Although we've inverted dependencies and significantly reduced coupling, constructors of **ViewModels** of our application are still responsible for creating instances of specific implementations of interfaces. It means that **ViewModels** are still a bit dependent on concrete classes. The **ViewModels** of real-world commercial applications could utilize more than a dozen different services. Each service, in turn, might have its own dependencies. So, even replacing one interface implementation with another might require dozens of changes in numerous files, increasing the risk of breaking the existing code.

Inversion of Control (IoC) is a design principle that helps solve this problem. It recommends inversing various types of controls to achieve loose coupling. Here, control means any responsibilities of a class other than its main responsibility. As you remember, business logic of a **View** is the main responsibility of a **ViewModel**, not controlling the life cycle of dependency objects. So, it would be great to get dependencies passed to a class so that the class doesn't need to take care of where dependency objects came from.

Dependency Injection

Dependency Injection (DI) is a design pattern, which is a way to achieve IoC between classes and their dependencies in practice. The idea is to inject dependencies using the constructor of a class.

Let's apply the IoC principle and the DI pattern to the **ViewModels** of our banking app. Modify constructors of **ViewModelBase** and **HomePageViewModel**, shown as follows, and then do the same for other **ViewModels**; use **Chapter_5/4_LearningMauiBankingApp_IoC_DI** application for this section if needed:

ViewModelBase.cs:

```
public ViewModelBase(INavigationService navigationService)
{
    _navigationService = navigationService;
}
```

HomePageViewModel.cs:

```
public HomePageViewModel(
    INavigationService navigationService,
    IBankCardManager bankCardManager)
    : base(navigationService)
{
    _bankCardManager = bankCardManager;
    OpenTransferModalCommand = new Command(OpenTransferModal);
}
```

Now **ViewModels** know nothing about concrete implementations of **INavigation Service** and **IBankCardManager**. So now, **ViewModels** can even be covered by unit tests separately from dependencies, replacing dependencies with mock objects.

Although we've inverted control over dependency objects, the following problems are there:

- A navigation service must instantiate all dependencies required for a **ViewModel** we desire to navigate. Besides, it must instantiate all dependencies of every dependency of a **ViewModel**. It doesn't sound like a responsibility of a navigation service.

- Even in the case of our tiny banking app, the code of the navigation service is about to become messy with such logic in it.

- In a real-world large commercial project with multiple classes depending on services like **IBankCardManager**, the configuration code becomes scattered across the app.

What if we could have a tool that returns an object of the desired class with all dependencies resolved, where each dependency has been resolved by the desired concrete type? A **Dependency Injection Container** is an answer.

A **Dependency Injection Container** is an **object** that knows how to instantiate and configure other objects. It manages object creation and its lifetime and also injects dependencies into the class.

.NET MAUI, unlike its predecessor, Xamarin, comes with a built-in DI container, so we just need to configure it to let the container know about the classes and abstractions that the container can instantiate.

Add the following code to the **CreateMauiApp** method of the **MauiProgram** class:

```
builder.Services.AddTransient<LoginPage>();
builder.Services.AddTransient<LoginPageViewModel>();

builder.Services.AddTransient<HomePage>();
builder.Services.AddTransient<HomePageViewModel>();

builder.Services.AddTransient<TransferModalPage>();
builder.Services.AddTransient<TransferModalPageViewModel>();

builder.Services.AddTransient<IBankCardManager, DummyBankCardManager>();
builder.Services.AddTransient<INavigationService,
HierarchicalNavigationService>();
```

In the context of the DI container, every registered class is called a service. The **builder.Services** property returns a reference to the object of type **IServiceCollection** that is responsible for storing registered DI services. As you can see, we've registered specific types for pages and **ViewModels**, and implementations for interfaces. So, the DI container will create an instance of **DummyBankCardManager** every time the **IBankCardManager** dependency is required. A service can be registered in one of three ways:

- The DI container creates a new instance for each dependency of a service registered as **Transient**.

- When a type registered as **Scoped**, the DI container creates and injects the same instance for every dependency of a specified type within the same context.. For example, in the case of injecting two dependencies of type **IBankCardManager** to the same **ViewModel**, only one **DummyBankCardManager** instance will be created and passed for both **ViewModel** parameters.

- For the service registered as **Singleton**, the DI container creates only one service instance that is injected everywhere it's required.

Each of the **AddTransient**, **AddScoped**, **AddSingleton** methods has multiple overloads providing a flexible registration mechanism that enables you not only to register a service in different ways but also define how exactly an instance of a specific service must be created. In addition, **IServiceCollection** allows the configuration of the built-in logger and options mechanism (options pattern in .NET).

After the required types have been registered, the DI container is ready to resolve our custom dependencies. Modify the constructor of the **App** class as follows:

```
public App(INavigationService navigationService)
{
    InitializeComponent();

    navigationService.Initialize<LoginPage, LoginPageViewModel>();
}
```

Then, let's make the navigation service use the DI container to instantiate pages and **ViewModels**. Add the constructor and modify the **CreatePage** method of the **HierarchicalNavigationService** class, as follows:

```
public class HierarchicalNavigationService : INavigationService
{
    private readonly IServiceProvider _serviceProvider;

    public HierarchicalNavigationService(IServiceProvider provider)
    {
        _serviceProvider = provider;
    }
    ...
    private ContentPage CreatePage<TPage, TViewModel>()
        where TPage : ContentPage
        where TViewModel : ViewModelBase
    {
        var page = _serviceProvider.GetService<TPage>();
        var viewModel = _serviceProvider.GetService<TViewModel>();
```

```
        page.BindingContext = viewModel;
        return page;
    }
}
```

IServiceProvider is a preregistered DI service that allows resolving instances of the required types *manually*. We've delegated the responsibility for controlling the life cycle of objects of pages, **ViewModels**, and their dependencies to the DI container, so classes of our application don't rely on concrete implementations. Instead, they rely on abstractions, and there is only one place, i.e., DI container configuration, where concrete implementations of abstractions are referenced.

Third-Party DI Container Integration (StrongInject)

There are several different DI container frameworks on the market that are chosen by companies for their applications instead of the container provided by Microsoft. The reasons might be different. Sometimes the old project that relies on a specific DI container must be migrated to the newest technology. Sometimes, a third-party container offers benefits and features important for a concrete application. Whatever the reason is, the key point is that sometimes we want to use a third-party DI container.

In this section, we are about to integrate a third-party DI container into our banking app using the **StrongInject** DI container framework as an example. **StrongInject** was chosen over a number of other frameworks because it differs from many other containers, offering some unique features that resolve a few important (especially for mobile applications) problems of traditional DI containers.

Here are a few advantages of **StrongInject**:

- **StrongInject** is a compile-time DI framework. Unlike other containers where an attempt to inject unregistered dependency causes a runtime exception, which is super annoying, **StrongInject** analyzes the code of an application during compilation and throws a compilation error, immediately notifying you about forgotten registration.

- Thanks to the utilized modern "Source Generators" feature of .NET, **StrongInject** doesn't use reflection, runtime code generation, and dictionary lookups. It means lower application startup time and better overall performance of an application.

The main idea of integration is that we create a **StrongInject** container class and ask the .NET MAUI container to use our **StrongInject** container instead of the default one to resolve a requested service and its dependencies.

Let's add the **StrongInject** DI container to our banking app. Use the **Chapter_5/ 6_LearningMauiBankingApp_Replace_DI** application if needed for this section.

First, install the following NuGet packages to the project:

- StrongInject

- StrongInject.Extensions.DependencyInjection

Next, go to **MauiProgram.cs** and modify DI services registrations using the **AddTransientServiceUsingContainer** extension method we got from the **StrongInject** framework, as follows:

```
builder.Services.AddTransientServiceUsingContainer<StrongContainer,
LoginPage>();

…

builder.Services.AddTransientServiceUsingContainer<StrongContainer,
INavigationService>();
```

This extension method "says" to the .NET MAUI container: "Hey, don't use your mechanisms to instantiate and manage the **INavigationService** type. Ask the **StrongContainer** class to make it for you instead." So, we need to add the **StrongContainer** class. Add it to the root of the project and fill in with the following code:

```
[Register(typeof(LoginPage))]

[Register(typeof(LoginPageViewModel))]

[Register(typeof(HomePage))]

[Register(typeof(HomePageViewModel))]

[Register(typeof(TransferModalPage))]

[Register(typeof(TransferModalPageViewModel))]

[Register(typeof(DummyBankCardManager), typeof(IBankCardManager))]

[Register(typeof(HierarchicalNavigationService),
typeof(INavigationService))]

public partial class StrongContainer :

    IContainer<IStrongServiceProvider>,

    IContainer<LoginPage>,

    IContainer<LoginPageViewModel>,
```

```
IContainer<HomePage>,

IContainer<HomePageViewModel>,

IContainer<TransferModalPage>,

IContainer<TransferModalPageViewModel>,

IContainer<IBankCardManager>,

IContainer<INavigationService>
{

    [Instance]
    private readonly IServiceProvider _serviceProvider;


    public StrongContainer(IServiceProvider serviceProvider)
    {

        _serviceProvider = serviceProvider;

    }

}
```

A **StrongInject** container is a factory that knows how to provide an instance of a service on demand and dispose of it once it's no longer needed. The code of a factory is generated during the compilation. That is why the class of the preceding container is marked as partial. In turn, the code we've written by hand is a registration that lets **StrongInject** know what and how it can instantiate.

This integration works both ways, allowing us to inject the **IServiceProvider** service preregistered in .NET MAUI container into the **StrongInject** container. So, the .NET MAUI DI container resolves the dependency of the **StrongInject** container while using it.

Congratulations! We've integrated a third-party DI container into our application.

Invoke platform code from shared code

There are cases when certain features are not available in cross-platform .NET MAUI API. In those situations, you can write your own API and handle things you need on a level of platform APIs. This requires knowledge of Apple's iOS and MacCatalyst APIs, Google Android APIs, and Microsoft Windows App SDK APIs.

Platform code can be invoked from cross-platform code by using conditional compilation or partial classes and partial methods. In this section, the second approach will be considered because of the more clean and structured resulting code it produces, which is good for commercial development.

Suppose we need to get the device screen brightness level. First, we need to create an empty partial class with a partial method **GetBrightness**, as follows:

```
namespace MyExampleMauiApplication.Services

{

    public partial class DeviceScreenManager

    {

        public partial double GetBrightness();

    }

}
```

Next, platform implementations must be added to the platforms child folders. The important thing here is that platform implementation must be in the same namespace and the same class that the cross-platform API was defined in. So, the platform implementations placed in platform-specific folders should look as follows:

For iOS

```
namespace MyExampleMauiApplication.Services

{

    public partial class DeviceScreenManager

    {

        public partial double GetBrightness()

        {

            return UIScreen.MainScreen.Brightness;

        }

    }

}
```

For Android

```
namespace MyExampleMauiApplication.Services

{

    public partial class DeviceScreenManager

    {

        public partial double GetBrightness()

        {

            var contentResolver = MainApplication.Current.
ContentResolver;

            var brightnessSettingName = Android.Provider.Settings.
```

```
System.ScreenBrightness;

        var nativeValue = Android.Provider.Settings.System.
GetInt(contentResolver, brightnessSettingName);
        return ConvertToLinearLinearFactor(nativeValue);
    }
  }
}
```

So, now the build system chooses the platform-specific implementation of **DeviceScreenManager** depending on the target platform, and **DeviceScreenManager** can be consumed in cross-platform code as any other class. In other words, since .NET provides full access to the platform-native API, we've created a cross-platform API for the feature that is not available in MAUI out of the box.

Since .NET MAUI apps can also be multi-targeted based on filename or folder, the platform implementations might not be placed into platforms folders. In such a case, a standard pattern is to include the platform name as an extension in the filename for the platform code file (that is, **DeviceScreenManager.Android.cs**). However, this approach requires adding a multi-targeting configuration added to the ***.csproj** file.

Gesture Recognizers

When it comes to user interactions, there is a set of UI controls like **Button** or **Picker** that are created specifically to handle user input. However, sometimes, there is a need to make other UI elements clickable or able to detect specific user input, such as swipe or pinch. .NET MAUI makes this possible, thanks to a set of gesture recognizers that can be applied to any UI element deriving from the **View** class.

Let us get back to our banking app and make money transfers more convenient. What if tiles of bank cards would be clickable so that once a user taps on a bank card, the transfer modal page shows up with a tapped card being preselected?

Since now we need to pass to the transfer page not only a collection of bank cards but also a number of the chosen card, we have to create a dedicated navigation parameter model. Add a new **TransferModalPageNavigationParameter** class to the **Models** folder and modify **TransferModalPageViewModel**, as follows. Don't forget to change the binding mode of "From Card" picker to "TwoWay" to make it able to react to the **SelectedFromCard** property changes. Use **Chapter_5/7_ LearningMauiBankingApp_Gestures** application if needed.

```
public class TransferModalPageNavigationParameter
{
    public IEnumerable<BankCard> BankCards { get; }
```

```csharp
    public long FromCardNumber { get; }

    public TransferModalPageNavigationParameter(
        IEnumerable<BankCard> bankCards, long fromCardNumber = 0)
    {
        BankCards = bankCards;
        FromCardNumber = fromCardNumber;
    }
}

public class TransferModalPageViewModel : ViewModelBase,
    IInitialize<TransferModalPageNavigationParameter>
{
...
    private BankCard _selectedFromCard;
    public BankCard SelectedFromCard
    {
        get => _selectedFromCard;
        set
        {
            _selectedFromCard = value;
            OnPropertyChanged(nameof(SelectedFromCard));
        }
    }
...

    public void Initialize(TransferModalPageNavigationParameter
navigationParameter)
    {
        Cards = navigationParameter.BankCards;
        SelectedFromCard = Cards.FirstOrDefault(x =>
            x.CardNumber == navigationParameter.FromCardNumber);
    }
}
```

Now, the transfer page is ready to be preconfigured. On **HomePage**, in turn, we need to create a new command property to handle taps on bank cards and add **TapGuestureRecognizer** to the Grid of bank card tiles. Modify **HomePageViewModel** by adding a new **SelectBankCardCommand** command in a way similar to the existing **OpenTransferModalCommand**, as follows:

HomePageViewModel.cs:

```csharp
public ICommand SelectBankCardCommand { get; }

...

SelectBankCardCommand = new Command<long>(OnBankCardSelected);

...

private async void OpenTransferModal()
{
    await _navigationService.NavigateToAsync<
        TransferModalPage,
        TransferModalPageViewModel,
        TransferModalPageNavigationParameter>(
        new TransferModalPageNavigationParameter(BankCards), true);
}


private async void OnBankCardSelected(long bankCardNumber)
{
    await _navigationService.NavigateToAsync<
        TransferModalPage,
        TransferModalPageViewModel,
        TransferModalPageNavigationParameter>(
        new TransferModalPageNavigationParameter(BankCards,
bankCardNumber),
        true);
}
```

As you can see, the command uses the command parameter, so we are going to pass the number of a chosen card straight from the gesture recognizer. Go to the **HomePage. xaml** file and modify the root **Grid** of the **BindableLayout.ItemTemplate**, which defines the visual template of bank cards.

There is a thing that needs to be explained here. In this book, **async void** methods will be used to make code examples simpler and to make you focus on a MAUI-specific things. However, it's important to know that **async void** methods are considered a bad practice because they are complicate testing and often a reason for hard-to-debug bugs. In complex commercial applications, "async void" methods are considered acceptable only for event handlers. In any other cases, async methods should return **Task** or **Task<T>**. To learn more about this topic and best async/await practices, read .NET specific literature.

Let's now make our bank cards tappable with **TapGestureRecognizer** as shown below:

```
...
<DataTemplate x:DataType="models:BankCard">
    <Grid WidthRequest="311" HeightRequest="214"
          RowDefinitions="1*, 1*">
        <Grid.GestureRecognizers>
            <TapGestureRecognizer
                Command="{Binding BindingContext.
SelectBankCardCommand, Source={x:Reference ValueableContentGrid}}"
                CommandParameter="{Binding CardNumber}"/>
        </Grid.GestureRecognizers>
...
```

Although we've added only one gesture recognizer, **GestureRecognizers** is a collection of type **IList<IGestureRecognizer>** so multiple gesture recognizers can be applied to the same UI element. The important thing here is that since the Grid is placed inside **ItemTemplate**, its default **BindingContext** is an object of type **BankCard**. Therefore, **CommandParameter** is bound to the **CardNumber** property without any additional configurations. However, the target of the command's binding is in the view model. Because of that, we've overridden the source of the command's binding and then specified the binding target property by the **SelectBankCardCommand** property of the source's **BindingContext**, which is **HomePageViewModel** since **ValueableContentGrid** control derives it from parent elements of the visual tree. As a result, tapping on the bank card opens the transfer modal page where the tapped card is set as "From Card" by default.

.NET MAUI provides the following gesture recognizers:

- **TapGestureRecognizer** is used for tap detection. In addition to **Command** and **CommandProperty**, it allows defining the number of taps required to recognize a tap gesture and detect whether the primary or secondary mouse button or both trigger the gesture on desktop operating systems. This gesture recognizer also has the **Tapped** event, the argument parameter of which provides additional information such as the position of a tap relative to other elements.

- **SwipeGestureRecognizer** detects when a finger is moved across the screen in a horizontal or vertical direction. Desired swipe direction and the threshold (minimum swipe distance) can be configured.

- **PointerGestureRecognizer** detects when the pointer enters, exits, and moves within a view. It provides a wide set of commands and events to handle different states of the pointer. However, pointer gesture recognition is only supported on iPadOS, MacCatalyst, and Windows platforms.

- **PinchGestureRecognizer** is usually used for performing interactive zoom. Since this recognizer was created to handle advanced UI/UX cases, it doesn't have commands. Instead, the recognizer provides the **PinchUpdated** event that is raised when the detected pinch gesture changes.

- **PanGestureRecognizer** detects the movement of fingers around the screen and can be used, for example, to move content next to a finger. The number of **TouchPoints** is configurable. The **PanUpdated** event is raised when the detected pan gesture changes.

- **DragGestureRecognizer** and **DropGestureRecognizer** enable UI elements and their associated data to be dragged from one onscreen location to another using continuous gesture. Drag and drop can take place in a single application or can start in one application and end in another. The drag source, which is the element on which the drag gesture is initiated, can provide data to be transferred by populating a data package object. When the drag source is released, a drop occurs. The drop target, which is the element under the drag source, then processes the data package.

LiteDB database

Almost every application needs some persistent data storage at least to store users' data and cache the data coming from a web API. LiteDB is a fast and lightweight embedded single-file NoSQL database for .NET applications that is mobile- and desktop-friendly.

LiteDb stores data as documents, which are JSON-like objects containing key-value pairs. Those JSON-like objects are called BSONs (Binary JSON). Documents are a schema-less data structure. Each document stores both its data and its structure and can be easily extended. LiteDB stores documents in collections. A collection is a group of related documents that have a set of shared indices. Collections are analogous to tables in relational databases. Although LiteDB is a document database, it supports references between collections of documents.

To keep its memory profile slim, the size of documents is limited to 1MB. It is more than enough for most use cases. However, consider the case when, let's say, every bank branch on a list in a mobile application contains a high-resolution photo of the main entry, so we have to store an image along with the address and contact data while caching the list of bank branches that came from the web API. For such a case, LiteDb provides FileStorage, a custom collection to store files and streams. FileStorage uses two special collections.

Local storage implementation

At this moment, we have been getting bank cards from **IBankCardManager**. However, **TransferModalPage** retrieves bank cards from the navigation parameter because it needs to operate on the same objects that **HomePage** uses. And this is a problem because now there might be more than one so-called source of truth for bank cards. What if some other page of the application, that is not opened from the HomePage, would require bank card data? The most obvious answer is to inject **IBankCardManager**. But in that case, it must be considered as a single way to get and manipulate bank cards. Moreover, we need to store data in some persistent storage, so the user gets the correct data even after the application restarts. Of course, in the case of making real money transfer and manipulating bank card data, we most likely would perform all the operations communicating with some server via the internet and would not store such important data locally. However, if you think about it more abstractly, you will find lots of similar cases.

Install the **LiteDB** NuGet package. The further implementation is valid for **LiteDB v5.0.15**. Next, add the following interface to the **Interfaces** folder, and then apply it to the **BankCard** class and add a constructor to the **BankCard** class, as shown here:

ILocalStorageItem.cs:

```
public interface ILocalStorageItem
{
    ObjectId LocalStorageId { get; set; }
}
```

BankCard.cs:

```
public class BankCard : NotifyPropertyChangedBase, ILocalStorageItem
{
    [BsonId]
    public ObjectId LocalStorageId { get; set; }

...


    [BsonCtor]
    public BankCard(ObjectId localStorageId, string alias, long
```

```
cardNumber, DateTime expirationDate, decimal balance)

    : this(alias, cardNumber, expirationDate, balance)

{

    LocalStorageId = localStorageId;

}

}
```

The **LocalStorageId** of type **ObjectId** here serves as the primary key to a LiteDB document. The document **Id** property must be marked with the **[BsonId]** attribute to let LiteDB know what property is the **Id**. The attribute is not required when an **Id** property follows the **<ClassName>Id** naming convention. However, since models to be saved often contain their business logic meaningful IDs, the good practice is to explicitly appoint property a LiteDB ID. Another thing here is a constructor marked as **[BsonCtor]**. This constructor is used by LiteDB while deserializing LiteDB document into an object.

Note one more thing. In large complex applications, it's better to create separate classes for DB entity and the class utilized in **ViewModels**, for example, **BankCardDbEntity** implementing the **ILocalStorageItem** and the **BankCardDesignModel** that doesn't contain DB-related ID and constructors. It's made to split the responsibility and increase maintainability of a codebase because complex applications like **DesignModel** may contain additional business logic-related code, which has nothing to do with database. In such a case, it's the responsibility of intermediate services like **BankCardManager** to map those models to each other, usually using extension methods or dedicated constructors of model classes.

Next, add the **LocalStorage** class, shown as follows, to the **Services** folder and register it as a singleton in the **StrongContainer** class. Don't forget to add an interface corresponding to the **LocalStorage** to the **Interfaces** folder.

Registration attribute for **StrongContainer.cs**:

```
[Register(typeof(LocalStorage), Scope.SingleInstance,
typeof(ILocalStorage))]
```

Registration for **MainProgram.cs**:

```
builder.Services.AddSingletonServiceUsingContainer<StrongContainer,
ILocalStorage>();
```

LocalStorage.cs:

```
public sealed class LocalStorage : ILocalStorage, IDisposable

{
```

```csharp
    private const string DatabaseFileName = "localDb.db";


    private readonly LiteRepository _localDatabase;
    private bool _disposed;


    public LocalStorage()
    {
        var filePath = FileSystem.Current.AppDataDirectory;
        filePath = Path.Combine(filePath, DatabaseFileName);
        var connectionString = $"Filename={filePath};Mode=Exclusive;";


        _localDatabase = new LiteRepository(connectionString);
    }


    public IEnumerable<T> GetAll<T>(Expression<Func<T, bool>> predicate
= null) where T : ILocalStorageItem
    {
        return predicate is null
            ? _localDatabase.Query<T>().ToList()
            : _localDatabase.Query<T>().Where(predicate).ToList();
    }


    public T FirstOrDefault<T>(Expression<Func<T, bool>> predicate =
null) where T : ILocalStorageItem
        => _localDatabase.FirstOrDefault(predicate);


    public void Insert<T>(T item) where T : ILocalStorageItem
        => _localDatabase.Insert(item);


    public void Insert<T>(IEnumerable<T> item) where T :
ILocalStorageItem
        => _localDatabase.Insert(item);


    public bool Update<T>(T item) where T : ILocalStorageItem
```

```
            => _localDatabase.Update(item);

    public bool Delete<T>(ObjectId id) where T : ILocalStorageItem
            => _localDatabase.Delete<T>(id);

    public bool DeleteAll<T>() where T : ILocalStorageItem
            => _localDatabase.Database.DropCollection(typeof(T).Name);

    public void Dispose()
    {
        if (!_disposed)
            _localDatabase.Dispose();

        _disposed = true;
    }
}
```

As you can see the **LocalStorage** class is mainly a wrapper for the **LiteRepository** class. The **LocalStorage** class creates and disposes the connection to the LiteDB database file and encapsulates access to the database while exposing only the necessary functionality. LiteDB creates collections of documents per stored type. So, the **GetAll<T>** method returns all stored objects of type **T**. The **FileSystem. Current.AppDataDirectory** property returns a path to the application folder, which is unique per platform. Constraining parameters type by **ILocalStorageItem** helps ensure that only classes which are LiteDB-ready (containing **LocalStorageId**) are passed to the methods.

Now it looks like we are ready to make the bank card manager service use our newly created local storage. To do this, modify **DummyBankCardManager** as follows:

```
public class DummyBankCardManager : IBankCardManager
{
    private readonly ILocalStorage _localStorage;

    public event EventHandler<IEnumerable<BankCard>> BankCardsChanged;

    public DummyBankCardManager(ILocalStorage localStorage)
    {
        _localStorage = localStorage;
    }
```

```csharp
public async Task<IEnumerable<BankCard>> GetBankCardsAsync()
{
    var localStorageCards = _localStorage.GetAll<BankCard>();

    if (localStorageCards is null || !localStorageCards.Any())
    {
        localStorageCards = CreateDummyCards();
        _localStorage.Insert(localStorageCards);
    }

    return await Task.FromResult(localStorageCards);
}


public Task<bool> TryMakeTransferAsync(BankCard fromCard, BankCard
toCard, decimal valueToTransfer)
{
    if (fromCard.Balance < valueToTransfer)
        return Task.FromResult(false);

    var storageFromCard = _localStorage.FirstOrDefault<BankCard>(x
=> x.LocalStorageId == fromCard.LocalStorageId);
    if (storageFromCard is null)
        return Task.FromResult(false);

    var storageToCard = _localStorage.FirstOrDefault<BankCard>(x =>
x.LocalStorageId == toCard.LocalStorageId);
    if (storageFromCard is null)
        return Task.FromResult(false);

    storageFromCard.Balance -= valueToTransfer;
    storageToCard.Balance += valueToTransfer;

    _localStorage.Update(storageFromCard);
```

```
        _localStorage.Update(storageToCard);
        var localStorageCards = _localStorage.GetAll<BankCard>();

        BankCardsChanged?.Invoke(this, localStorageCards);
        return Task.FromResult(true);
    }

    private IEnumerable<BankCard> CreateDummyCards()
    {
        return new List<BankCard>
        {
            new BankCard("Main card", 1882824500100505, new
DateTime(2029, 5, 1), 3253.45m),
            new BankCard("Emergency card", 4004799964524057, new
DateTime(2028, 2, 1), 8500m),
            new BankCard("Savings card", 4576241367871031, new
DateTime(2025, 10, 1), 4300m),
        };
    }
}
```

The main idea is that we've made our bank card manager responsible for getting and manipulating our bank card balance value. So, now, **TryMakeTransferAsync** must be called in the **OnTransferCommandCalled** method of **TransferModalPageViewModel** instead of doing mathematics. The **TryMakeTransferAsync**, in turn, does not only perform calculations and update bank cards in the local storage but also invokes the **BankCardsChanged** event to notify any subscriber about changes. You might also notice that **GetBankCardsAsync** now checks if cards exist in the database and creates new ones only when the database is empty.

Here are tasks for you to finish this upgrade of the application; use **Chapter_5/ 8_LearningMauiBankingApp_LocalStorage** if needed:

- Remove the **BankCards** property from **TransferModalPageNavigation Parameter** and make **TransferModalPage** get back cards from the **IBankCardManager** service.

- Call **TryMakeTransferAsync** in **TransferModalPageViewModel** instead of doing mathematics in the **OnTransferCommandCalled** method.

- Register **IBankCardManager** as a singleton to ensure that event subscribers subscribe to the same object.

- Subscribe to the **BankCardsChanged** manager in **HomePageViewModel** to update the **BankCards** property with modified bank cards.

Conclusion

Congratulations! Thanks to the applied MVVM pattern, **Inversion of Control**, **Dependency Injection**, and navigation service, our application is easy to maintain, test, and extend. Also, we've improved user experience using **Gesture Recognizer**. Now you even know that thanks to full access to the platform API, almost everything is possible in .NET MAUI.

All this means that you and our banking app are ready to dive deeper into UI development. In the next chapter, we will dive deeper into UI development. You will also get familiar with more advanced elements and tools that are used in real-world applications.

Points to remember

- The **CanExecute** method of the command is called to check whether it is allowed to call the **Execute** method.

- High-level modules should not depend on low-level modules. Both modules should depend on abstractions instead.

- Dependency Injection (DI) is a design pattern, which is a way to achieve **Inversion of Control**.

- .NET MAUI cross-platform API can be easily extended, thanks to the possibility of reaching any platform-specific API.

- Gesture recognizers help make almost any UI element interactive.

Questions

1. What is the main problem MVVM addresses?

2. What is the basic idea of MVVM?

3. What are the responsibilities of each of the layers of MVVM?

4. Why is it a bad practice to invoke navigation from the **View** layer instead of **ViewModel**?

5. What are the differences between services registered as **Transient**, **Singleton**, and **Scoped**?

Join our book's Discord space

Join the book's Discord Workspace for Latest updates, Offers, Tech happenings around the world, New Release and Sessions with the Authors:

https://discord.bpbonline.com

Chapter 6

Deep Dive into UI Design

Introduction

This chapter covers some of the more advanced UI development topics, knowledge about which, based on the author's experience, is of the highest priority when developing custom UI cross-platform applications.

It's highly recommended to refer to the book repository in case of any doubts or confusion. Besides, the official .NET MAUI documentation could significantly enhance your knowledge about nearly half a hundred UI controls available in .NET MAUI.

Structure

In this chapter, we will cover the following topics:

- Handling System Themes
- Custom Themes with DynamicResources
- Multilanguage support
- CarouselView
- IndicatorView

- VisualState Manager

- VisualState Triggers

- Animations

- ContentView

- Custom Controls

- FlexLayout

- Triggers

- OnPlatform and OnIdiom

- Brushes

- Shadows

- Behaviors

- CollectionView

- Customizing native controls

Objectives

In this chapter, we are about to dive deeper into UI development. Most of the chapter is about UI controls, pages, views, and layouts. However, it also covers topics describing different approaches that could help you bring modern sophisticated UI designs to life. Let's get started!

Handling system themes

One of the recent decade's most significant UI design trends is the possibility of switching between so-called **Light** and **Dark** modes. It's not a new idea though. Individual programs had provided similar functionalities long before smartphones became essential, everyday gadgets. However, as people spent more and more time in front of screens, it became clear that interface color schemes preferred by the majority of users can be divided into two groups: light and dark. So, major operation systems vendors introduced the option of switching UI color schemes between **Light** and **Dark**. Besides, some applications allow additional independent color schemes or multiple variations of dark and light themes. .NET MAUI enables you to handle both scenarios.

The **Application** class (inherited by the **App** class) contains the set of the following members to handle light and dark themes during runtime:

- The **PlatformAppTheme** property returns the enum of type **AppTheme** indicating the theme currently set in an operating system. This enumeration defines three members: **Light**, **Dark**, and **Unspecified**. The last one is returned when a platform or version of a platform doesn't support themes.

- The **RequestedTheme** property returns the **AppTheme** enum indicating the current theme to be used for the application. **RequestedTheme** equals **PlatformAppTheme** as long as the **UserAppTheme** value is **Unspecified**.

- The **UserAppTheme** property enables you to force of a specific theme, regardless of which system theme is currently operational.

- The **RequestedThemeChanged** event is raised when the **RequestedTheme** changes.

The current instance of the **Application** class can be reached using the **Application. Current** static property.

AppThemeBinding is a binding class that subscribes the **RequestedThemeChanged** event to assign a corresponding value to the property of UI control depending on the requested theme. This binding can be used in XAML code in the same way as regular binding, which we've learned about in the previous chapter. Thanks to the eponymous markup extension, **AppThemeBinding** is used to create the object of type **AppThemeBinding**. The markup extension contains three properties:

- The values of the **Light** and **Dark** properties are used when the system theme is light or dark, respectively.

- The value of the **Default** property is used when the system theme is light/ dark, but the **Light**/**Dark** property wasn't specified.

It's worth knowing that the properties of **AppThemeBinding** aren't bindable. So, **DynamicResources** can't be used to define **Light**, **Dark**, and **Default** values.

Let us make our banking app handle light and dark system themes. First, add images from the **LearningMauiBankingApp_Assets/Dark** folder of the book repository to the **Resources/Images** folder of the app project. Don't forget to apply **MauiImage build action** to them. Then, add the following set of color resources to **App. xaml** right after the existing color resources. For this section, use the **Chapter_6/1_ LearningMauiBankingApp_DarkLight** application from the book repository if needed:

```
<Color x:Key="DarkPrimaryTextColor">#FFFFFF</Color>

<Color x:Key="DarkSecondaryTextColor">#8E8E93</Color>

<Color x:Key="DarkPrimaryBackgroundColor">#1C1C1E</Color>

<Color x:Key="DarkSecondaryBackgroundColor">#000000</Color>
```

Next, apply the **AppThemeBinding** binding to the **TextColor** property of the **Welcome** label of the **LoginPage** using the **AppThemeBinding** markup extension, as shown here:

```
TextColor="{AppThemeBinding Light={StaticResource LightPrimaryTextColor},
Dark={StaticResource DarkPrimaryTextColor}}"
```

AppThemeBinding can also be used within styles. For example, open the **App.xaml** file and modify the setter of the **TextColor** property of the **PrimaryContentLabelStyle** style, as follows:

```
<Setter Property="TextColor" Value="{AppThemeBinding Light={StaticResource
LightPrimaryTextColor}, Dark={StaticResource DarkPrimaryTextColor}}"/>
```

Now, apply **AppThemeBinding** in the same way to every single place where colors are set. As a result, you will see that the colors in the application change depending on the selected system theme.

Images can be handled in the same way. Logical names of images (that is, **light_background.png**) can still be hardcoded in XAML or defined as string resources, just like colors. However, there is also a widely used alternate approach. Values can be assigned to properties of a static class and then used within the **x:Static** markup extension instead of the **StaticResource** markup extension. This approach has gained popularity because the attempt of using a non-existing static property name will cause a build error, while using a non-existing resource key will not. And this small detail makes a difference in big commercial projects, making the developer's job easier, saving time, and decreasing the number of bugs to fix.

So, let's add such a static class. Create a new **AppConstants** folder in our project and put the new **ImageId** class into it. The following code snippet shows properties for two images. Populate the class with the rest of the properties in the same way as it was done for background images:

```
public static class ImageId
{
    public static string LightBackground { get; } = "light_background.
png";
    public static string DarkBackground { get; } = "dark_background.
png";

    ...
}
```

The following code snippet shows how those strings can be consumed in XAML of the **LoginPage** to set different background images depending on current theme. Refactor other places where images are used by applying the same approach. As a result, you will see that the images in the application change depending on the selected system theme. Besides, any typo or attempt to use non-existing property will throw a build error:

```
xmlns:const="clr-namespace:LearningMauiBankingApp.AppConstants"
```

```
<Image     Source="{AppThemeBinding     Light={x:Static     const:ImageId.
LightBackground},     Dark={x:Static     const:ImageId.DarkBackground}}"
Aspect="AspectFill"/>
```

.NET MAUI also includes a few extension methods of the **BindableObject** class that help simplify the creation of **AppThemeBinding** in C# code. Those methods have the following signatures:

```
void     SetAppTheme<T>(this     BindableObject     self,     BindableProperty
targetProperty, T light, T dark);
```

```
void     SetAppThemeColor(this     BindableObject     self,     BindableProperty
targetProperty, Color light, Color dark);
```

The **SetAppTheme** method establishes **AppThemeBinding** for a property of any type backed by **BindableProperty**. **SetAppThemeColor**, in turn, uses the **SetAppTheme** method and simplifies **AppThemeBinding** creation for properties of type **Color**.

Custom themes with DynamicResources

As we learned from *Chapter 4, In and Out of UI Development*, **DynamicResources** are resources that can be applied to the bindable property of a UI control to change its value dynamically at runtime. Once the resource with the appropriate **x:Key** changes, a new value is applied to the target property of a control.

Another useful feature is **MergedResources**, a property of the **ResourceDictionary** class that refers the collection of other **ResourceDictionaries**. It means that you can, for example, create multiple separated **ResourceDictionaries** and "attach" them to the main resource dictionary of the **App** class. This might be helpful in multiple ways. For example, you can put different kinds of resources to separate files to make the XAML code of your resources less messy and then merge them in **App.xaml**. Or you can create separate resource dictionaries for each color scheme and replace one **ResourceDictionary** with another within the **MergedResources** collection. And then, you just need to utilize the **DynamicResource** markup extension instead of **StaticResource** to make UI controls apply the new colors once the new color scheme applies.

To implement this, we first need to create separate resource dictionaries for theme-dependent resources and then add the default one as a merged resource dictionary. So, add the new **Themes** folder and create a new resource dictionary XAML called **DefaultColorScheme** in it. Next, move all color resources from

App.xaml to **DefaultColorScheme.xaml**, as follows; use the **Chapter_6/2_ LearningMauiBankingApp_DynamicResources** application if needed:

```
<ResourceDictionary xmlns="http://schemas.microsoft.com/dotnet/2021/
maui"

              xmlns:x="http://schemas.microsoft.com/winfx/2009/xaml"

              x:Class="LearningMauiBankingApp.Themes.DefaultColorScheme">

    <Color x:Key="LightPrimaryTextColor">#000000</Color>

    <Color x:Key="LightSecondaryTextColor">#8E8E93</Color>


    <Color x:Key="LightPrimaryBackgroundColor">#FFFFFF</Color>

    <Color x:Key="LightSecondaryBackgroundColor">#F5F5F5</Color>


    <Color x:Key="DarkPrimaryTextColor">#FFFFFF</Color>

    <Color x:Key="DarkSecondaryTextColor">#8E8E93</Color>


    <Color x:Key="DarkPrimaryBackgroundColor">#1C1C1E</Color>

    <Color x:Key="DarkSecondaryBackgroundColor">#000000</Color>

</ResourceDictionary>
```

Now, create one more resource dictionary called **AlternativeColorScheme** with the same color resources, but replace hex color values with any colors you prefer. Next, modify **App.xaml** as follows:

```
xmlns:themes="clr-namespace:LearningMauiBankingApp.Themes"

...

<Application.Resources>

    <ResourceDictionary>

        <ResourceDictionary.MergedDictionaries>

            <themes:DefaultColorScheme/>

        </ResourceDictionary.MergedDictionaries>


        <!--Styles-->

        <Style x:Key="PrimaryHeaderLabelStyle" TargetType="Label">

...
```

As you can see, the behavior of the application remains the same, but color resources are placed in a separate file. To switch between themes, we would need a new service called **ThemeManager**. Create the following service and then register it as transient. Don't forget about the **IThemeManager** interface. In addition, create the new **Enums** folder and put the following enum to it:

```
public enum ColorScheme
{
    Default,
    Alternative
}
```

This enum will be used as an abstraction of application color scheme because of few reasons. First, an application might have numerous different themes. Second, it's better when **ViewModel** know nothing about concrete resource dictionary class. Now, implement the following **ThemeManager**:

```
public class ThemeManager : IThemeManager
{
    private readonly IServiceProvider _serviceProvider;
    private readonly IDictionary<ColorScheme, Type> _
colorSchemeResources = new Dictionary<ColorScheme, Type>();

    public ColorScheme CurrentTheme => GetCurrentTheme();

    public ThemeManager(IServiceProvider serviceProvider)
    {
        _serviceProvider = serviceProvider;

        _colorSchemeResources.Add(ColorScheme.Default,
typeof(DefaultColorScheme));
        _colorSchemeResources.Add(ColorScheme.Alternative,
typeof(AlternativeColorScheme));
    }

    public void SwitchThemeTo(ColorScheme colorScheme)
    {
        if (CurrentTheme == colorScheme)
            return;
```

```
        var globalMergedDictionaries = GetGlobalMergedDictionaries();

        var currentThemeResources = GetCurrentThemeResources();

        var currentResourcesIndex = globalMergedDictionaries.
IndexOf(currentThemeResources);

        var newThemeResources = (ResourceDictionary) _serviceProvider.
GetService(_colorSchemeResources[colorScheme]);

        globalMergedDictionaries.Insert(currentResourcesIndex,
newThemeResources);

        globalMergedDictionaries.Remove(currentThemeResources);

    }


    private ColorScheme GetCurrentTheme()

    {

        var globalMergedDictionaries = GetGlobalMergedDictionaries();

        return _colorSchemeResources.First(x =>
globalMergedDictionaries.Any(y => x.Value == y.GetType())).Key;

    }


    private ResourceDictionary GetCurrentThemeResources()

    {

        var globalMergedDictionaries = GetGlobalMergedDictionaries();

        return globalMergedDictionaries.Single(x => _
colorSchemeResources.Values.Contains(x.GetType()));

    }


    private ObservableCollection<ResourceDictionary>
GetGlobalMergedDictionaries()

        => (ObservableCollection<ResourceDictionary>)App.Current.
Resources.MergedDictionaries;

}
```

This manager knows exactly what **ResourceDictionary** type relates to what **ColorScheme**, thanks to the **_colorSchemeResources** dictionary. The **SwitchThemeTo** method applies the specified **ColorScheme**. The **CurrentTheme** property returns the currently active color scheme. Now, add a new **SettingsPage** to the project containing the **Button** to switch themes and consume **IThemeService** in the command handler, as follows:

```
if (_themeManager.CurrentTheme is ColorScheme.Alternative)

    _themeManager.SwitchThemeTo(ColorScheme.Default);

else

    _themeManager.SwitchThemeTo(ColorScheme.Alternative);
```

Finally, replace the top bar placeholder of the **HomePage** with the following button, providing a way to navigate to the **SettingsPage**:

```
<ImageButton Grid.Row="0"

        Margin="0,0,16,0"

        Style="{StaticResource SmallImageButtonStyle}"

        HorizontalOptions="End"

        VerticalOptions="Center"

        Source="{AppThemeBinding Light={x:Static const:ImageId.
LightSettingsIcon}, Dark={x:Static const:ImageId.DarkSettingsIcon}}"

        Command="{Binding OpenSettingsCommand}"/>
```

You might notice that we haven't used **DynamicResources** yet. From this moment, you can replace any **AppThemeBinding** that handles color with **DynamicResource**, and the color would change once **ThemeManager** replaces a dictionary.

However, what if we want to have multiple custom themes, each handling both light mode and dark mode? Well, it requires additional effort. Unfortunately, **DynamicResource** can't be used within **AppThemeBinding**. It can't track whether the values provided for Light and Dark themes have been changed. Fortunately, there are at least three possible solutions:

- Save information about a selected theme in the local DB or application preferences dictionary (see *Application Preferences* section of *Chapter 7, Essentials and Community Toolkit*) and ask a user to restart the application. In the constructor of the **App** class, in turn, replace the color scheme resource dictionary according to the saved information to prepare proper resources before any page is initialized.

- Recreate pages presented in the navigation stack. In this case, new resources are also applied during page initialization. Or, for example, simply navigate to the home page and remove all previous pages from the navigation stack. The key point is to recreate **AppThemeBindings** with the current values of resources.

- Add an identical **Style** that uses **AppThemeBindings** along with **StaticResources** for each custom theme and consume this style using **DynamicResource**.

The last option can be adopted as follows:

```
<!--The same Style must be in every resource dictionary-->
<Style x:Key="PageStyle" TargetType="Page">
    <Setter Property="BackgroundColor"
            Value="{AppThemeBinding Light={StaticResource
LightSecondaryBackgroundColor},
                                    Dark={StaticResource
DarkSecondaryBackgroundColor}}"/>
</Style>


<!--Style consumption-->
Style="{DynamicResource PageStyle}"
```

Unlike the **Light** and **Dark** properties of **AppThemeBinding**, the **Style** property of controls can consume dynamic resources, so the entire style will be refreshed once the resource dictionary is replaced, changing the value of the **PageStyle** resource. So, **AppThemeBindings** used within the style will also be refreshed. Try this approach with the newly created **SettingsPage**.

Multilanguage support

Applications are often made for a specific country, so texts can be simply hard coded. However, in the case of global software products, multiple localization support is one of the most important things. .NET MAUI supports standard .NET localization mechanism based on the ***.resx** resource. In this section, we will bring multilanguage/localization support to our banking app. The application from the repository that reflects this section is **Chapter_6/3_LearningMauiBankingApp_ Multilanguage**.

Resource ***.resx** files are translated prior to the execution of the consuming application; in other words, they represent translated content at rest. A resource filename most commonly contains a locale identifier and takes on the **[TypeName]. [Locale].resx**. The ***.resx** file with no locale part is a file containing translations in the default language. For global applications, usually, English is used as a default language. Default translations are applied when an application doesn't support the locale that the user has set on a device. The locale part can contain language code only (that is, "en") or both language and region codes (that is, "en-UK"), providing support for country specifics.

Let us add a new **Localization** folder to the project of our banking app and create two ***.resx** files with the following content in them. Use built-in resx designer or any third-party resx editor you like. For the sake of this book, Polish is used as an alternate language. You can choose any language you are comfortable with:

Strings.resx	
Key	Value
LoginPage_Welcome	Welcome
LoginPage_UsernamePlaceholder	Username
LoginPage_PasswordPlaceholder	Password
LoginPage_LoginButton	Login

Table 6.1: *Localization Resource File (Strings.resx) Key-Value Pairs for Login Page*

Refer to the following *Table 6.2:*

Strings.pl.resx	
Key	Value
LoginPage_Welcome	Witaj
LoginPage_UsernamePlaceholder	Nazwa użytkownika
LoginPage_PasswordPlaceholder	Hasło
LoginPage_LoginButton	Zaloguj się

Table 6.2: *Localization Resource File (Strings.pl.resx) Key-Value Pairs for Login Page*

Based on the data from the ***.resx** files, the *.**Designer.cs** files generated contain static properties corresponding to aliases provided in the **Key** column. So, now, we can use them in XAML as follows:

```
xmlns:localization="clr-namespace:LearningMauiBankingApp.Localization"
...
<Entry x:Name="PasswordEntry"
    Placeholder="{x:Static localization:Strings.LoginPage_
PasswordPlaceholder}"
    IsPassword="True"
    Text="{Binding Password, Mode=OneWayToSource}"/>
```

Additional platform-specific configuration is needed to let the operating system and application distribution services (like Apple AppStore) know about supported languages. Having this information, an operating system can, for example, allow users to set specific language per application. Let's make such a configuration for iOS and Android. Open the **Platforms/iOS/info.plist** file in the source code/text editor and specify **CFBundleLocalizations** and **CFBundleDevelopmentRegion**, as follows:

```
<dict>
    ...
    <key> CFBundleLocalizations</key>
    <array>
        <string>en</string>
        <string>pl</string>
    </array>
    <key> CFBundleDevelopmentRegion</key>
    <string>en</string>
</dict>
```

CFBundleLocalizations specifies the list of supported languages, while **CFBundleDevelopmentRegion** defines the default locale.

On Android, manual selection of app language was introduced in Android 13, so first, we need to open **AndroidManifest.xml** in "Source Code Editor" and set **android:targetSdkVersion** to 33 (API Level). Then, create a new **Platforms/ Android/Resources/xml** folder and add the following **locales_config.xml** file to it; don't forget to set **Build Action** to **AndroidResource** for this file:

```
<locale-config xmlns:android="http://schemas.android.com/apk/res/
android">
    <locale android:name="en"/> <!-- English -->
    <locale android:name="pl"/> <!-- Polish -->
</locale-config>
```

Then, get back to **AndroidManifest.xml** and add the information about the config, as follows:

```
<application android:localeConfig="@xml/locales_config"
android:allowBackup="true" android:icon="@mipmap/appicon" ...
```

Thanks to those configurations, a specific language can be applied to **LearningMauiBankingApp** in the system settings of iOS and Android (*Figure 6.1*):

Figure 6.1: Per-application localization configuration

The task for you: Go through the XAML files of the application and replace all hardcoded texts with localization resources.

Alternatively, localization can be changed in runtime, which can be more suitable for some kinds of applications. In such a case, we have to implement a service to handle localization switching, retrieving information about current localization. The chosen localization must be stored by the application (refer to the *Application Preferences* section of *Chapter 7, Essentials and Community Toolkit*) to be set at the next application start.

The main idea of the mechanism presented as follows is to bind the property of UI control to a property of localization resource and update it once a localization service switches the language. Here's a service that must be registered as a singleton (single instance):

```
public class LocalizationManager : ILocalizationManager,
INotifyPropertyChanged
{
    public event PropertyChangedEventHandler PropertyChanged;
    public CultureInfo CurrentLocalization => Strings.Culture;
```

```csharp
    public string this[string resourceKey] =>
            Strings.ResourceManager.GetString(resourceKey, Strings.
Culture);

    public void SetCulture(CultureInfo culture)
    {
        Strings.Culture = culture;
        PropertyChanged?.Invoke(this, new
PropertyChangedEventArgs(null));
    }
}
```

The other part of the mechanism is the following markup extension, which uses the indexer property of **LocalizationManager** to create a binding to string localization resource:

```csharp
[ContentProperty(nameof(Key))]
public class LocalizationBindingExtension :
IMarkupExtension<BindingBase>
{
    public string Key { get; set; }

    public BindingBase ProvideValue(IServiceProvider serviceProvider)
    {
        var localizationManager = StrongContainer.ServiceProvider.
GetService<ILocalizationManager>();
        return new Binding
        {
            Path = $"[{Key}]",
            Source = localizationManager,
            Mode = BindingMode.OneWay
        };
    }

    object IMarkupExtension.ProvideValue(IServiceProvider
serviceProvider)
```

```
    {
        return ProvideValue(serviceProvider);
    }
}
```

Note that this markup extension uses the **StrongContainer.ServiceProvider** static property to resolve localization manager service, so don't forget to add such a property to the **StrongInject** class.

This approach was applied to **SettingsPage** of our banking app. Two buttons, shown as follows, are responsible for switching languages, while their texts are consumed using the **LocalizationBinding** markup extension:

```
xmlns:markups="clr-namespace:LearningMauiBankingApp.MarkupExtensions"

...

<Button Text="{markups:LocalizationBinding SettingsPage_
SwitchToEnglishButton}"
        Margin="20,10,20,0"
        Style="{StaticResource RegularButton}"
        Command="{Binding SwitchToEnglishCommand}"/>


<Button Text="{markups:LocalizationBinding SettingsPage_
SwitchToPolishButton}"
        Margin="20,10,20,0"
        Style="{StaticResource RegularButton}"
        Command="{Binding SwitchToPolishCommand}"/>
```

SettingsPage_SwitchToEnglish and **SettingsPage_SwitchToPolish** are keys of localization resources.

Localization is a huge challenge and includes extra effort while preparing UI designs, resolving corner cases, and culture-specific and platform-specific issues. So, it's highly recommended to carefully read localization-related documentation for each platform that an application is supposed to be run on.

CarouselView

CarouselView is one of the most powerful controls of .NET MAUI, thanks to a wide range of available adjustment opportunities. The purpose of **CarouselView** is to present a collection of data items in a scrollable layout, where the currently shown item can be selected by a user swiping through or programmatically. The main feature of **CarouselView** is the slideshow-like UX manner it acts in. **CarouselView** displays a single item at a time and automatically aligns this element on a screen.

Up to this moment, we used the regular **HorizontalStackLayout** wrapped into **ScrollView** to display bank cards. Although it served its purpose, it's not the user experience most users expect. So, replace the scroll view bank card container on the home page of our banking app with the following code; use the **Chapter_6/4_ LearningMauiBankingApp_CarouselView** application from the repository if needed:

```xml
<StackLayout Grid.Row="1" VerticalOptions="Center" Spacing="20">
    <CarouselView ItemsSource="{Binding BankCards}"
                PeekAreaInsets="45,0"
                Loop="False">
        <CarouselView.ItemsLayout>
            <LinearItemsLayout Orientation="Horizontal"
                            ItemSpacing="15"
                            SnapPointsType="MandatorySingle"
                            SnapPointsAlignment="Center"/>
        </CarouselView.ItemsLayout>
        <CarouselView.EmptyView>
            <ContentView>
                <Border StrokeShape="RoundRectangle 15,15,15,15"
                        BackgroundColor="DarkGrey"
                        Margin="40,0">
                    <Label Style="{StaticResource
PrimaryHeaderLabelStyle}"
                            Text="{x:Static localization:Strings.
HomePage_CardsLoading}"
                            VerticalOptions="Center"
HorizontalOptions="Center"/>
                </Border>
            </ContentView>
        </CarouselView.EmptyView>
        <CarouselView.ItemTemplate>
            <DataTemplate x:DataType="models:BankCard">
                <Grid RowDefinitions="1*, 1*">
```

```
            <Grid.GestureRecognizers>

                ...

            </Grid>

        </DataTemplate>

    </CarouselView.ItemTemplate>

</CarouselView>

</StackLayout>
```

The **ItemSource** and **ItemTemplate** properties specify a source collection of data items and the look of each displayed item, just as in **BindableLayout**. However, note that we are not specifying the **Grid** size of an item anymore. This is because we want collection view to do it for us. As mentioned earlier, **CarouselView** displays one (current) item at a time on a screen. The rest of the elements are off-screen at this time. The **PeakAreaInsets** property is used to make those off-screen items partially visible, informing the user that there is at least one more element to scroll to. So, the value we've set ("45, 0") moves off-screen items into the visible area. In addition, each item's size is adjusted automatically, making **CarouselView** items look proportional. However, it would look weird without spacing between items. This is where the **LinearItemsLayout** assigned to the **ItemsLayout** property comes into the picture.

The proper configuration of those parameters is crucial when it comes to achieving the proper look and feel on devices with different screen sizes. **LinearItemsLayout** contains the following properties:

- Orientation specifies the direction in which items are expanded; **Horizontal** and **Vertical** options are available. Orientation must be specified explicitly. Otherwise, an exception is thrown.

- Spacing specifies the size of a gap between items, which is especially useful in conjunction with the **PeakAreaInsets** parameter.

- **SnapPointsType** specifies the behavior of snap points when scrolling.

- **SnapPointsAlignment** specifies how snap points are aligned with items.

Another feature we've used is an empty view represented by the **EmptyView** property. **EmptyView** is a view specified by a programmer that is displayed when the **ItemsSource** collection is null or empty. To demonstrate how it works, let's simulate a delay while getting bank cards from **DummyBankCardManager**. Replace the return statement of the **GetBankCardsAsync** method with the following code:

```
await Task.Delay(1000);

return localStorageCards;
```

Besides, **EmptyView** can be specified by a simple string or can be set to a custom type whose template is specified within **EmptyViewTemplate**. Here's an example:

```
<CarouselView ItemsSource="{Binding BankCards}">
    <CarouselView.EmptyView>
        <models:BankCardPlaceholder CardNumber="XXXX XXXX XXXX XXXX"/>
    </CarouselView.EmptyView>
    <CarouselView.EmptyViewTemplate>
        <DataTemplate x:DataType="models:BankCard">
            <VerticalStackLayout>
                <Label Text="{Binding CardNumber}"/>
                <Label Text="Loading..."/>
            </VerticalStackLayout>
        </DataTemplate>
    </CarouselView.EmptyViewTemplate>
</CarouselView>
```

When it comes to interaction, **CarouselView** provides the following set of properties, events, and methods to refine the behavior of the control and response to user interactions:

- The **CurrentItem** property with **TwoWay** backing bindable property enables you to get and set the current item being displayed.

- The **CurrentItemChangedCommand** property and the **CurrentItemChanged** event are called when the current item changes. **CurrentChangedCommandParameter** is passed as the command's argument.

- The **Position** property of type **int** with **TwoWay** backing bindable property enables you to get the index of **CurrentItem** and set the current item being displayed.

- The **PositionChangedCommand** property and the **PositionChanged** event are called when the position changes. **PositionChangedCommandParameter** is passed as the command's argument.

- **IsBounceEnabled** specifies whether the **CarouselView** will bounce at a content boundary. The default value is **true**.

- **IsSwipeEnabled** determines whether a user can change the current item with a swipe gesture. The default value is **true**.

- **Loop** determines whether **CarouselView** provides looped access while swiping through the items list.

- The **VisibleViews** property of type **ObservableCollection<View>** contains visual elements that are currently visible. In our case, the collection contains the Grid object of the currently displayed bank card created based on the **ItemTemplate** XAML description.

- The **HorizontalScrollBarVisibility** and **VerticalScrollBar Visibility** properties specify when scroll bars are visible.

- The **ItemsUpdatingScrollMode** property specifies the scrolling behavior when new items are added to **CarouselView**.

- The **IsDragging** property indicates whether the **CarouselView** is scrolling.

- The **IsScrollAnmated** property specifies whether an animation will occur when the current item is changed.

- The **ScrollToRequested** event is fired when the **ScrollTo** method is invoked.

- The **Scrolled** event is fired to indicate that scrolling occurred.

- The **ScrollTo** method enables request scrolling to the specific index or item programmatically. Both overloads have additional arguments to specify how this scrolling should be done.

All those properties are backed by **BindableProperty** objects.

The **CarouselView** defines four visual states: **CurrentItem**, **PreviousItem**, **NextItem**, and **DefaultItem**. The **VisualStateManager** feature of .NET MAUI will be covered further in this chapter.

CarouselView supports incremental data virtualization as the user scrolls through items. It means **CarouselView** lets you know when the user approaches the end of the items collection, so you, for example, can request the next chunk of data from web API and add it to the **ItemsSource** collection. Such an approach helps improve the overall performance significantly. However, keep in mind that it's not recommended to use **CarouselView** to represent a potentially infinite amount of data. **CollectionView**, which can be considered as the brother of **CarouselView** (both inherit **ItemsView** class), is recommended when the size of data collection is hard to predict. The following properties control incremental data loading:

- The **RemainingItemsThresholdReached** event and **RemainingItems Threshold ReachedCommand** are called when a carousel is scrolled so far that **RemainingItems Threshold** is reached.

- The **RemainingItemsThreshold** property of type int is a threshold of items that are not visible yet, at which the **RemainingItemsThresholdReached** event will be fired and **RemainingItemsThresholdReachedCommand** will be executed. In other words, it is the number of items between the last item and the current item. This number should be chosen depending on the business logic of the application and predicted data loading speed to provide a smooth user experience.

IndicatorView

As mentioned earlier, **CarouselView** is often used in conjunction with **IndicatorView**, which indicates the overall number of items and current position in a **CarouselView**. To make a connection between **IndicatorView** and **CarouselView**, the **x:Name** value must be assigned to **IndicatorView** and then passed to the **IndicatorView** property of **CarouselView**.

Modify the bank card info section of the **HomePage** of our application, as follows, to see how it works in practice; use the **Chapter_6/4_LearningMauiBankingApp_CarouselView** application from the repository if needed:

```
<StackLayout Grid.Row="1" VerticalOptions="Center" Spacing="20">

    <CarouselView ItemsSource="{Binding BankCards}"

                  IndicatorView="Indicators"

                  PeekAreaInsets="45,0"

                  Loop="False">

    ...

    </CarouselView>


    <IndicatorView x:Name="Indicators"

                   IndicatorSize="8"

                   HorizontalOptions="Center"

                   IndicatorColor="{AppThemeBinding
Light={StaticResource LightPrimaryBackgroundColor}, Dark={StaticResource
DarkPrimaryBackgroundColor}}"

                   SelectedIndicatorColor="{DynamicResource
AccentColor}"/>

</StackLayout>
```

Here, we use **IndicatorView** along with **CarouselView** to provide a visual indication of what bank card visual element is currently displayed. However, **IndicatorView** has its own **ItemsSource** and **Position** properties, so **IndicatorView** can be used as a standalone element when needed. Besides, it has its own customization possibilities represented by the following set of class members:

- The **ItemsSource** property is the collection of data that indicators will be displayed for. This property is set automatically when **IndicatorView** is connected to **CarouselView**.

- The **Position** property specifies the currently selected item index. This property uses **TwoWay** binding by default. It is set automatically when **IndicatorView** is connected to **CarouselView**.

- The **Count** property returns the number of indicators.

- The **MaximumVisible** property specifies the maximum number of visible indicators.

- The **HideSingle** property defines whether the indicator must be hidden whenonly one exists.

- The **IndicatorColor** property specifies the color of indicators whose position is not equal to the **Position** property value.

- The **SelectedIndicatorColor** property specifies the color of the currently selected item.

- The **IndicatorSize** property specifies the size of indicators.

- The **IndicatorShape** property of enumeration type **IndicatorShape** specifies the shape of indicators. Possible values are **Circle** or **Square**.

- **IndicatorTemplate** of type **DataTemplate** enables you to define the custom appearance of indicators just like any other custom **DataTemplate** we've described before.

Visual State Manager

The .NET MAUI Visual State Manager introduces a way of changing the visual appearance of UI elements depending on their underlying state. For example, what if we want to change an appearance of a button when it's disabled? There are at least three obvious ways to do so: handling it in the code-behind of a view, applying a trigger (triggers will be covered further in this chapter), and using a visual state manager.

The **VisualStateManager** is a static class that contains the **VisualStateGroups** attached property that can be set for any UI element derived from the **VisualElement** class. Besides, **VisualStateManager** defines **VisualStateGroup** named **CommonStates** with the default set of four visual states that are supported by all controls derived from **VisualElement**:

- **Disabled** is active when the value of the **IsEnabled** property is **false**.

- **PointerOver** is active when a visual element is not disabled and the pointer is over the element.

- **Focused** is active when an element isn't in one of the previous states and the element is focused.

- **Normal** is active when none of the states mentioned earlier is active. In the case of handling at least one of the mentioned states, the **Normal** visual state (whether empty or not) must be added to a visual group.

The visual state manager allows you to define entirely in XAML how visual elements react to a different state. Besides, unlike triggers, visual states within state groups guarantee that only one state in each group is the current state.

In addition to the set of default states defined in the base VisualElement class, some individual UI controls define their own visual states. Here is a table of visual states defined in .NET MAUI:

UI Control	States
VisualElement	Normal, Disabled, Focused, PointerOver
Button	Pressed
ImageButton	Pressed
RadioButton	Checked, Unchecked
Switch	On, Off
CollectionView	Selected
CheckBox	IsChacked
CarouselView	DefaultItem, CurrentItem, PreviousItem, NextItem

Table 6.3: Visual states defined in .NET MAUI

Let us now use Visual State Manager to make the previous and next bank cards of our banking app carousel view look different from the current one. It means we need to attach the **VisualStateGroup** property to the root element of **ItemTemplate**, letting **CarouselView** know that its children are ready to react to position changes. Modify the **ItemTemplate** of bank cards **CarouselView** as follows; use the **Chapter_6/5_LearningMauiBankingApp_VisualStateManager** application from the repository for this section if needed:

```
<CarouselView.ItemTemplate>

    <DataTemplate x:DataType="models:BankCard">
```

```
    <Grid RowDefinitions="1*, 1*">
        <Grid.GestureRecognizers>

            ...

        </Grid.GestureRecognizers>
        <VisualStateManager.VisualStateGroups>
            <VisualStateGroup Name="CommonStates">
                <VisualState Name="CurrentItem"/>
                <VisualState Name="PreviousItem">
                    <VisualState.Setters>
                        <Setter Property="Opacity" Value="0.5" />
                        <Setter Property="Scale" Value="0.9" />
                    </VisualState.Setters>
                </VisualState>
                <VisualState Name="NextItem">
                    <VisualState.Setters>
                        <Setter Property="Opacity" Value="0.5" />
                        <Setter Property="Scale" Value="0.9" />
                    </VisualState.Setters>
                </VisualState>
            </VisualStateGroup>
        </VisualStateManager.VisualStateGroups>


        <Image Source="{Binding Balance,
Converter={converters:AccountBalanceToCardBackgroundImage}}"
                Aspect="AspectFit"
                Grid.RowSpan="2"/>

        ...

    </Grid>
    </DataTemplate>
</CarouselView.ItemTemplate>
```

As you can see, values are set similarly to styles, using setters. So, the previous and next items of the carousel are scaled down and semi-transparent now. Note that scaling down adds a kind of natural spacing between items, so the value of the **ItemsSpacing** property of **LinearItemsLayout** must be readjusted; set it to zero.

VisualStateManager can also be used within **Styles**. Moreover, **VisualState Setter** can change the properties of elements other than the element **VisualStateGroups** is attached to. Those capabilities give us a great opportunity to introduce some validation states to **LoginPage** with minimum effort and without handling appearance changes in C#.

Open the **LoginPage** of our banking app and add the following style resources to it:

```
<ContentPage.Resources>
    <ResourceDictionary>
        <Style TargetType="Entry" x:Key="UsernameEntryStyle">
            <Setter Property="VisualStateManager.VisualStateGroups">
                <VisualStateGroupList>
                    <VisualStateGroup Name="ValidityStates">
                        <VisualState Name="Valid"/>
                        <VisualState Name="Invalid">
                            <VisualState.Setters>
                                <Setter TargetName="PasswordEntry"
                                        Property="Entry.IsEnabled"
                                        Value="False" />
                            </VisualState.Setters>
                        </VisualState>
                    </VisualStateGroup>
                </VisualStateGroupList>
            </Setter>
        </Style>
        <Style TargetType="Entry" x:Key="PasswordEntryStyle">
            <Setter Property="VisualStateManager.VisualStateGroups">
                <VisualStateGroupList>
                    <VisualStateGroup Name="CommonStates">
                        <VisualState Name="Normal"/>
                        <VisualState Name="Disabled">
                            <VisualState.Setters>
                                <Setter Property="Opacity"
                                        Value="0.3" />
                            </VisualState.Setters>
```

```
                        </VisualState>
                    </VisualStateGroup>
                </VisualStateGroupList>
            </Setter>
        </Style>
        <Style x:Key="LoginButtonStyle" TargetType="Button"
BasedOn="{StaticResource RegularSmallButton}">
            <Setter Property="VisualStateManager.VisualStateGroups">
                <VisualStateGroupList>
                    <VisualStateGroup Name="CommonStates">
                        <VisualState Name="Normal"/>
                        <VisualState Name="Disabled">
                            <VisualState.Setters>
                                <Setter Property="Opacity" Value="0.3"
/>
                            </VisualState.Setters>
                        </VisualState>
                        <VisualState Name="Pressed">
                            <VisualState.Setters>
                                <Setter Property="Scale" Value="0.9" />
                            </VisualState.Setters>
                        </VisualState>
                    </VisualStateGroup>
                </VisualStateGroupList>
            </Setter>
        </Style>
    </ResourceDictionary>
</ContentPage.Resources>
```

Then, modify entries, button, and code-behind as follows to apply styles and make validation work:

LoginPage.xaml:

```
<Entry x:Name="UsernameEntry"
       Style="{StaticResource UsernameEntryStyle}"
```

```xml
        TextChanged="OnUsernameEntryTextChanged"

        Margin="0,40, 0, 10"

        Placeholder="{x:Static localization:Strings.LoginPage_
UsernamePlaceholder}"

        ReturnType="Next"

        Completed="OnClientIdEntryCompleted"

        ClearButtonVisibility="WhileEditing"

        IsSpellCheckEnabled="False"

        Keyboard="Plain"

        Text="{Binding Username, Mode=OneWayToSource}"/>


<Entry x:Name="PasswordEntry"

        Style="{StaticResource PasswordEntryStyle}"

        Placeholder="{x:Static localization:Strings.LoginPage_
PasswordPlaceholder}"

        IsPassword="True"

        Text="{Binding Password, Mode=OneWayToSource}"/>


<Button x:Name="LoginButton"

        Text="{x:Static localization:Strings.LoginPage_LoginButton}"

        Margin="0, 25, 0, 0"

        HorizontalOptions="Center"

        Style="{StaticResource LoginButtonStyle}"

        Command="{Binding LoginButtonCommand}"/>
```

LoginPage.xaml.cs:

```csharp
public LoginPage()
{
    InitializeComponent();
    ValidateEntry(UsernameEntry);
}


private void OnUsernameEntryTextChanged(object sender,
TextChangedEventArgs e)
```

```
    => ValidateEntry((Entry)sender);


private void ValidateEntry(Entry entry)
{
    if (string.IsNullOrEmpty(entry.Text))
        VisualStateManager.GoToState(entry, "Invalid");
    else
        VisualStateManager.GoToState(entry, "Valid");
}
```

For the username entry, we've defined a custom visual state group called **ValidityStates** that contains two states: **Valid** and **Invalid**. Another thing you might notice is that **Setter** controls not the property of username entry but the **IsEnabled** property of the **PasswordEntry** UI control. When it comes to code-behind, we actually ask **VisualStateManager** to apply the **Invalid** or **Valid** visual state to **UsernameEntry**. The **Invalid** state of **UsernameEntry** sets the **False** value for the **IsEnabled** property of **PasswordEntry**, and .NET MAUI applies the **Disabled** visual state to **PasswordEntry** as a reaction to that false value. As a result, **PasswordEntry** is non-interactive and semi-transparent when **UsernameEntry** is in an **Invalid** visual state.

Note that here, validation logic that checks if text value null or empty has been placed in the code behind. Such a case can be considered internal behavior logic of a view. However, validation logic must be moved to the **ViewModel** layer when validation logic is based on advanced scenarios, for example, checking if provided username meets some rules specific to business-domain.

Visual State Triggers

Visual state triggers are a group of classes derived from the **StateTriggerBase** class that define the conditions under which a **VisualState** should be applied. State triggers are added to the **StateTriggers** collection of a **VisualState**. When a collection contains more than one state trigger and multiple triggers are simultaneously active, then the one declared first in the XAML markup takes precedence. Besides, state triggers can be set in a **Style** or directly on elements. So, state triggers introduce an alternative way of activating visual states.

There are seven built-in state triggers in .NET MAUI:

- **StateTrigger** triggers visual state change when the **IsActive** bindable property of type **bool** changes value. So, the visual state is activated when the binding returns true.

- **AdaptiveTrigger** has the **MinWindowHeight** and **MinWindowWidth** properties of type **double**. The trigger activates its visual state when the current window height and width satisfy those minimum values. Properties can be used independently or in conjunction with each other.

- **CompareStateTrigger** has the **Property** and **Value** properties. The visual state is activated when the **Property** value is equal to a specific value of the **Value** property.

- **DeviceStateTrigger** triggers its visual state when an application is running on a platform specified for the **Device** property (that is, "iOS").

- **OrientationStateTrigger** triggers its visual state when the new orientation of the device matches the orientation specified for the **Orientation** property of the trigger.

- **SpanModeStateTrigger** and **WindowSpanModeStateTrigger** are helpful for applications targeting dual-screen devices, such as Microsoft Surface Duo, allowing users to adjust the UI depending on the current configuration of screens.

Let's consider the application of state triggers by making the layout of **LoginPage** of our banking app respond on device orientation. **AdaptiveTrigger** is a proper choice in this case. Put **UsernameEntry** and **PasswordEntry** to **Grid** and apply visual states as follows; use the **Chapter_6/6_LearningMauiBankingApp_StateTriggers** application from the repository in case of any doubts:

```
<Grid RowSpacing="10" ColumnSpacing="10">

    <VisualStateManager.VisualStateGroups>

        <VisualStateGroup Name="OrientationStates">

            <VisualState Name="Portrait">

                <VisualState.StateTriggers>

                    <AdaptiveTrigger MinWindowWidth="0"/>

                </VisualState.StateTriggers>

                <VisualState.Setters>

                    <Setter Property="Margin" Value="0, 40, 0, 0"/>

                    <Setter Property="RowDefinitions" Value="*,*"/>

                    <Setter Property="ColumnDefinitions" Value="*"/>

                    <Setter TargetName="PasswordEntry" Property="Grid.
Row" Value="1"/>

                    <Setter TargetName="PasswordEntry" Property="Grid.
Column" Value="0"/>
```

```
                    </VisualState.Setters>
            </VisualState>
            <VisualState Name="Landscape">
                <VisualState.StateTriggers>
                    <AdaptiveTrigger MinWindowWidth="800"/>
                </VisualState.StateTriggers>
                <VisualState.Setters>
                    <Setter Property="Margin" Value="100, 0"/>
                    <Setter Property="RowDefinitions" Value="*"/>
                    <Setter Property="ColumnDefinitions" Value="*,*"/>
                    <Setter TargetName="PasswordEntry" Property="Grid.
Row" Value="0"/>
                    <Setter TargetName="PasswordEntry" Property="Grid.
Column" Value="1"/>
                </VisualState.Setters>
            </VisualState>
        </VisualStateGroup>
    </VisualStateManager.VisualStateGroups>
    <Entry x:Name="UsernameEntry"

            ...
    <Entry x:Name="PasswordEntry"

            ....

</Grid>
```

As you can see, the **Portrait** and **Landscape** visual states change the configuration of the **Grid** they are attached to and the configuration of **PasswordEntry**. When the window width value is between 0 and 800 device-independent units, the orientation is considered the portrait. Therefore, Grid is defined as two-row one-column, and **PasswordEntry** is put to the second row. Otherwise, Grid is defined as a single-row two-column and **PasswordEntry** is put to the second column. The reason why we've chosen **AdaptiveTrigger** over **OrientationTrigger** is that **OrientationTrigger** doesn't apply any visual state reacting to the initial state of the application. So, a device must be rotated when an application is running to make the trigger apply a visual state.

Of course, **AdaptiveTrigger** can be used to handle much more advanced scenarios, making your app look good on different types of devices with a wide range of screen sizes from mobile apps to wide curved desktop screens.

Animations

You probably noticed that the visual states we applied to carousel view bank cards are applied discreetly with no animation. Although it works, it doesn't look smooth and fancy. Unfortunately, the **Setter** class **VisualState** utilizes simply applies the specified value to a property. It cannot make animations. However, what if we turn the bank card item markup of the item template into a custom control and add an ability to animate changing its opacity and scale? To do this, we need to break down a few topics: animations and custom MAUI controls.

.NET MAUI animations are done thanks to the **Animation** class, which is the fundamental building block of all animations. An animation concept is built around the idea of progressively changing a property of UI control from one value to another over a period of time. The **Animation** class can contain a single animation or a combination of animations.

The **Animation** constructor has the following signature:

```
Animation(Action<double> callback, double start = 0.0, double end = 1.0,
Easing easing = null, Action finished = null)
```

- The **callback** parameter of delegate type **Action<double>** is a callback that is called multiple times during the animation run to set the new value of type double to the animatable property of UI control.

- The **start** and **end** parameters are the start and end values of the animatable property. So, the callback parameter is a value that is progressively changed from the start value to the end value over the runtime of animation.

- The **easing** parameter of enum type **Easing** allows you to select a transfer function that controls how animation speeds up and slows down as it's running.

- The **finished** delegate parameter is called once the animation has been completed.

For example, the 3-second animation that animates the **Opacity** of some image from 1.0 to 0.5 can be defined and launched as follows:

```
var animation = new Animation(v => myImage.Opacity = v, 1, 0.5);

animation.Commit(this, "MyAnimationName", 16, 3000);
```

The **Commit** method actually starts an animation and declares the following named and optional parameters:

- The **owner** (first) parameter identifies the owner of the animation. This can be the visual element on which animation is applied, or another visual element, such as the page.

- The **name** (second) parameter gives any custom name to the animation. This name, combined with the owner, uniquely identifies the animation and can be used to determine whether the animation is running or needs to be canceled (**AnimationIsRunning** and **AbortAnimation** extension methods). .NET MAUI also uses this name to abort the animation before starting the new one when you start the animation with the same name while the previous one is running.

- The **rate** (third) optional parameter is the number of milliseconds between each call to the callback defined in the **Animation** constructor. The default value is 16.

- The **length** (fourth) optional parameter defines animation duration in milliseconds. The default value is 250 ms.

- The **easing** (fifth) optional parameter of the enum type **Easing** defines the easing function.

- The **finished** (sixth) optional parameter defines a callback to be executed when the animation has been completed. As you remember, the constructor of the **Animation** class has finished the callback parameter as well. In the case of a single animation, if **finished** callbacks are specified in both the **Animation** constructor and the **Commit** method, only the callback of the **Commit** method will be executed.

- The **repeat** (seventh) optional parameter is a callback that allows the animation to be repeated. It's called at the end of the animation. The **callback** method must return true for the animation to repeat.

As it was said, the **Animation** class can have a combination of animations. It means the child's animation could be added to the **Animation** class. Let's consider two equivalent pieces of C# code, as follows:

```
//First:
var combinedAnimation = new Animation()
{
    { 0, 0.7, new Animation(x => myImage.Opacity = x, 1, 0.5) },
    { 0.4, 1, new Animation(x => myLabel.Scale = x, 1, 0.8) }
};
combinedAnimation.Commit(this, "UpdateAppearance", length: 1000);


//Second
```

```
var combinedAnimation = new Animation();
animation.Add(0, 0.7, new Animation(x => myImage.Opacity = x, 1, 0.5));
animation.Add(0.4, 1, new Animation(x => myLabel.Scale = x, 1, 0.8));
combinedAnimation.Commit(this, "UpdateAppearance", length: 1000);
```

Here, we have an animation with two simple child animations that reduce the **Opacity** of some image element and the **Scale** of some label element. The duration of the whole set of animations is 1 second (since the length is defined at 1000ms). However, the key point here is that the **beginAt** and end **finishAt** parameters are **0** and **0.7**, respectively, for **Opacity** reduction animation. It means that opacity reduction animation will start at 0% of the set of animations duration and finish at 70% of the duration. The timeline in the following figure visualizes the combined animation:

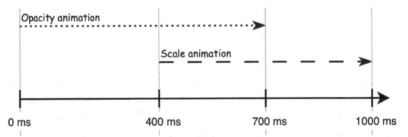

Figure 6.2: Two-child combined animation timeline

The power of animating UI elements with the **Animation** class is that you can create any custom animation or combination of custom animations with any way of calculating the animated value for any property of an element. But what if you need to make some simple animation of one property? The .NET MAUI provides a set of **VisualElement** class extension methods that are shortcuts, using the **Animation** class and the commit method inside. For example, here's how opacity animation with the **FadeTo** extension method can be done:

```
await myImage.FadeTo(0.5);
```

Such an animation extension methods are awaitable and usually take a few named and optional parameters, such as target value, animation length, and easing function. Here's a list of the available extension methods:

- **FadeTo** animates the **Opacity** property of a **VisualElement**.

- **RelScaleTo** applies an animated incremental increase or decrease to the **Scale** property of a VisualElement.

- **RotateTo** animates the **Rotation** property of a VisualElement.

- **RelRotateTo** applies an animated incremental increase or decrease to the **Rotation** property of a VisualElement.

- **RotateXTo** animates the **RotationX** property of a VisualElement.

- **RotateYTo** animates the **RotationY** property of a VisualElement.

- **ScaleTo** animates the **Scale** property of a VisualElement.

- **ScaleXTo** animates the **ScaleX** property of a VisualElement.

- **ScaleYTo** animates the **ScaleY** property of a VisualElement.

- **TranslateTo** animates the **TranslationX** and **TranslationY** properties of a VisualElement.

- **CancelAnimations** cancels all the mentioned animations that are running at the moment.

ContentView

The **ContentView** is a control that enables the creation of custom, reusable controls by putting your custom content to the content property, just like you put your custom content on the page.

Since the **ContentView** class derives from the **TemplatedView** class, which defines the **ControlTemplate** vendable property, multiple appearances of your custom controls can be specified in separate files and switched during runtime.

Another benefit of **ContentView** is encapsulation. For example, instead of inheriting **ContentView** and putting **Grid** into the **Content** of **ContentView**, we can simply inherit and extend the **Grid** itself. However, such an approach is not recommended since the client view/page using such a custom control will get easy access to all properties of the **Grid**, increasing the risk of incorrect use of custom control and bugs.

Custom Controls

Let's now apply newly received knowledge and turn the **HomePage** bank card tile into a custom control. As you remember, we want the bank card tile opacity and scale be animated. Besides the animation must be triggered by the value of **IsSelected** property.

First, create a new **Controls** folder in the project and add a new .NET MAUI ContentView (XAML) file named **BankCardTile** to it, just like we added pages. This will be our custom **BankCardTile** UI control. As you can see, VisualStudio has created similar pair of ***.xaml** and ***.xaml.cs** files that, however, derive from the **ContentView** class instead of **ContentPage**. Next, move the Grid from **ItemTemplate** of HomePage's CarouselView to the content of **BankCardTile**. As a result, your **BankCardTile.xaml** file must look as follows; use the **Chapter_6/7_ LearningMauiBankingApp_CustomControls** application for this section if needed:

```
<ContentView xmlns="http://schemas.microsoft.com/dotnet/2021/maui"
             xmlns:x="http://schemas.microsoft.com/winfx/2009/xaml"
             xmlns:converters="clr-namespace:LearningMauiBankingApp.
Converters"
             xmlns:models="clr-namespace:LearningMauiBankingApp.Models"
             x:DataType="models:BankCard"
             x:Class="LearningMauiBankingApp.Controls.BankCardTile">
    <Grid x:Name="RootContainer" RowDefinitions="1*, 1*">
        <Image Source="{Binding Balance,
Converter={converters:AccountBalanceToCardBackgroundImage}}"
               Aspect="AspectFit"
               Grid.RowSpan="2"/>

        ...

    </Grid>
</ContentView>
```

Then, modify the **BankCardTile.xaml.cs** as shown here, specifying the desired behavior of our custom control:

```
public partial class BankCardTile : ContentView
{
    public static BindableProperty IsSelectedProperty =
BindableProperty.Create(
        nameof(IsSelected),
        typeof(bool),
        typeof(BankCardTile),
        propertyChanged: OnIsSelectedPropertyChanged);

    private const double UnselectedOpacity = 0.5;
    private const double UnselectedScale = 0.9;


    public bool IsSelected
```

```
    {
        get => (bool) GetValue(IsSelectedProperty);
        set => SetValue(IsSelectedProperty, value);
    }


    public BankCardTile()
    {
        InitializeComponent();
        UpdateAppearance(false);
    }


    private static void OnIsSelectedPropertyChanged(BindableObject view,
object oldValue, object newValue)
    {
        ((BankCardTile)view).UpdateAppearance(true);
    }


    private void UpdateAppearance(bool animate)
    {
        if (!animate)
        {
            if (IsSelected)
            {
                RootContainer.Opacity = 1;
                RootContainer.Scale = 1;
            }
            else
            {
                RootContainer.Opacity = UnselectedOpacity;
                RootContainer.Scale = UnselectedScale;
            }
            return;
        }
```

```
Animation animation;
if (IsSelected)
{
    animation = new Animation()
    {
        { 0, 1, new Animation(x => RootContainer.Opacity = x,
RootContainer.Opacity, 1) },
        { 0, 1, new Animation(x => RootContainer.Scale = x,
RootContainer.Scale, 1) }
    };
}
else
{
    animation = new Animation()
    {
        { 0, 1, new Animation(x => RootContainer.Opacity = x,
RootContainer.Opacity, UnselectedOpacity) },
        { 0, 1, new Animation(x => RootContainer.Scale = x,
RootContainer.Scale, UnselectedScale) }
    };
}

    animation.Commit(this, nameof(UpdateAppearance));
    }
}
```

As you can see, we've defined a new **IsSelected** bindable property and the **OnIsSelectedPropertyChanged** delegate that calls the **UpdateAppearance** method to change the **Opacity** and **Scale** properties of the root **Grid** layout (**RootContainer**) of the control depending on the **IsSelected** value. Now, go back to the **HomePage**, and modify the **CarouselView.ItemTemplate** code using the newly created **BankCardTile** UI control, as follows:

```
xmlns:controls="clr-namespace:LearningMauiBankingApp.Controls"

...

<CarouselView.ItemTemplate>
```

```xml
<DataTemplate x:DataType="models:BankCard">
    <controls:BankCardTile>
        <controls:BankCardTile.GestureRecognizers>
            <TapGestureRecognizer Command="{Binding BindingContext.
SelectBankCardCommand, Source={x:Reference ValueableContentGrid}}"
                                  CommandParameter="{Binding
CardNumber}"/>
        </controls:BankCardTile.GestureRecognizers>
        <VisualStateManager.VisualStateGroups>
            <VisualStateGroup Name="CommonStates">
                <VisualState Name="CurrentItem">
                    <VisualState.Setters>
                        <Setter Property="IsSelected" Value="True" />
                    </VisualState.Setters>
                </VisualState>
                <VisualState Name="PreviousItem">
                    <VisualState.Setters>
                        <Setter Property="IsSelected" Value="False" />
                    </VisualState.Setters>
                </VisualState>
                <VisualState Name="NextItem">
                    <VisualState.Setters>
                        <Setter Property="IsSelected" Value="False" />
                    </VisualState.Setters>
                </VisualState>
            </VisualStateGroup>
        </VisualStateManager.VisualStateGroups>
    </controls:BankCardTile>
</DataTemplate>
</CarouselView.ItemTemplate>
```

And here's a point. Now, the **VisualStateManager** changes the value of the **IsSelected** property of **BankCardTile**. **BankCardTile**, in turn, changes its appearance, animating the **Opacity** and **Scale** properties of the content layout as a reaction to the new value.

The task for you: Replace all banking service buttons (for example, **Transfer** Button) with custom reusable control. The control must define two bindable properties of the type of string (**Text** and **Image**), providing a way to customize the description and the image of the inner image button. Name this control **BankingServiceButton**, and don't forget to move **BankingServiceImageButtonStyle** and **BankingServiceButtonDescriptionStyle** to the **BankingServiceButton** resource dictionary. Check out the sample application of this section if needed.

FlexLayout

As mentioned earlier, the layouts big three contains **StackLayout**, **Grid**, and **FlexLayout**. **FlexLayout** is a layout control based on the **Cascading Style Sheets (CSS)** Flexible Box Layout Module widely used in front-end web development. The idea of this layout is to arrange children elements in a flexible manner so that children of different sizes automatically arrange in a way to fit available space and adapt to different screen/window sizes. Besides, a set of parameters allow the configuration of the behavior of the layout engine and the direction in which children will be arranged. Probably the most iconic examples of **FlexLayout** usage are a gallery of photos on your smartphone and a file explorer on your computer where images are arranged and rearranged automatically, adapting to children's size and the available space.

The default **direction** of **FlexLayout**, also called the **main axis**, is horizontal. The direction can be overridden by defining the **Direction** property with one of the following **FlexDirection** enum values:

- **Row** (default value) indicates that children should be stacked horizontally (the main axis is horizontal, and the cross axis is vertical).

- **RowReverse** indicates that children should be stacked horizontally in reverse order.

- **Column** indicates that children should be stacked vertically (the main axis is vertical, and the cross axis is horizontal).

- **ColumnReverse** indicates that children should be stacked vertically in reverse order.

The **Wrap** property value determines whether **FlexLayout** will move children to the new line when a single line space is not enough. The following options are available:

- **NoWrap** indicates that children are laid out in a single line.

- **Wrap** indicates that items are laid out in multiple lines if needed.

- **Reverse** is like **Wrap**, but items are laid out in reverse order.

The **AlignContent**, **AlignItems**, and **JustifyContent** properties determine how the layout engine distributes space between and around children:

- **JustifyContent** specifies how space is distributed along the main axis.

- **AlignItems** specifies how space is distributed along the cross axis between and around children relative to each other.

- **AlignContent** specifies how space is distributed along the cross axis between and around children that have been laid on multiple lines. In other words, it determines how the space between lines is managed.

For the sake of learning, let's replace a grid, keeping the set of **BankingServiceButton** controls of the **HomePage** with a flex layout, as follows:

```
<!--Buttons-->
<ScrollView Grid.Row="2">
    <FlexLayout Wrap="Wrap"
                AlignItems="Start"
                JustifyContent="SpaceAround"
                AlignContent="Center">
        <FlexLayout.Resources>
            <Style TargetType="controls:BankingServiceButton">
                <Setter Property="Margin" Value="5"/>
                <Setter Property="WidthRequest" Value="100"/>
            </Style>
        </FlexLayout.Resources>


        <!--Transfer Button-->
        <controls:BankingServiceButton Text="{x:Static
localization:Strings.HomePage_TransferButton}"
                                       Image="{AppThemeBinding
Light={x:Static const:ImageId.LightTransferIcon}, Dark={x:Static
const:ImageId.DarkTransferIcon}}"/>

        ...

    </FlexLayout>
</ScrollView>
```

Since the screen of the end user's device may not be large enough to fit all FlexLayout's children, the **ScrollView** is used as a container for the **FlexLayout**. So, buttons now are available even on devices like iPhone 5s, where FlexLayout arranges buttons within two columns instead of three.

The next thing is the button style we've added to the **FlexLayout**. A **FlexLayout** layout doesn't have predefined columns and rows, so its layout engine doesn't control the size of child elements according to their **HorizontalOptions** and **VerticalOptions** values. Besides, it doesn't allow users to specify the minimum spacing between rows and columns. That is why **Margin** and **WidthRequest** are specified with style. Otherwise, the width of each **BankingServiceButton** would be defined based on the description label width, and there is a chance of buttons having no gap between each other.

Now let's consider the configuration of **FlexLayout** itself. The **Start** value has been chosen for the **AlignItems** property to make all buttons in a row vertically aligned by the upper edge of button controls when description label text takes more than one line. The **Center** value has been chosen for the **AlignContent** property to ensure that the whole content of FlexLayout is vertically aligned by the center of the area occupied by FlexLayout when the device screen is so tall that the available area is higher than needed. The **SpaceAround** value of the **JustifyContent** property makes the layout engine distribute children horizontally in a way they have a distance from the edges of **FlexLayout** and are equally spaced from each other. It's highly recommended to spend some time experimenting with different configurations of **FlexLayout** to see how it reacts to them. You can also find free "Flexbox playground" tools on the internet to get a better understanding of how specific properties affect the behavior of **FlexLayout**.

You might be curious to know how **FlexLayout** can be used to represent the collection of data. Since **FlexLayout** derives the **Layout** class as other layout controls, it supports the **BindableLayout** feature. So, you can use **BindableLayout.ItemsSource**, **BindableLayout.ItemsTemplate**, and other attached properties, just like we did with **StackLayout**.

The **FlexLayout** control also offers the following set of attached properties that can be used by children for alignment and sizing purposes of a particular child element:

- The **FlexLayout.AlignSelf** property overrides the value **AlignItems** set on **FlexLayout**, changing the way the layout engine distributes space between and around a specific child.

- The **FlexLayout.Order** property enables you to change the order in which children are arranged.

- The **FlexLayout.Basis** property defines the size of the child on the main axis (width in the case of row direction). The size can be set in device-independent units or percents where 100% is the width of space occupied by FlexLayout (for example, **FlexLayout.Basis="30%"**).

- The **FlexLayout.Grow** property of a child is respected when the **Wrap** property of **FlexLayout** is set to **NoWrap** or a column of children has a shorter height than the FlexLayout. The **Grow** property, in those cases, indicates how to apportion the remaining space among the children. When **Grow** property is used for two or more children, the leftover space is apportioned between them all. In that case, the bigger **Grow** property value is, the bigger portion of space the child gets.

- The **FlexLayout.Shrink** property of a child is respected when the **Wrap** property of **FlexLayout** is set to **NoWrap** and the aggregate width of a row of children is greater than the width of the **FlexLayout**, or the aggregate height of a single column of children is greater than the height of the **FlexLayout**. Normally, **FlexLayout** will display these children by constricting their sizes. The **Shrink** property can indicate which children are given priority in being displayed at their full sizes.

All this might sound like a description of a great, almost universal tool. However, you have to remember that every extra calculation which needs to be done while rendering a view affects performance. FlexLayout performs significantly more calculations in comparison to Grid and StackLayouts. Performance drop may not be noticeable with a small number of items to be rendered. However, with a big enough number of complex visual items, the difference may be significant, especially on low-end Android devices. So, the general advice is to prefer Grid and StackLayouts to FlexLayout if possible.

Triggers

Apart from visual state triggers, a group of regular triggers serves a similar purpose, allowing you to express actions declaratively in XAML. The difference is that those triggers don't require **VisualStateManager** and can be applied to any UI control deriving **VisualElement** class directly by filling the **Triggers** collection with triggers you need. **Triggers** can apply values to properties using **Setters** or execute actions defined in classes derived from **TriggerAction** class. Let's consider what triggers are there and what each of them can be used for.

A **Trigger** applies value when the value of a specified property meets a specified condition. The **Trigger** shown in the following code snippet changes the text color to green when the entry is focused. When the **Entry** loses focus, **TextColor** changes back to **Black**. The **Trigger** handling the **False** value isn't required here, but it is considered a good practice to handle both **True** and **False** states of a property since there were cases in the past when the property may not be set back to initial state (that is, **Black**) when the condition (**IsFocused** is **True**) wasn't met:

```
<Entry Text="My text" TextColor="Black">
    <Entry.Triggers>
        <Trigger TargetType="Entry" Property="IsFocused" Value="True">
            <Setter Property="TextColor" Value="Green" />
        </Trigger>
        <Trigger TargetType="Entry" Property="IsFocused" Value="False">
            <Setter Property="TextColor" Value="Black" />
        </Trigger>
    </Entry>
</Entry>
```

An **EventTrigger** applies a set of actions in response to an event. In other words, an **EventTrigger** enables applying reusable event handlers to events of UI controls without handling them in code-behind. Let's use **EventTrigger** to improve **LoginPage** validations in our banking app. First, we must create a **TriggerAction** class containing simple password validation logic. Create a new folder called **Triggers** and put the **PasswordValidationTriggerAction** class, shown as follows, in it; use **Chapter_6/9_LearningMauiBankingApp_Triggers** for this section if needed:

```
public class PasswordValidationTriggerAction : TriggerAction<Entry>
{
    public VisualElement ElementToDisable { get; set; }


    protected override void Invoke(Entry sender)
    {
        ElementToDisable.IsEnabled = sender.Text.Length >= 8;
    }
}
```

Now set the **IsEnabled** property of **LoginButton** to **False** to make it disabled by default, and modify the **PasswordEntry** property of **LoginPage** as follows, applying the newly created trigger action:

```
xmlns:triggers="clr-namespace:LearningMauiBankingApp.Triggers"


<Entry x:Name="PasswordEntry"
        Style="{StaticResource PasswordEntryStyle}"
```

```
        Placeholder="{x:Static localization:Strings.LoginPage_
PasswordPlaceholder}"

        IsPassword="True"

        Text="{Binding Password, Mode=OneWayToSource}">
    <Entry.Triggers>
        <EventTrigger Event="TextChanged">
            <triggers:PasswordValidationTriggerAction
ElementToDisable="{x:Reference LoginButton}"/>
        </EventTrigger>
    </Entry.Triggers>
</Entry>
```

With this **EventTrigger** being applied, once the **TextChanged** event is raised, the **Invoke** method of the **PasswordValidationTriggerAction** class is called, changing the **IsEnabled** property value of **LoginButton**.

A **DataTrigger** is used to react on the value of a property of another control or **BindingContext** (that is, ViewModel object). To demonstrate the power of both **DataTrigger** and **TriggerActions**, let's add the following hint label above the **LoginButton** of **LoginPage** and the new **FadeTriggerAction**:

FadeTriggerAction.cs:

```
public class FadeTriggerAction : TriggerAction<VisualElement>
{
    public double TargetOpacity { get; set; }

    protected override void Invoke(VisualElement sender)
    {
        sender.FadeTo(TargetOpacity, 500);
    }
}
```

LoginPage.xaml:

```
<Label Text="Magic hint"
       HorizontalOptions="Center"
       Margin="0,15,0,0"
       Opacity="0"
```

```
        TextColor="{StaticResource AccentColor}"
        Style="{StaticResource PrimaryContentLabelStyle}">
    <Label.Triggers>
        <DataTrigger TargetType="Label" Binding="{Binding IsFocused,
Source={x:Reference PasswordEntry}}" Value="True">
            <DataTrigger.EnterActions>
                <triggers:FadeTriggerAction TargetOpacity="1"/>
            </DataTrigger.EnterActions>
            <DataTrigger.ExitActions>
                <triggers:FadeTriggerAction TargetOpacity="0"/>
            </DataTrigger.ExitActions>
        </DataTrigger>
    </Label.Triggers>
</Label>
```

As you can see, our magic hint is fully transparent by default. When the focus is moved to **PasswordEntry** (the **IsFocused** property changes to **True**), the trigger calls the **Invoke** method of **TriggerActions** stored in the **EnterActions** collection, if any. When the focus is moved out from **PasswordEntry**, **ExitActions** are executed. As a result, the hint **Label** appears and disappears with animation when **PasswordEntry** is focused on and unfocused. Note that it's up to you what way to use: **TriggerActions**, **Setters**, or both at the same time.

A **MultiTrigger** is similar to both **Trigger** and **DataTrigger** because it can handle both types of conditions. The difference is that **MultiTrigger** supports multiple conditions to be satisfied. A **MultiTrigger** condition can be described using **BindingCondition** and **PropertyCondition**. **PropertyCondition** acts as a condition of the **Trigger**.

The **MultiTrigger** shown in the following code snippet shows the **Grid** only when the user's geolocation is near a service point and the device is currently online:

```
<Grid x:name="IndoorServices" IsVisible="False">
    <Grid.Triggers>
        <MultiTrigger TargetType="Grid">
            <MultiTrigger.Conditions>
                <BindingCondition Binding="{Binding IsUserInside}"
Value="True"/>
                <BindingCondition Binding="{Binding
InternetAccessStatus}" Value="Online"/>
```

```
        </MultiTrigger.Conditions>
        <Setter Property="IsVisible" Value="True" />
      </MultiTrigger>
    </Grid>
  </Grid>
```

OnPlatform and OnIdiom

There are situations sometimes when the value of UI control property must differ depending on the runtime platform. There are two popular reasons for that. The first is that certain UI elements are rendered differently by different platforms. For example, a custom font required by the UI designer might have a different line height on Android, so the value of the **LineHeight** property of **Label** must be decreased, but for Android only. The second popular reason is a desire to implement certain features of an application considering the specifics of the platform. For example, you might be required to display the list of discovered Bluetooth devices in your application. While it's possible to retrieve such a list on Android, it's impossible to do so on Apple due to security restrictions. So, it might be helpful to change certain parts of UI on a per-platform basis.

The **OnPlatformExtension** class represented by the **OnPlatform** markup extension defines the following properties:

- **Default** is a default value to be applied in case a specific value wasn't set for the platform the application is currently running on. The **Default** property is marked with the **ContentProperty** attribute so that the **Default=** part can be eliminated when **Default** is the first argument.

- **Android, iOS, MacCatalyst, Tizen**, and **WinUI** are properties to be used for platform-specific properties.

- **Converter** and **ConverterParameter** are properties similar to the ones **Binding** has. In general, the XAML parser expects that values assigned to the properties listed earlier have the type of target UI control property. However, sometimes it might be helpful to make a custom type conversion.

Here's an example of how line height might be changed for certain platforms only using the **OnPlatform** markup extension:

```
<Label LineHeight="{OnPlatform 1, Android=0.73, MacCatalyst=1.05}"/>
```

The **OnIdiom** markup extension does the same thing as **OnPlatform**, but based on the idiom of the device the application is running on. .NET MAUI differentiatessmartphone, tablet, desktop, TV, and watch idioms.

When it comes to C# code, you can use the **DeviceInfo** class from the **Microsoft. Maui.Devices** namespace to determine the platform (**Platform** property of **DevicePlatform** enumeration type) and idiom (**Idiom** property of **DeviceIdiom** enumeration type) the application is running on.

Brushes

We already know how to apply **Colors** to the background of UI elements. There is another, more sophisticated way for background coloring. Since the **Background** property of type **Brush** is declared in **VisualElement**, **Brush** background can be applied to any control.

.NET MAUI Brush is an abstract class that three built-in MAUI **Brushes** inherit:

- **SolidColorBrush**, which paints an area with a solid color. Color can be assigned instead of **SolidColorBrush**. In that case, MAUI creates a brush of the specified color for you.

- **LinearGradientBrush,** which paints an area with a linear gradient.

- **RadialGradientBrush**, which paints an area with a radial gradient.

Let us look at **RadialGradientBrush** in action by adding a bottom bar with the ".NET MAUI" label on it. Use the **Chapter_6/10_LearningMauiBankingApp_ Brush** application from the repository if needed. Add a new **Accent1Color** resource of color **#FFD60A** to themes, and then replace the bottom bar placeholder grid with the following piece of code:

```
<!--Bottom bar-->
<Border Grid.Row="3"
        Margin="15,0, 15, 10"
        StrokeShape="RoundRectangle 30,30,30,30">
    <Border.Background>
        <RadialGradientBrush x:Name="BottomBarBrush" Center="0,1"
Radius="0.4">
            <GradientStop Offset="0" Color="{DynamicResource
Accent1Color}" />
            <GradientStop Offset="1" Color="{DynamicResource
AccentColor}" />
        </RadialGradientBrush>
    </Border.Background>
```

```
<Grid>
    <Label Style="{StaticResource PrimaryHeaderLabelStyle}"
            TextColor="{AppThemeBinding Light={StaticResource
LightPrimaryTextColor}, Dark={StaticResource DarkPrimaryTextColor}}"
            Text=".NET MAUI"
            FontSize="30"
            TranslationY="{OnPlatform 0, Android=3}"
            VerticalOptions="Center"
            HorizontalOptions="Center"/>
</Grid>
</Border>
```

In the case of **RadialGradientBrush**, there are two properties defining the main configuration:

- The **Center** property of type **Point** represents the center point of the circle for the radial gradient. The default value is (0.5,0.5) which means the center of the gradient is in the center of the painted area.

- The **Radius** property of type double specifies the radius of a gradient in a range from 0 to 1.

GradientStops can be considered the building blocks of any gradient brush since **GradientStop** specifies the color and its location along the gradient axis.

- The **Color** property specifies the color of **GradientStop**.

- The **Offset** property of type float represents the location of the gradient stop within the gradient vector. Valid values are in the range of 0-1. The closer **Offset** is to 1, the closer the color is to the end of the linear gradient, or the further the color is from the center of the radial gradient.

You might notice that we have given the name to brush. Let's make our bottom bar even more cooler and animate our gradient. Put the following animation to the **OnNavigatedTo** life cycle method of **HomePage** and see what happens:

```
new Animation()
{
    { 0, 0.6, new Animation(x => BottomBarBrush.Radius = x, 0.01, 0.4,
Easing.CubicOut) },
    { 0.5, 1, new Animation(x => BottomBarBrush.Center = new Point(x, 1
- x), 0.5, 0, Easing.CubicInOut) },
}.Commit(this, nameof(OnNavigatedTo), length: 3000);
```

Shadows

Another popular thing helping the UI look and feel more sophisticated is **Shadow**. Shadow can be defined for any UI control derived from VisualElement. The **Shadow** class defines the following properties backed by **BindableProperties**:

- **Radius** defines the radius of the blur; the default value is 10.

- **Brush** of type **Brush** is used to colorize the shadow. At the time the book was written, **Shadow** supports a **SolidColorBrush** only.

- **Opacity** indicates the opacity of the shadow.

- **Offset** of type **Point** represents the position of the light source that creates the shadow.

Let us try to apply shadow to the brand new bottom bar of our HomePage. Modify the bottom bar code as follows; use the **Chapter_6/11_LearningMauiBankingApp_ Shadows** application if needed:

```
<!--Bottom bar-->
<Border Grid.Row="3"

        ...>

    <Border.Background>

        ...

    </Border.Background>
    <Border.Shadow>

        <Shadow Brush="Black"

                Offset="{OnPlatform Default='8,8', Android='20,20'}"

                Radius="{OnPlatform 6, Android=40}"

                Opacity="{OnPlatform 0.4, Android=0.5}" />

    </Border.Shadow>

    ...

</Border>
```

You must be curious why all core properties of shadow are set using the **OnPlatform** markup extension. Unfortunately, the ways shadows are calculated by platforms are drastically different, and .NET MAUI doesn't provide API to eliminate this difference. So, if your goal is to achieve the same look on every platform, it would take some time to discover appropriate values for each platform you target.

Behaviors

The power of behaviors is in enabling you to change the behavior of UI controls without having to subclass them. Instead, the functionality is implemented in a reusable class called **Behaviors** and attached to any control derived from **VisualElement**.

Behaviors are created by deriving from the **Behavior** or **Behavior<T>** class when **T** is a type of control to which the behavior is about to be applied. **Behavior** contains two virtual methods to be overridden:

- The **OnAttached** virtual method is called right after the behavior is attached to a control. The method receives a reference to the control to which it is attached. This method is used to register event handlers if needed and perform any other setup needed for the purpose of the **Behavior**.

- The **OnDetachingFrom** virtual method is called when the behavior is about to be removed from the control. This method also receives reverence to the control and is used to perform any required cleanup, such as unregistering from events and closing possible connections.

The following code snippet shows how validation behavior can be created and attached to an **Entry**:

LettersValidationBehavior.cs:

```
public class AllLettersValidationBehavior : Behavior<Entry>
{
    protected override void OnAttachedTo(Entry entry)
    {
        entry.TextChanged += OnEntryTextChanged;
        base.OnAttachedTo(entry);
    }

    protected override void OnDetachingFrom(Entry entry)
    {
        entry.TextChanged -= OnEntryTextChanged;
        base.OnDetachingFrom(entry);
    }

    private void OnEntryTextChanged(object sender, TextChangedEventArgs args)
```

```
    {
        bool isValid = args.NewTextValue.All(Char.IsLetter);
        ((Entry)sender).TextColor = isValid ? Colors.Black : Colors.Red;
    }
}
```

XAML Markup:

```
<Entry Placeholder="Surname">
    <Entry.Behaviors>
        <myBehaviors:AllLettersValidationBehavior/>
    </Entry.Behaviors>
</Entry>
```

It's important to know that despite Behavior being derived from **BindableObject**, MAUI doesn't set its **BindingContext** because the same instance of behavior can be shared with multiple controls through styles.

CollectionView

The **CollectionView** control is the most powerful tool when it comes to representing collections of data that require scrolling or selection. Being a brother of **CarouselView**, **CollectionView** has several features we already know from **CarouselView**, such as **EmptyView**, incremental data virtualization as the user scrolls, or the possibility to scroll programmatically to a specific item. The collection of data is also assigned in the same way, using the **ItemsSource** and **ItemTemplate** properties that we are already familiar with. There are features though that are worth highlighting. Besides, when it comes to displaying big scrollable lists of data, it's recommended to choose **CollectionView** over the conjunction of **StackView**, **BindableLayout**, and **ScrollView** because of performance reasons.

The **CollectionView** control enables you to control its layout by choosing the way items are arranged with the **ItemsLayout** and **ItemSizingStrategy** properties. **LinearItemsLayout**, which can be assigned to the **ItemsLayout** proper,ty is similar to the one we used for **CarouselView**. It controls the orientation of items (vertical or horizontal), snap points, and item spacing. **GridItemsLayout**, on the other hand, enables you to arrange items in a grid, specifying the number of columns or rows and item spacing using the following bindable properties:

- The **Orientation** property represents the orientation to be used by the layout engine; the available options are **Vertical** or **Horizontal**.

- The **VerticalItemSpacing** and **HorizontalItemSpacing** properties of type **double** represent the vertical and horizontal empty space around each item.

- The **Span** property of type **int** represents the number of columns or rows depending on the value of the **Orientation** property.

The following XAML markup snippet shows how items could be arranged in three columns:

```
<CollectionView.ItemsLayout>

    <GridItemsLayout Orientation="Vertical"

                     HorizontalItemSpacing="3"

                     VerticalItemSpacing="5"

                     Span="3"/>

</CollectionView.ItemsLayout>
```

When it comes to the **ItemsSizingStrategy** property, there are two values available:

- **MeasureAllItems** is a default value that means each item is measured individually.

- **MeasureFirstItems** means only the first item is measured, and all subsequent items are given the same size as the first item. Use this option when it's expected that all items have the same size since it impacts performance positively.

CollectionView can also have a header and footer displayed at the top and the bottom of the control. They might be configured using the following set of properties:

- The **Header** and **Footer** properties of type **object** are used to specify simple hardcoded strings, bindings, or views that will be displayed.

- **HeaderTemplate** and **FooterTemplate** of type **DataTemplate** are used to format the **Header** and **Footer** respectively using **DataTemplates** and **DataTemplateSelector**.

CollectionView allows interaction with items by single and multiple selections offering an advanced set of properties, command properties, and events to be used.

- The **SelectionMode** property enables you to choose one of three available options: **None**, **Single**, and **Multiple**; here, **None** means items selection is disabled.

- **SelectionChangedCommand** is executed when the selected item changes. The **SelectionChangedCommandParameter** is used as a command parameter then.

- **SelectedItem** represents the selected item in the list. This property has a default binding mode of **TwoWay** and can be used to select an item programmatically, which is helpful when some item needs to be pre-selected.

- **SelectedItems** of type **IList<object>** represents the collection of selected items. This property can also be used to select items programmatically. The default binding mode is **OneWay**.

- **SelectedChanged** event is fired when the **SelectedItem** property changes. The event argument object that accompanies the event contains two collections, i.e., **PreviousSelection** and **CurrentSelection**, containing references to the current and previously selected sets of items.

The last remarkable feature specific to **CollectionView** is grouping. Grouping enables you to specify a custom group header and footer to be displayed before and after a group. To make grouping happen, a data set must be grouped in a specific way using a group model class. Let us imagine we have a list of historical payment transactions to display grouped by date. The following **Transaction** and **TransactionGroup** classes show how such a set of data must be grouped:

```
public class Transaction
{
    public DateTime TimeStamp { get; set; }
    public string Title { get; set; }
    public decimal MoneyTotal { get; set; }
}


public class TransactionGroup : List<Transaction>
{
    public DateTime TransactionsDate { get; }

    public TransactionGroup(DateTime transactionsDate)
    {
        TransactionsDate = transactionsDate;
    }
}
```

As you can see, we extend the **List** class with the **TransactionsDate** property that is used for group header proposes, as follows:

```
<CollectionView ItemsSource="{Binding Transactions}"
                IsGrouped="true">
    <CollectionView.GroupHeaderTemplate>
        <DataTemplate>
            <Grid>
                <Label Text="{Binding TransactionsDate, StringFormat='
{0:dd/MM/yyyy}'}"/>
            </Grid>
        </DataTemplate>
    </CollectionView.GroupHeaderTemplate>
    <CollectionView.ItemTemplate>
        <DataTemplate>
            <HorizontalStackLayout>
                <Label Text="{Binding Title}"/>
                <Label Text=" - "/>
                <Label Text="{Binding Money}"/>
            </HorizontalStackLayout>
        </DataTemplate>
    </CollectionView.ItemTemplate>
</CollectionView>
```

The properties that control how grouping is presented are as follows:

- **IsGrouped** of type bool specifies whether or not grouping is used. The default value is **false**.

- **GroupHeaderTemplate** and **GroupFooterTemplate** of type **DataTemplate** can be used to describe the custom appearance of the group header and footer.

Customizing native controls

As you already know, by default, each control is styled while maintaining the original characteristics of platform-native controls. As a result, sometimes controls may look different and cross-platform API doesn't provide a way to make a control look the same because, as mentioned earlier, some features on one platform are not present on another. Besides, based on the author's experience, in most cases, those differences are not meaningful, since cross-platform applications usually strive to provide as much a unified UI design as possible.

Entry control is the most iconic example of this (*Figure 6.3*), since the question, "How can we disable underline on Android Entry?" is probably the most popular question for people who are starting their cross-platform development journey:

Figure 6.3: *The same Entry control looks different on iOS and Android*

The solution is to extend the configuration of the **Mapper** of **EntryHandler**, introducing a native control customization. The following code shows how to disable both Android's underline and iOS's border for every **Entry** control in your application:

```
EntryHandler.Mapper.AppendToMapping("MyCustomization", (handler, view)
=>
{
#if ANDROID
    handler.PlatformView.Background = null;
#elif IOS || MACCATALYST
    handler.PlatformView.BorderStyle = UITextBorderStyle.None;
#endif
});
```

There are three methods provided to customize handlers:

- **AppendToMapping** modifies the mapper of a handler after the .NET MAUI mappings have been applied.

- **ModifyMapping** modifies an existing mapping.

- **PrependToMapping** modifies the mapper of a handler before the .NET MAUI mappings have been applied.

All three methods require two arguments: a string key and an **Action** that performs the handler customization. The important thing here is that the string-based key must be unique for modified control and doesn't have to correspond to the name of a property exposed by a cross-platform control. This is because the key values of MAUI mappings are based on property names of a control, for example, **nameof(IEntry. Text)**.

Since handler customization affects all controls of the same type, you can subclass a standard MAUI control and then introduce handler customization affecting your custom control only. Here's an example:

```
internal class MyCarouselView : CarouselView
{
}
```

```
CarouselViewHandler.Mapper.AppendToMapping(nameof(MycarouselView),
(handler, view) =>
{
    if (view is MyCarouselView)
    {
        //Your customizations
    }
});
```

The **AppendToMapping** method should be called somewhere in your code prior to the control being used. For example, in the **MauiProgram.CreateMauiApp** or **App.OnStart** method.

Another way to customize platform native control with the handler is to get access to the handler using the following members of .MAUI control:

- The **Handler** property returns the current handler that provides an access to the native control via the **PlatformView** property.

- The **HandlerChanged** event is raised after the handler for cross-platform control has been created, indicating that the native control is available. The handler of this event is a good place to subscribe to events of native control or perform the customizations required by the page where a concrete instance of the control is used.

- **HandlerChanging** is raised when a new handler is about to be created and when an existing handler (if any) is about to be removed. The argument object accompanying the event contains the **NewHandler** and **OldHandler** properties. When the **OldHandler** property isn't null, all native control events must be unsubscribed and other cleanup should be performed to avoid memory leaks.

Conclusion

Congratulations! With such an amount of knowledge being applied in practice, you can already implement quite complex applications targeting different platforms and users around the globe. Presenting collections of data in different ways is not a challenge anymore, and the user's eye will surely be delighted with the visual effects. Besides, you know how to do all of this while keeping your codebase maintainability on a high level.

In the next chapter, we will concentrate on small tools, approaches, and features that make a big difference though for both development workflow and user satisfaction.

Points to remember

- AppThemeBinding doesn't support DynamicResources.
- ResourceDictionaries can be put into separate files.
- Multilanguage support can require additional configuration per platform.
- IndicatorView can be a standalone UI element.
- VisualState can change the properties of all elements other than the element its group is attached to.
- The DeviceInfo class can be used to determine runtime platform and idiom in C#.
- Shadows are handled differently by different platforms.
- Behaviors are reusable extensions of UI control behavior.
- Use CollectionView over BindableLayout for better performance when presenting a big collection of data.

Questions

1. What is the difference between AppThemeBinding and Binding?
2. What is the power of MergedDictionaries?
3. Can VisualStateManager be used to execute actions?
4. Can the Animation class perform multiple animations at the same time?
5. What are the differences between FlexLayout and CollectionView?
6. What is the difference between OnPlatform and OnIdiom?
7. How can we disable underline on Android Entry?

CHAPTER 7

Essentials and Community Toolkit

Introduction

This chapter will introduce you to two extremely important libraries. To be precise, while both came from being third-party Xamarin libraries, one of them became an integral part of .NET MAUI. Since those libraries contain many features, the main purpose of this chapter is to introduce you to the main ideas of libraries and show how some of the features can be used in practice so that you can easily explore the rest of the features on your own.

Structure

In this chapter, we will cover the following topics:

- Essentials library Overview
- Connectivity
- Text-to-Speech (TTS)
- Gyroscope
- Application preferences
- Secure storage

- Community Toolkit library overview

- Snackbar

- InvertedBoolConverter

- NumericValidationBehavior

- ValidationBehavior abstract class

- ColorAnimationExtensions

- UserStoppedTypingBehavior

- AsyncRelayCommand

Objectives

The first half of the chapter is about the **Essentials** library, and the second is about **Community Toolkit**. We will continue mixing theory with practical use cases and examine how Essentials and Community Toolkit together make .NET MAUI an even more powerful and versatile framework for creating engaging applications.

Essentials library overview

A set of classes, initially called Xamarin Essentials Library, was introduced to provide developers with simple, cross-platform APIs to access commonly used device features across iOS, Android, UWP, Tizen, and watchOS platforms like accelerometer, file system, geolocation, and many more. Over time, Microsoft continued to add new APIs and features to Xamarin Essentials, often by including the most popular third-party open-source libraries made by the Xamarin community. In Xamarin, the **Essentials** library has its own namespace and is delivered as an external NuGet package. While creating the new generation of the framework, MAUI, Microsoft announced that the **Essentials** library would be extended, enhanced, and included in .NET MAUI as an integral part of the MAUI platform. Now this set of cross-platform APIs is called **Platform-integration**.

Here's the set of API and helper classes available at the moment that make up what we call **Essentials**:

- The **Accelerometer** class lets you monitor the device's accelerometer sensor, which indicates the acceleration of the device in three-dimensional space.

- The **AppActions** class lets you create and respond to app shortcuts from the app icon.

- The **AppInfo** class provides platform-specific information about your application, such as package name, build number, requested theme (Dark or

Light), and so on. The **AppInfo.ShowSettingsUI** method opens a page of settings maintained by the operating system for the application.

- The **Barometer** class lets you monitor the device's barometer sensor, which measures pressure.

- The **Battery** class contains a set of properties and events, letting you check and monitor the device's battery and power source information. It can be useful, for example, to avoid background processing while the device is in energy-saver mode.

- The **Browser** class provides a cross-platform API to display a web page inside an application.

- The **Clipboard** class lets you copy and paste text to the system clipboard between applications and monitor clipboard changes.

- The **Compas** class provides access to the device's compass sensor to monitor the device's magnetic north heading.

- The **Connectivity** class lets you monitor for changes in the device's network conditions, check the current network access, and how it's currently connected. For example, you can use this class to limit the application capabilities when the internet isn't available or a mobile cellular is used.

- The **Contacts** class lets a user get information about a specific contact or all contacts.

- The **DeviceDisplay** class provides capabilities to check and monitor device-related information like dimensions, refresh rate, density, and so on. Besides, the **KeepScreenOn** property value can be adjusted to determine whether the screen should be kept on.

- The **DeviceInfo** class provides information about the device, such as platform, idiom, manufacturer, and model.

- The **Email** class provides a way to send emails using the default email client.

- The **FilePicker** class lets a user pick a single file or multiple files from the device's storage.

- The **FileSystem** class provides a way to access the package files and locations of the device folders.

- The **Flashlight** class provides an API to control the device's camera flashlight.

- The **Geocoding** class provides functionality to geocode a placemark to positional coordinates and reverse geocode coordinates to a placemark.

- The **Geolocation** class contains the set of methods and events to retrieve the device's current geolocation and listen for geolocation coordinates changes. In addition, the **Location** and **LocationExtensions** classes define the **CalculateDistance** methods that calculate the shortest distance between two geographic points along the surface of the Earth.

- The **Gyroscope** class provides an API to enable you to monitor the device's gyroscope sensor.

- The **HapticFeedback** class provides an API to control haptic feedback on the device.

- The **Launcher** class API enables an application to open a URI by the system. It's primarily used when deep linking another application's custom URI schemes.

- The **Magnetometer** class provides APIs to detect the device's orientation relative to Earth's magnetic field in microteslas.

- The **MainThread** class enables you to enforce running a specified block of code on the main (UI) thread. Additionally, it allows us to determine whether a currently running code is running on the main thread.

- The **Map** class enables an application to open the installed map application to a specific location. And it allows selecting the navigation mode, such as **Driving** and **Walking**, if needed.

- The **MediaPicker** class API lets a user pick or take a photo or video on the device.

- The **OrientationSensor** class lets you monitor the orientation of a device in three-dimensional space.

- The **Permissions** class provides an API to check and request runtime permissions, such as access to the device's media gallery, sensors, and microphone.

- The **PhoneDialer** class enables you to open a phone number in the dialer.

- The **Platform** class contains a bunch of useful static platform-specific helper methods.

- The **Preferences** class provides a cross-platform API to store application preferences in a persistent key/value store.

- The **SecureStorage** class provides a cross-platform API to store simple key/value pairs of secret data securely using platform-specific mechanisms like Android Keystore and iOS KeyChain.

- The **SemanticScreenReader** class, being a component of the accessibility subsystem, enables an application to announce audible text to the user using a screen reader provided by the operating system.

- The **Share** class provides an API to share files or text data with other applications on the device.

- The **Sms** class enables an application to open a default SMS application with a specified message to send to a recipient.

- The **TextToSpeech** class enables an application to speak back text from the device utilizing the text-to-speech engines provided by platforms.

- The **UnitConverters** helper class provides a bunch of methods to convert units from one system to another.

- The **VersionTracking** helper class provides several properties and methods to track the versions of an application and check, for example, if the current launch is the first launch for the current build or version.

- The **Vibration** class provides a cross-platform API to make the device vibrate for the specified time.

- The **WebAuthenticator** class is a web navigation API to be used for authentication with external web services that use browser-based flows and callbacks (e.g., OAuth).

- While developing applications, it is important to remember and consider that despite cross-platform APIs **Essentials** classes provide, some devices or platforms may not support particular **Essentials** features due to hardware or operating system limitations. More information about each API can be found in the .NET MAUI documentation at **https://learn.microsoft.com/en-us/dotnet/maui/platform-integration/**.

Connectivity

Since most applications rely on a device having access to the internet, it's important to be able to check network access state and monitor network access state changes.

Connectivity is a static proxy class that provides access to connectivity features. It contains the following static members:

- The **Current** property of type **Iconnectivity** returns an existing static instance of the **ConnectivityImplementation** class or creates one if needed. **ConnectivityImplementation** performs all the work.

- The **NetworkAccess** property of enum type **NetworkAccess** is a shortcut that returns **Current.NetworkAccess**. It returns the current state of the connection to the internet.

- The **ConnectionProfiles** property of type **Ienumerable<Connection Profile>** is a shortcut that returns active connectivity types for a current device that are retrieved via the **Current.ConnectionProfiles.Distinct** method.

- The **ConnectivityChanged** event is a shortcut for the **Current. ConnectivityChanged** event that is raised when network access or profile has changed.

The **NetworkAccess** falls into the following states:

- **Unknown**: Unable to determine internet connectivity

- **None**: No connectivity available

- **Local**: Local network access only

- **ConstrainedInternet**: Indicates captive portal connectivity, where local access to a web portal is provided but access to the internet requires specific credentials to be provided via a portal

- **Internet**: Local and internet access; it's important to say that connectivity works different on different platforms. Because of that, **Internet** state only guarantees that a connection is available. For example, the device may be connected to Wi-Fi, but the router is disconnected from the internet; internet access may be reported in such cases

The **ConnectivityProfile** enum, in turn, represents the following profiles:

- **Bluetooth**: The Bluetooth data connection

- **Cellular**: The mobile/cellular data connection

- **Ethernet**: The Ethernet data connection

- **WiFi**: The WiFi data connection

- **Unknown**: Unknown type of connection

Let's now utilize the **Connectivity** class to notify the user of our banking app about lost and restored internet connection.

First of all, in the case of Android, make sure the access network state permission entry is added to the **Platforms/Android/AndroidManifest.xml** file, as shown here:

```
<uses-permission android:name="android.permission.ACCESS_NETWORK_STATE"
/>
```

Now, open the **App.xaml.cs** file and add the following code to it; use the **Chapter_7/1_LearningMauiBankingApp_Connectivity** application from the book repository if needed:

```
private NetworkAccess _lastKnownNetworkAccess;


protected override void OnStart()
{
    _lastKnownNetworkAccess = Connectivity.NetworkAccess;
    Connectivity.ConnectivityChanged += OnConnectivityChanged;
    base.OnStart();
}


protected override void OnResume()
{
    Connectivity.ConnectivityChanged += OnConnectivityChanged;
    base.OnResume();
}


protected override void OnSleep()
{
    Connectivity.ConnectivityChanged -= OnConnectivityChanged;
    base.OnSleep();
}


private async void OnConnectivityChanged(object sender,
ConnectivityChangedEventArgs e)
{
    //return if ConnectionProfiles collection has been changed, not
NetworkAccess
    if (_lastKnownNetworkAccess == e.NetworkAccess)
        return;
```

```
Connectivity.ConnectivityChanged -= OnConnectivityChanged;


if (e.NetworkAccess == NetworkAccess.Internet)
    await MainPage.DisplayAlert(
        Localization.Strings.ConnectivityAlert_InternetOkTitle,
        Localization.Strings.ConnectivityAlert_InternetOkMessage,
        Localization.Strings.ConnectivityAlert_ButtonText);
else
    await MainPage.DisplayAlert(
        Localization.Strings.ConnectivityAlert_NoInternetTitle,
        Localization.Strings.ConnectivityAlert_NoInternetMessage,
        Localization.Strings.ConnectivityAlert_ButtonText);


_lastKnownNetworkAccess = e.NetworkAccess;


Connectivity.ConnectivityChanged += OnConnectivityChanged;
}
```

This code subscribes to the **ConnectivityChanged** event once the application is started or resumed from the background and shows the notification alert on a currently visible page, informing the user when internet access is lost or resumed. Don't forget to add appropriate localization strings.

Now, let's prevent the user from clicking the **Login** button when the internet is not accessible. To do this, we would create a reusable behavior that disables the UI control when the internet isn't available. So, add a new folder called **Behaviors** to the project and add the following class to it:

```
public class NoInternetDisableBehavior : Behavior<VisualElement>
{
    private VisualElement _bindable;
    private NetworkAccess _lastKnownNetworkAccess;

    protected override void OnAttachedTo(VisualElement bindable)
    {
        base.OnAttachedTo(bindable);
        _bindable = bindable;
```

```
    _lastKnownNetworkAccess = Connectivity.NetworkAccess;
    Connectivity.ConnectivityChanged += OnConnectivityChanged;
}


protected override void OnDetachingFrom(VisualElement bindable)
{
    base.OnDetachingFrom(bindable);
    Connectivity.ConnectivityChanged -= OnConnectivityChanged;
}


private void OnConnectivityChanged(object sender,
ConnectivityChangedEventArgs e)
{
    if (_lastKnownNetworkAccess == e.NetworkAccess)
        return;

    _lastKnownNetworkAccess = e.NetworkAccess;
    Connectivity.ConnectivityChanged -= OnConnectivityChanged;

    if (e.NetworkAccess == NetworkAccess.Internet)
        _bindable.IsEnabled = true;
    else
        _bindable.IsEnabled = false;

    Connectivity.ConnectivityChanged += OnConnectivityChanged;
}
}
```

Next, add this behavior to the **Login** button of the **LoginPage**, as follows. As a result, the **Login** button must be disabled once the internet isn't accessible:

```
<Button x:Name="LoginButton"
        ...>
    <Button.Behaviors>
        <behaviors:NoInternetDisableBehavior/>
```

```
    </Button.Behaviors>
</Button>
```

Text-to-Speech (TTS)

The **TextToSpeech** class is like **Connectivity** when it comes to architecture. It's also a static class providing access to a single instance of **TextToSpeech** util and a number of shortcut class members. Here are the members of the **TextToSpeech** static class:

- The **Default** property of type **ITextToSpeech** returns an existing static instance of the **TextToSpeechImplementation** class or creates one if needed.

- The **GetLocalesAsync** method returns a list of locales supported by text-to-speech.

- The **SpeakAsync** method speaks the given text through the device's speech-to-text engine. The method expects a string argument and two optional parameters: **SpeechOptions** and **CancelationToken**. **SpeechOptions** is used to override text-to-speech settings, and **CancelationToken** can be used to stop text-to-speech speaking.

Let us now welcome a user with text-to-speech when they navigate from **LoginPage** to **HomePage**. Use the **Chapter_7/2_LearningMauiBankingApp_TTS** application if needed. To avoid utilizing static classes in the view model, register the **ITextToSpeech** in **StrongContainer.cs** by adding the following property to it, and then inject the **ITextToSpeech** into the **LoginPageViewModel**:

```
[Instance]
public static ITextToSpeech TextToSpeechInstance => TextToSpeech.
Default;
```

Now, strong inject will return **TextToSpeech.Default** every time **ITextToSpeech** needs to be injected.

Finally, modify the **OnLoginButtonClicked** method of **LoginPageViewModel**, as follows, to speak the welcome text before the user is navigated to the **HomePage**:

```
private async void OnLoginButtonClicked()
{
    await _textToSpeech.SpeakAsync($"{Localization.Strings.TTS_
WelcomeBack} {Username}");

    await _navigationService.NavigateToAsync<HomePage,
HomePageViewModel>();
}
```

Of course, you must add **TTS_WelcomeBack** localization strings for every language application support. By default, text-to-speech selects a language engine that fits the application language and culture, and this works well along with localization strings. However, the **SpeakAsync** method enables applications to specify custom settings by passing an object of the **SpeechOptions** class. Here's how locale, pitch, and volume (all optional) can be changed with **SpeechOptions**:

```
var locales = await TextToSpeech.GetLocalesAsync();

var plTtsLocale = locales.FirstOrDefault(x => x.Language.ToLower() ==
"pl-pl");


await TextToSpeech.SpeakAsync(
    $"{Localization.Strings.TTS_WelcomeBack} {Username}",
    new SpeechOptions()
    {
        Locale = plTtsLocale,
        Pitch = 1.5f, //higher voice tone (default is 1, range is 0-2)
        Volume = 1f //Lower volume level (default is 0.5, range is 0-1)
    });
```

As you can see, this piece of code gets the Polish locale from the list of available text-to-speech locales and uses it while speaking the welcome message. You must be careful here because Polish (in this particular case) text-to-speech engine isn't able to speak other languages correctly. So, when your application uses, for example, English, it will try to speak the text of English localization treating it as Polish. So, you must make sure the text to be spoken is in the right language while the text-to-speech locale is chosen manually.

There are a few important things that need to be mentioned. First, text-to-speech doesn't support background audio playback, so the application needs to be foregrounded to make text-to-speech work. Second, it's recommended to wrap text-to-speech calls into try-catch because the **TextToSpeech** class can throw an exception if text-to-speech isn't supported by a device. Third, the device shouldn't be in silent mode, otherwise the speech will not be heard.

Gyroscope

The **Gyroscope** static class allows developers to access the gyroscope sensor to detect and react to device rotation and orientation changes. Just like previously learned classes, the **Gyroscope** class is a proxy that provides several static class members:

- The **Default** property of type **IGyroscope** returns an existing static instance of the **GyroscopeImplementation** class or creates one if needed.

- The **IsMonitoring** property of type **bool** indicates whether the gyroscope is actively being monitored. The property returns the value of the **Default. IsMonitoring** property.

- The **IsSupported** property of type **bool** indicates whether the gyroscope is supported on the current device. The property returns the value of the **Default.IsSupported** property.

- The **Start** and **Stop** methods are responsible for starting and stopping monitoring changes to the gyroscope sensor. The **Start** method requires an argument of enum type **SensorSpeed** that specifies the gyroscope sensor data update rate. Those methods also call the corresponding methods of **GyroscopeImplementation** returned by the **Default** property.

To see how **Gyroscope** can be utilized, let's make the bottom bar of **HomePage** rotate as the user rotates the device; use **Chapter_7/3_LearningMauiBankingApp_ Gyroscope** if needed.

First of all, let's register the **Gyroscope** class in the **StrongInject** container. Add the following property to **StrongContainer**:

```
[Instance]
public static IGyroscope GyroscopeInstance => Gyroscope.Default;
```

Next, give the bottom bar **Border** element the **BottomBar** name and modify the **HomePage.xaml.cs** as shown:

```
public partial class HomePage : ContentPage
{
    private readonly IGyroscope _gyroscope;
    private DateTime _lastVisibleBottomBarRotationChange;

    public HomePage(IGyroscope gyroscope)
    {
        _gyroscope = gyroscope;
        InitializeComponent();
    }

    protected override void OnNavigatedTo(NavigatedToEventArgs args)
```

...

```csharp
protected override void OnAppearing()
{
    if (_gyroscope.IsSupported)
    {
        _gyroscope.ReadingChanged += OnGyroscopeReadingChanged;
        _gyroscope.Start(SensorSpeed.Fastest);
    }
    base.OnAppearing();
}


protected override void OnDisappearing()
{
    if (_gyroscope.IsSupported)
    {
        _gyroscope.ReadingChanged -= OnGyroscopeReadingChanged;
        _gyroscope.Stop();
    }
    base.OnDisappearing();
}


private void OnGyroscopeReadingChanged(object sender,
GyroscopeChangedEventArgs e)
{
    if (this.AnimationIsRunning(nameof(ResetBotomBarRotation)))
        return;

    const double maxRotationXY = 8;
    const double maxRotationZ = 4;
    const double velocityCoeficient = 0.5;
    TimeSpan resetRotationFreePlayWait = TimeSpan.
FromMilliseconds(250);
```

```
        var velocityX = e.Reading.AngularVelocity.X;
        var velocityY = e.Reading.AngularVelocity.Y;
        var velocityZ = e.Reading.AngularVelocity.Z;


        var newRotationX = BottomBar.RotationX + velocityX *
velocityCoeficient;
        var newRotationY = BottomBar.RotationY - velocityY *
velocityCoeficient;
        var newRotationZ = BottomBar.Rotation - velocityZ *
velocityCoeficient;


        MainThread.BeginInvokeOnMainThread(() =>
        {
            if (Math.Abs(newRotationX) <= maxRotationXY)
                BottomBar.RotationX = newRotationX;


            if (Math.Abs(newRotationY) <= maxRotationXY)
                BottomBar.RotationY = newRotationY;


            if (Math.Abs(newRotationZ) <= maxRotationZ)
                BottomBar.Rotation = newRotationZ;
        });


        if (IsDeviceRotatingSignificantly(velocityX, velocityY,
velocityZ))
        {
            _lastVisibleBottomBarRotationChange = DateTime.Now;
        }
        else if (DateTime.Now - _lastVisibleBottomBarRotationChange >=
resetRotationFreePlayWait)
        {
            ResetBotomBarRotation();
            _lastVisibleBottomBarRotationChange = DateTime.Now;
        }
```

```
    }


    private bool IsDeviceRotatingSignificantly(double velocityX, double
velocityY, double velocityZ)
    {
        const double rotationFreePlayVelocityLimit = 0.08;


        return Math.Abs(velocityX) > rotationFreePlayVelocityLimit
            || Math.Abs(velocityY) > rotationFreePlayVelocityLimit
            || Math.Abs(velocityZ) > rotationFreePlayVelocityLimit;
    }


    private void ResetBotomBarRotation()
    {
        new Animation()
        {
            { 0, 1, new Animation(x => BottomBar.RotationX = x,
BottomBar.RotationX, 0) },
            { 0, 1, new Animation(x => BottomBar.RotationY = x,
BottomBar.RotationY, 0) },
            { 0, 1, new Animation(x => BottomBar.Rotation = x,
BottomBar.Rotation, 0) }
        }.Commit(this, nameof(ResetBotomBarRotation), length: 400,
easing: Easing.CubicInOut);
    }
}
```

In addition, add the following permission to the **AndroidManifest.xml** file. This permission is required for applications targeting Android 12 and higher that gather motion sensor data at a rate higher than 50 Hz:

```
<uses-permission android:name="android.permission.HIGH_SAMPLING_RATE_
SENSORS"/>
```

Although the preceding code may seem complicated, there are a few things that happen here. First of all, we've overridden the **OnAppearing** and **OnDisappearing** life cycle methods to start and stop the gyroscope if it's supported.

Next, the **ResetBotomBarRotation** method returns all rotation parameters to zero. This method is called when gyroscope velocities are not considered significant for at least 250ms. It means the device is more or less stationary (for example, when laying on a table). When the **ResetBotomBarRotation** animation is run, gyroscope data is not processed.

Then, new rotation values are calculated: **velocityCoefficient** is used to slow the rotation moves down a little while keeping it smooth, and **maxRotationXY** and **maxRotationZ** are used to constrain rotation so that the bottom bar doesn't overlap with other UI elements.

Finally, new values are assigned to BottomBar UI control using another **Essentials** library class: **MainThread**. The **BeginInvokeOnMainThread** method forces assignments to be executed on a UI thread. It's important because it's not guaranteed that the **ReadingChanged** event is invoked on the main thread. The only exception is when the gyroscope was started with the **SensorSpeed.UI** argument.

Application preferences

The **Preferences** static class provides an API to store application preferences in a key-value store. It utilizes storages provided by platforms. The **Preferences** class relies on NSUserDefaults on iOS, SharedPreferences on Android, and **ApplicaionDataContainer** on Windows. The idea of a static proxy class is the same here. Here are the **Preferences** class members:

- The **Default** property of type **IPreferences** returns an existing static instance of the **PreferencesImplementation** class or creates one if needed.

- The **Set** method sets a value for a given key. The **sharedName** optional parameter can be used to share preferences across extensions or to a watch application.

- The **Get** method gets a value for a given key or the specified default value if the key doesn't exist in storage.

- The **Remove** method removes the key and its associated value if it exists.

- The **Clear** method removes all keys and values.

- The **ContainsKey** method indicates whether the specified key exists.

The values of simple types, string, and **DateTime** can be stored with **Preferences**. Be careful when storing a string because this API is not supposed to store large amounts of text. Besides, on Android, the **Auto Backup** feature needs to be disabled if you want preferences to be removed from the device along with the application. Don't use **Preferences** to store secret data like passwords.

The task for you: The following **ApplicationPreferences** service wraps the **Preferences** class, simplifying and encapsulating access to the application preferences. Introduce this service to our banking app. Then, use it to save the **Username** value before navigating to **HomePage**, and fulfil the **Username** entry with the previously stored **Username** preference at the startup of the application. Here are a few hints for you:

- Override the **OnNavigatedTo** method in the **LoginPageViewModel** class.

- Don't forget to register the **IPreferences** instance and the **IApplicationPreferences** transient class in **StrongContainer**.

- Don't forget to change the binding mode to **TwoWay** for the **Text** property of the **UsernameEntry** UI control.

- Don't forget to modify the **Username** property of **LoginPageViewModel** so that it calls **OnPropertyChanged**.

- Use the **Chapter_7/4_LearningMauiBankingApp_Preferences** application if needed.

```
public class ApplicationPreferences : IApplicationPreferences
{
    private readonly IPreferences _preferences;

    public ApplicationPreferences(IPreferences preferences)
    {
        _preferences = preferences;
    }

    public string Username
    {
        get => _preferences.Get(nameof(Username), string.Empty);
        set => _preferences.Set(nameof(Username), value);
    }
}
```

Secure storage

The **SecureStorage** class provides the API similar to the **Preferences**. The difference is that **SecureStorage** is designed to store sensitive information like authentication tokens, passwords, or API keys securely on the device. It does so by utilizing the following platform-specific secure storage mechanisms:

- **iOS, MacCatalyst, tvOS, and watchOS**: Secure Storage uses the iOS Keychain, a secure, encrypted storage system provided by Apple for storing sensitive data. Keychain items are encrypted, and access to the Keychain is usually restricted to the app that created the item. If needed, data can be shared between apps from the same developer using the **Keychain Access Groups** feature.

- **Android**: **Secure Storage** uses the **SharedPreferences** in conjunction with the Android Keystore system The encrypted data is stored in **SharedPreferences**, while a unique encryption key is stored in **Keystore**. Access to stored data is restricted to the app that created the data.

- **Windows**: **Secure Storage** uses the **Windows.DataProtection** API on Windows devices to encrypt the data using a combination of the user's **Windows** credentials and a system-specific secret generated by the **Windows Data Protection API**. The encrypted data is then stored in the app's local storage protected by file system permissions.

Here are some tips for working with SecureStorage:

- When developing on the iOS simulator, it's recommended to add the **Entitlements.plist** file to the iOS platform folder, enable Keychain entitlement, and set **Custom Entitlements** (iOS Bundle Signing in project preferences) to this entitlements file.

- It's recommended to wrap the **GetAsync** and **SetAsync** methods into try-catch blocks.

- In the case of **Preferences**, don't store large amounts of text in **Secure Storage**.

Community Toolkit library overview

As the popularity of Xamarin was growing, the community came up with several widely adopted components, extensions, and helpers that help reduce boilerplate code, improve productivity significantly, improve code quality, and enhance overall user experience. The .NET MAUI Community Toolkit, being a successor of the Xamarin Community Toolkit, is still a free, community-driven open-source library with several extremely useful features. Moreover, .NET MAUI Community Toolkit contains some features that Xamarin Community Toolkit does not.

Community Toolkit is delivered via NuGet. There are three toolkit packages available:

- The **CommunityToolkit.Maui** package is a collection of **Animations**, **Behaviors**, **Converters**, XAML markup extensions, and **Custom Controls**. After the package is installed, the **UseMauiCommunityToolkit** extension method must be called on the **MauiAppBuilder** class when bootstrapping an application in the **MauiProgram.cs** file.

- The **CommunityToolkit.Maui.Markup** package is a part of the toolkit that provides a set of extension methods to simplify building UI while using C# only. The library promotes a declarative way of creating UI in C#, which leads to cleaner and more understandable code. To use the markup toolkit, the **UseMauiCommunityToolkit** markup extension method must be called on **MauiAppBuilder** in the **MauiProgram.cs** file.

- The **CommunityToolkit.Maui.MediaElement** package contains **MediaElement** control for playing video and audio from web sources, embedded resources, and files from the local filesystem. The **UseMauiCommunityToolkitMediaElement** extension method must be called on **MauiAppBuilder** in the **MauiProgram.cs** file to use **MediaElement**.

The following **xmlns** must be added to your view or page when using the **Community Toolkit** in XAML:

```
xmlns:mct=http://schemas.microsoft.com/dotnet/2022/maui/toolkit
```

Snackbar

The **Snackbar** is a timed alert that usually appears at the bottom of the screen and is dismissed manually or after a configurable duration of time. In a significant number of cases, the **Snackbar** can be an appropriate replacement for the classic alert dialogs.

Natively, the **Snackbar** is only available on Android. In the case of other platforms, container views are used (UIView on iOS/MacCatalyst and ToastNotification on Windows).

The following code shows how **Snackbar** can be used instead of alerts in our banking app to inform users about connectivity state changes (**Chapter_7/5_ LearningMauiBankingApp_Snackbar application**):

```
private async void OnConnectivityChanged(object sender,
ConnectivityChangedEventArgs e)
{
    //return if ConnectionProfiles collection has been changed, not
NetworkAccess
    if (_lastKnownNetworkAccess == e.NetworkAccess)
        return;
```

```csharp
    Connectivity.ConnectivityChanged -= OnConnectivityChanged;


    var font = Microsoft.Maui.Font.OfSize("Poppins-Regular", 16);


    var snackbarOptions = new SnackbarOptions
    {
        BackgroundColor = (Color) (RequestedTheme == AppTheme.Dark
            ? Resources["DarkPrimaryBackgroundColor"]
            : Resources["LightPrimaryBackgroundColor"]),
        TextColor = (Color)(RequestedTheme == AppTheme.Dark
            ? Resources["DarkSecondaryTextColor"]
            : Resources["LightSecondaryTextColor"]),
        ActionButtonTextColor = (Color)(RequestedTheme == AppTheme.Dark
            ? Resources["DarkPrimaryTextColor"]
            : Resources["LightPrimaryTextColor"]),
        CornerRadius = new CornerRadius(15),
        Font = Microsoft.Maui.Font.OfSize("Poppins-Regular", 16),
        ActionButtonFont = Microsoft.Maui.Font.OfSize("Poppins-Bold", 14)
    };


    var duration = TimeSpan.FromSeconds(5);
    var messageText = string.Empty;
    var actionButtonText = Localization.Strings.ConnectivityAlert_
ButtonText;


    var cancelationToken = new CancellationTokenSource();
    Action buttonAction = () => cancelationToken.Cancel();


    if (e.NetworkAccess == NetworkAccess.Internet)
        messageText = Localization.Strings.ConnectivityAlert_
InternetOkMessage;
    else
        messageText = Localization.Strings.ConnectivityAlert_
```

```
NoInternetMessage;

    var snackbar = Snackbar.Make(
            messageText,
            bittonAction,
            actionButtonText,
            duration,
            snackbarOptions);

    await snackbar.Show(cancelationToken.Token);

    _lastKnownNetworkAccess = e.NetworkAccess;

    Connectivity.ConnectivityChanged += OnConnectivityChanged;
}
```

The **Make** method of the **Snackbar** class creates a new instance of **Snackbar**, configuring it using the following parameters:

- The **message** parameter of **string** type is displayed as a main message.

- The optional parameter **action** of type **Action** is a delegate that is called when the **Snackbar** button is pressed.

- The optional parameter **actionButtonText** of type **string** specifies the text of the **Snackbar** button.

- The optional parameter **duration** of type **TimeSpan** defines the amount of time for which **Snackbar** disappears. When the duration is not specified, the default value, 3 seconds, is used.

- The optional parameter **visualOptions** of type **SnackbarOptions** is a configuration of **Snackbar** appearance.

As you might notice, the **SnackbarOptions** class allows you to configure various visual parameters:

- Message character spacing (**CharacterSpacing** property)

- Message text font and color (**Font** and **TextColor** properties)

- Action button text font and color (**ActionButtonFont** and **ActionButtonTextColor** properties)

- **Snackbar** background color (**BackgroundColor** property)
- The radius of corners (**CornerRadius** property)

There are two ways to show the **Snackbar**. The first option is to create it using the **Make** method and then call the asynchronous **Show** method that displays the **Snackbar** at the bottom of the screen. The second option is to call the asynchronous **DisplaySnackbar** extension method on any UI element (derived from **VisualElement**) that creates the instance of the **Snackbar** and shows it by anchoring it to this UI element.

Manually, the **Snackbar** can be dismissed by calling the **Dismiss** method or by using the cancelation token passed to the **Show** or **DisplaySnackbar** methods.

Here are a few important notes:

- Only one instance of **Snackbar** can be displayed at a time.
- The **Snackbar** class provides a few static members to monitor life cycle, such as the **IsShown** property and two events: **Shown** and **Dismissed**.
- The API allows the modification of **Snackbar** by creating a subclass and overriding methods, or a custom **Snackbar** can be created by implementing the **ISnackbar** interface.

InvertedBoolConverter

InvertedBoolConverter can be nominated for the most popular community toolkit feature award. This very simple but extremely helpful value converter allows you to invert the value of a boolean property that comes from a binding source.

The following code snippet shows how **InvertedBoolConverter** can be used to make a label visible only when the **IsUserLogged** property of **ViewModel** is **false**:

```
<ContentPage xmlns="http://schemas.microsoft.com/dotnet/2021/maui"
             xmlns:x="http://schemas.microsoft.com/winfx/2009/xaml"
             xmlns:mct=http://schemas.microsoft.com/dotnet/2022/maui/
toolkit
             x:Class="ExampleApp.Pages.ExamplePage">
    <ContentPage.Resources>
        <ResourceDictionary>
            <mct:InvertedBoolConverter x:Key="InvertedBoolConverter" />
        </ResourceDictionary>
    </ContentPage.Resources>
```

...

```
    <Label Text="Guest mode is active. Please log in."
           IsVisible="{Binding IsUserLogged,
                        Converter={StaticResource
InvertedBoolConverter}}" />
```

...

```
</ContentPage>
```

NumericValidationBehavior

The **NumericValidationBehavior**, along with other validation behaviors, is another useful tool provided by the community toolkit. It's used to determine whether text input is a valid numeric value and apply different styles depending on the validation result.

The following code (**Chapter_7/6_LearningMauiBankingApp_Validation Behavior**) shows how **NumericValidationBehavior** can be applied to the entry of **TransferModalPage** to change the color of text when the provided value is bigger than the amount of money available:

```
xmlns:mct=http://schemas.microsoft.com/dotnet/2022/maui/toolkit
```

...

```
<Style x:Key="InvalidValueTransferEntryStyle" TargetType="Entry">
    <Setter Property="TextColor" Value="{DynamicResource
Accent1Color}"/>
</Style>
```

...

```
<Entry x:Name="TransferValueEntry"
       Placeholder="$1000"
       Keyboard="Numeric">
    <Entry.Behaviors>
        <mct:NumericValidationBehavior
            MinimumDecimalPlaces="0"
            MaximumDecimalPlaces="2"
            MinimumValue="0"
            MaximumValue="{Binding SelectedFromCard.Balance}"
```

```
        Flags="ValidateOnValueChanged"
        InvalidStyle="{StaticResource
InvalidValueTransferEntryStyle}"/>

  </Entry.Behaviors>
</Entry>
```

NumericValidationBehavior provides the following set of bindable properties:

- The **MinimumDecimalPlaces** and **MaximumDecimalPlaces** properties specify the number of decimal places that will be allowed.

- The **MinimumValue** and **MaximumValue** properties specify the range of allowed numeric values.

ValidationBehavior abstract class

The **NumericValidationBehavior** and other validation behaviors derive the base abstract **ValidationBehavior** class. **ValidationBehavior**, being a public class, also simplifies the creation of your own validators. Here are the bindable properties that come from the abstract **ValidationBehavior** class:

- The **Flags** property of enum type **ValidationFlags** specifies how to handle validation, for example, **ValidateOnAttaching**, **ValidateOnFocusing**, **ValidateOnUnfocusing**, **ValidateOnValueChanged**, or **ForceMakeValid WhenFocused**. Besides, a few validation flags can be applied; XAML example: **"ValidateOnValueChanged, ValidateOnUnfocusing"**.

- The **IsValid** and **IsNotValid** properties indicate whether the current value is considered valid.

- The **IsRunning** property indicates whether the validation is in progress.

- **ForceValidateCommand** is a blank property that allows you to add a forced validation feature to your custom validation behavior.

- The **InvalidStyle** and **ValidStyle** properties take styles to be applied to the control when the value is considered invalid or valid.

- The **Value** property is used to override the value to validate.

- **ValuePropertyName** of type string allows a developer to override the property whose value will be used as the value to validate.

Apart from styles, the **ValidationBehavior** class ensures that all validation behaviors support **VisualStateManager** by applying **Valid** or **Invalid** visual states to the UI element behavior is attached to.

ColorAnimationExtensions

ColorAnimationExtensions provides a set of extension methods for animating color properties. The extension methods allow you to specify the start and end colors for the animation, and the duration, easing function, and any additional animation parameters that you might need to make smooth animated color transitions.

ColorAnimationExtensions provides the following extension methods:

- **BackgroundColorTo** animates the **BackgroundColor** property of a control derived from VisualElement.

- **TextColorTo** animates the **TextColor** property of the text in a label, button, or other text-based views.

For example, the following code snippet animates the **BackgroundColor** property of a button, applying the red color in 2 seconds:

```
await MyButton.BackgroundColorTo(Color.FromArgb("#FF0000"), length: 2000);
```

UserStoppedTypingBehavior

UserStoppedTypingBehavior is used when we wish to perform some action when a user stopped writing instead of performing it using the **TextChanged** subscription. The typical use case is searching or filtering. The filtering operation can be quite time-consuming, especially when the application's business logic requires a web API to be called. So, there is no reason to fire the filtering procedure every time text changes.

UserStoppedTypingBehavior allows you to bind the **Command** property and a delay time in milliseconds. Let's make our banking app speak the username once a user stopped typing it. Use **Chapter_7/7_LearningMauiBankingApp_ UserStopperTyping** from the repository if needed. First, add the following command to the **ViewModel**:

```
LoginPageViewModel:
public ICommand SpeakCommand { get; }


//define the command in the constructor
SpeakCommand = new Command<string>(Speak);


private void Speak(string textToSpeak)
{
    _textToSpeech.SpeakAsync(textToSpeak);
}
```

Then, modify the **UsernameEntry** as shown below:

```
xmlns:mct="http://schemas.microsoft.com/dotnet/2022/maui/toolkit"

...

<Entry x:Name="UsernameEntry"
        Style="{StaticResource UsernameEntryStyle}"
        ...>
    <Entry.Behaviors>
        <mct:UserStoppedTypingBehavior
            Command="{Binding SpeakCommand}"
            CommandParameter="{Binding Text, Source={x:Reference
UsernameEntry}}"
            MinimumLengthThreshold="2"
            StoppedTypingTimeThreshold="800"/>
    </Entry.Behaviors>
</Entry>
```

Now the **UserStoppedTypingBehavior** calls the **SpeakCommand** and uses the **Text** value of **UsernameEntry** as a parameter. Additionally, it calls the command only if the length of the text is greater than two characters and 800ms have passed since the user stopped typing the text.

This behavior contains one more property: the **ShouldDismissKeyboard Automatically** property of type **bool** specifies if the on-screen keyboard will be dismissed along with calling the command.

AsyncRelayCommand

The **CommunityToolkit** has one more important NuGet package called **CommunityToolkit.MVVM**. This library isn't MAUI-specific. It's built to be used across different .NET frameworks that adopt the MVVM pattern. This library contains several useful MVVM-oriented tools, for example, **AsyncRelayCommand**, which solves the problem of "async void" command handler methods, mentioned in *Chapter 5, Layering With MVVM*.

As you remember, regular **Commands** don't support asynchronous operations. So, we were forced to use "async void", which is considered a bad practice because of the extremely high risk of unhandled exceptions this approach leads to.

AsyncRelayCommand and **AsyncRelayCommand<T>**, on the other hand, extend regular commands by providing support for Task-returning delegates. Using Task-returning delegates allows exceptions to be captured and observed within the **Task** context. If an exception is thrown during the execution of an asynchronous Task, it is stored in the Task and can be handled later, when the Task is awaited.

Install the **CommunityToolkit.MVVM** NuGet, replace all async void command handlers with **async Task** ones, and replace **Commands** with **AsyncRelayCommands**; use the **Chapter_7/8_LearningMauiBankingApp_AsyncRelayCommand** application if needed. Here is how, for example, the **LoginButtonCommand** of the **LoginPageViewModel** can be modified with **AsyncRelayCommand**:

```
LoginButtonCommand = new AsyncRelayCommand(OnLoginButtonClickedAsync);

...

private async Task OnLoginButtonClickedAsync()
{
    ....
```

In addition to asynchronous operations support, the **AsyncRelayCommand** **AsyncRelayCommand<T>** provides the following useful functionalities:

- They can wrap asynchronous functions with an additional **CancellationToken** parameter to support cancelation, and they expose the **CanBeCanceled** and **IsCancellationRequested** properties, and the **Cancel** method.

- They expose an **ExecutionTask** property, which can be used to monitor the progress of a pending operation and an **IsRunning**, which can be used to check when an operation completes. This is particularly useful to bind a command to UI elements, such as loading indicators.

The full CommunityToolkit.MVVM documentation can be found at **https://learn.microsoft.com/en-us/dotnet/communitytoolkit/mvvm/**.

Conclusion

Congratulations. We've completed a significant part of our journey. .NET MAUI **Essentials** and **Community Toolkit** have become indispensable helpers for professional developers over the years. In addition to their practical usefulness, the set of tools also demonstrates the power of the community and its willingness to help. Explore each tool available to make your work more productive and possibly make your own contribution to the MAUI Community Toolkit in the future.

Here's a challenging task for you: Our settings page still doesn't have a back button and the selected theme is not saved as an application preference. Since you already know a lot, enhance the banking app as follows:

- Make the application save the selected theme in application preferences so that the selected theme is set when the application is started.

- Modify the layout of **SettingsPage** and add the custom button for navigating back to the **HomePage**.

Points to remember

- Essentials is an integral part of .NET MAUI, while MAUI Community Toolkit is delivered via NuGet.

- Essentials provide cross-platform helpers and APIs to access commonly used device features.

- Use the **MainThread** class to enforce running a specified block of code on the main (UI) thread.

- Some of Essentials features may not work on every platform or device.

- Do not store texts longer than a few words in **Preferences** and **Secure Storage**.

- Do not store secret information in preferences.

- Use **AsyncRelayCommand** for asynchronous operations.

Questions

1. Why is it important to be careful while manually defining text-to-speech locale?

2. What data types are supported by **Preferences** and **Secure Storage**?

3. What makes **Secure Storage** secure in comparison to **Preferences**?

Join our book's Discord space

Join the book's Discord Workspace for Latest updates, Offers, Tech happenings around the world, New Release and Sessions with the Authors:

https://discord.bpbonline.com

CHAPTER 8
Accessibility

Introduction

Accessibility in software development is a practice of making digital content easier to use for all users, especially those with disabilities, impairments, and limitations. The World Health Organization (WHO) claims that an estimated 1.3 billion people (or 16% of the global population) experience significant disabilities. This is a huge amount of people every modern society led by principles of human rights and equality feels responsible for. Accessibility technologies help them be socially inclusive and unlock their human potential through art, building careers, and contributing to science, and so on.

For example, *Dr. Mona Minkara*, a computational chemist and an Assistant Professor of Bioengineering at the Northeastern University, has been blind since the age of seven. A doctor said to her parents that it wasn't worth spending a penny on her education. Despite her disability, thanks to the supportive environment and accessibility technologies, she earned a degree and has been a significant contributor to the world of science using computational methods to study complex molecular systems. Moreover, her blindness helped her solve problems nobody else did because she developed her own mathematic-based technique for doing research job that classically requires sight.

Structure

In this chapter, we will cover the following topics:

- Overview
- Font sizing
- Screen readers overview
- Enable TalkBack
- Enable VoiceOver on Mac
- Enable VoiceOver on iPhone/iPad
- Enable Narrator on Windows
- Accessibility tree
- Semantic properties
- Description
- Hint
- HeadingLevel
- SetSemanticFocus and Announce
- SemanticOrderView
- Exclude from the accessibility tree
- Good practices

Objectives

In this chapter, you will be familiarized to the main ideas of accessibility and the accessibility tree. We will also explore the main accessibility tools and accessibility-related .NET MAUI APIs.

Overview

Accessibility support in software is beneficial for both society and businesses. Considering the viewpoint of individuals and the daily life of society, we can identify at least three sectors significantly affected by accessibility:

- **Equal access**: Accessibility ensures that people with disabilities have equal access to information, services, and opportunities available on websites and mobile applications. This access is essential for promoting equality and preventing discrimination.

- **Independence**: Accessible technologies enable people with disabilities to perform tasks independently, reducing the need for assistance from others. This independence can lead to increased self-confidence and a greater sense of autonomy.

- **Social inclusion**: Accessibility promotes social inclusion by enabling people with disabilities to participate in various aspects of society, such as education, employment, and social activities. It helps break barriers and fosters a sense of belonging and acceptance.

There are also reasons why accessibility support is important for businesses:

- **Wider audience reach**: By making digital content accessible, businesses and organizations can expand their audience, as accessible design often benefits not only people with disabilities but also older adults or individuals using less capable devices.

- **Improved user experience**: Accessible design principles generally lead to a better overall user experience, as they encourage simple and clear navigation, consistent layouts, and user-friendly interfaces. This improved user experience can benefit all users, not just those with disabilities.

- **Corporate social responsibility**: Providing accessible digital experiences demonstrates a commitment to social responsibility and ethical business practices, which can improve a company's reputation and customer loyalty.

- **Legal compliance**: Many countries have enacted laws and regulations to ensure that digital content is accessible to people with disabilities, for example, the **Americans with Disabilities Act (ADA)** in the United States and the Equality Act in the United Kingdom. These legal frameworks require businesses, organizations, and governments to provide accommodations and ensure accessibility for people with disabilities.

One of the most famous guidelines in terms of accessibility is the **Web Content Accessibility Guidelines (WCAG)**. WCAG is a set of guidelines developed by the **World Wide Web Consortium (W3C)** to help make web content more accessible to people with disabilities. WCAG is organized around four main principles, which are often referred to by the acronym **P-O-U-R**. These principles are as follows:

- **Perceivable**: This means users must be able to access the information through at least one of their senses. Examples of making content perceivable include providing text alternatives for non-text content, using captions for audio, and ensuring that text is easy to read. Additionally, in the case of mobile and cross-platform applications, it's important to design UI layouts that work well on both small mobile screens and larger desktop displays.

- **Operable**: This means all interactive elements should be accessible using various input methods, such as a keyboard, mouse, or touchscreen. This includes ensuring that all interactive elements are accessible using various input methods, such as touchscreens, keyboards, or voice commands. Provide clear navisay, ion mechanisms, and ensure that users can easily control time-sensitive content or media playback.

- **Understandable**: This means content should be presented in a clear and concise manner, and the user interface should be designed to minimize confusion and ambiguity. Use clear, concise language and consistent design elements, such as buttons and icons, to minimize confusion. Anticipate potential user errors and provide helpful guidance or error messages to help users recover from mistakes.

- **Robust**: Applications must be compatible with a wide variety of devices, operating systems, and assistive technologies. Ensure that your application can adapt to different screen sizes, orientations, and input methods, and test it with various assistive technologies, such as screen readers and speech recognition software.

More information about WCAG can be found at **https://www.w3.org/WAI/standards-guidelines/wcag/**.

Font sizing

Accessibility font scaling is a feature provided by operating systems that allows users to increase or decrease the size of the text displayed on their screens to improve readability. This feature is particularly useful for people with visual impairments or for those who have difficulty reading small text.

By default, the font scaling feature involves every single application installed. In practice, it can be considered a font size coefficient that the operating system applies to all texts of your application. So, it's important to ensure that the interface remains usable and visually appealing when the font size changes. For example, buttons and labels must have a flexible size to be able to grow or shrink, and the spacing between elements may need to be adjusted to maintain readability and usability. Therefore, avoid using absolute sizes when it comes to layouts; use **ScrollView**. Also, test how an application looks with different scaling applied; apply the **MaxLines** and **LineBreakMode** properties. The experience of UI designers and developers says that finding the compromise between aesthetic appearance and usability shouldn't be underestimated, especially when it comes to applications with fully custom UI and UX.

However, if you decided to not support font scaling, it can be disabled by setting the **FontAutoScalingEnabled** property on text-based controls to false.

Screen readers overview

When it comes to actual accessibility tools, screen readers are often crucial to people with visual impairments or reading difficulties. They are software applications that enable people to access and interact with digital content on various types of devices, including desktops, smartphones, tablets, smartwatches, and smart TVs. Screen readers usually offer auditory descriptions of on-screen controls, assisting users in navigating the app and referring to controls like images, which lack input or text. They can be operated through touchscreens, trackpads, or keyboards using gestures.

Screen readers can be third-party applications or built-in operating system tools like the following:

- **Narrator**, which is a built-in screen reader provided by Windows OS.

- **TalkBack**, which is a built-in screen reader of Google's Android, Wear OS, and Android TV.

- **VoiceOver**, which is a built-in screen reader of Apple's macOS, iOS, watchOS, and tvOS.

- **Orca**, which is the most popular open-source screen reader for Linux distributions like Ubuntu and Fedora.

While all screen readers serve the same purpose, there are certain differences between them:

- User interface and navigation methods differ between platforms. Because of that switching from one platform to another is chelenging. When it comes to comparison, users often claim that on mobile devices, VoiceOver is more consistent, intuitive, and easy to learn than TalkBack. When it comes to desktop operating systems, users often claim that Apple's VoiceOver and Microsoft's Narrator are comparable. While VoiceOver can be easier to learn for beginners, the Narrator might be more useful when it comes to specific software like audio production programs.

- VoiceOver is well integrated with Apple's ecosystem and works seamlessly across all Apple operating systems and devices. When it comes to TalkBack, users often complain about inconsistency, lack of predictability, and compatibility issues due to differences in a wide range of device vendors and poor backward compatibility between OS versions in comparison to VoiceOver. In all fairness, it should be said that VoiceOver isn't perfect and has its own bugs that don't exist on TalkBack.

- Each screen reader may have unique features specific to their operating system, device, or ecosystem. For example, VoiceOver on AppleWatch has a feature called **Taptic Time** that uses haptic feedback to communicate the time discreetly. On the other hand, users point out useful fingerprint gestures and speaking password features that TalkBack provides.

Enable TalkBack

There are three ways to enable the **TalkBack** screen reader. Follow these steps to turn on the **TalkBack** screen reader using the **Settings** app:

1. Open the **Settings** app.

2. Select the **Accessibility** menu and head to the **TalkBack** submenu.

3. Turn **Use TalkBack** on.

4. Select **OK**.

Follow the given steps to turn on the TalkBack using the volume keys:

1. Press and hold both volume keys for 3 seconds.

2. To confirm that you want to turn TalkBack on or off, press both volume keys again for 3 seconds.

Say "Hey Google, Turn off/on TalkBack" to turn off/on the screen reader with GoogleAssistant.

In case of any doubts, check the user manual of your device since the steps may vary depending on the vendor of a specific device.

Enable VoiceOver on Mac

There are a few ways to turn on/off the **VoiceOver** on Mac:

1. Press *Command-F5* to turn the **VoiceOver** on or off.

2. Activate Siri and say, *"Turn VoiceOver on"* or *"Turn VoiceOver off"*.

3. If your Mac or Magic Keyboard has Touch ID, press and hold the "Command" key while quickly pressing Touch ID thrice.

Follow these steps to activate/deactivate VoiceOver via system settings:

1. Choose **Apple Menu** and select **System Settings**.

2. Click **Accessibility** in the sidebar.

3. Click **VoiceOver** on the right.

4. Turn **VoiceOver** on or off.

Enable VoiceOver on iPhone/iPad

Perform the following steps to turn **VoiceOver** on/off via the **Settings** app:

1. Open the **Settings** app.

2. Go to the **Accessibility** → **VoiceOver** submenu.

3. Turn the setting on or off.

Here are the other ways:

1. Activate Siri and say *Turn on VoiceOver* or *Turn off VoiceOver*.

2. If you've set up the **Accessibility** shortcut, triple-click the side button or the **Home** button (depending on your iPhone/iPad model).

3. Use the accessibility icon in **Control Center** if you've set up one.

Enable Narrator on Windows

The Narrator screen reader can be enabled in two ways:

1. Press the *Windows* key + *Ctrl* + *Enter* together.

2. Press the *Windows* key + *Ctrl* + *N* together to open the **Narrator** settings, and then turn on the toggle under **Use Narrator**.

Accessibility Tree

We are already familiar with the concept of a **Visual Tree** of an application, which is a hierarchical representation of the UI elements as they are rendered on the screen. A **Visual Tree** includes every visual element that contributes to the final appearance of the application, such as controls and layout containers.

The **Accessibility Tree** is a hierarchical representation of the user interface that is specifically generated for assistive technologies like screen readers. An **Accessibility Tree** is derived from a **Visual Tree**, but it only includes elements that are relevant to accessibility. Each element in the **Accessibility Tree** is represented as a node, which has information about the element's role (for example, **Button**), state (for example, disabled), and its properties like text or value. As the UI changes due to user interaction or programmed behavior, the **Accessibility Tree** is updated to reflect the current state of the UI.

Developers influence the generation of the **Accessibility Tree** by providing semantic information for UI elements or explicitly excluding particular elements from the **Accessibility Tree**.

Semantic properties

Many accessibility requirements are addressed by assistive technology products installed by users or through tools and settings available within the operating system. Such functionality includes screen readers, screen magnification, and high-contrast settings.

As we've learned, different operating systems come with different screen readers, each with unique behavior and configurations. Most screen readers read the text linked to control upon receiving focus, helping users orient themselves while navigating the app. Some screen readers can even read the entire app interface when a page appears, providing users with all the information on the page before they attempt to navigate.

Most screen readers automatically read any text associated with a control that gains accessibility focus. As a result, controls like **Label** or **Button**, which have a **Text** property set, are accessible to users. However, **Image**, **ImageButton**, **ActivityIndicator**, and others might not be part of the accessibility tree due to the absence of associated text.

.NET Multi-platform App UI (.NET MAUI) supports two methods for accessing the accessibility experience of the underlying platform. Semantic properties are the .NET MAUI approach for incorporating accessibility values in apps and are the recommended method. Automation properties, on the other hand, are the Xamarin. Forms approach for including accessibility values in apps but have been superseded by semantic properties. In both approaches, the default accessibility order of controls corresponds to the order in which they appear in XAML or are added to the layout. However, various layouts may have additional factors influencing the accessibility order. For example, StackLayout's accessibility order also depends on its orientation, while Grid's accessibility order is based on its row and column arrangement.

Note that when **WebView** displays a website, it's the responsibility of the website to support accessibility. When a **WebView** displays a website that is not accessible, it won't be accessible in a .NET MAUI app.

Semantic properties are used to specify information about the controls that should gain accessibility focus and the text that should be audibly read to the user. These are attached properties that can be applied to any element to configure the accessibility APIs of the underlying platform.

It's important to remember that rather than attempting to enforce identical behavior across all platforms, semantic properties depend on the accessibility experience offered by each individual platform.

The **SemanticProperties** class defines three attached properties: **Description**, **Hint**, and **HeadingLevel**.

Description

The **Description** attached property of type **string** is a short descriptive text that a screen reader uses to announce an element. This should be set for elements that are important for understanding the content or interacting with the UI.

The following XAML markups show how the **Description** property can be used to announce the password entry:

```
<Entry SemanticProperties.Description="Provide your password" />
```

```
<Label x:Name="EntryLabel" Text="Provide your password" />
<Entry SemanticProperties.Description="{Binding Text,
Source={x:Reference EntryLabel}}" />
```

There are a few important things to remember in terms of the **Description** property:

- Avoid setting the **Description** property on a **Label** control since this will stop the **Text** property from being spoken by the screen reader.

- On iOS, if you set the **Description** property on any control with children, the screen reader will be unable to reach the children. This is because iOS doesn't provide accessibility features that allow navigation from a parent element to a child element.

Hint

The **Hint** attached property of type string provides additional context to the **Description** property, such as the purpose of control or additional guidance.

The following markup shows how the **Hint** property can be used in the context of the **BankCardTile** control from our banking app:

```
<controls:BankCardTile SemanticProperties.Description="{Binding Alias,
StringFormat='{0} card'}"
                       SemanticProperties.Hint="Tapa it to make a transfer" />
```

It can also be set from the code-behind, just like any other attached property. Consider this example:

```
SemanticProperties.SetHint(MyPasswordEntry, "Enter a password here");
```

There are a few Android-related specifics here:

- It's not recommended to use the **Hint** property for **Entry** control on Android. Both **Hint** and **Entry.Placeholder** map to the same platform property, causing a conflict.

- On Android, the **Hint** property behaves differently on text-based controls and controls without text. For controls with text values, the hint is not displayed and is read after the text value, while for controls like **Switch**, the **Hint** is displayed with the control.

HeadingLevel

The **SemanticProperties.HeadingLevel** attached property helps structure the content in a way that is easy to understand and navigate for users using screen readers. Heading levels are similar to those in HTML. Screen readers rely on heading levels to provide the content with a clear structure. Also, some screen readers enable users to quickly jump between headings.

It is worth saying that you can rely on the **HeadingLevel** property in the case of Windows only because the Windows OS offers nine levels of headings, while Android and iOS/MacCatalyst only offer a single heading. Therefore, only on Windows, the **HeadingLevel** value is mapped to the correct heading level. The heading level can be easily set in XAML markup as follows:

```
<Label Text="Hello World" SemanticProperties.HeadingLevel="Level2"/>
```

SetSemanticFocus and announce

The **SetSemanticFocus** extension method, available for any UI control implementing the **IView** interface, forces a screen reader to focus on a specific UI element. Here's an example:

```
myTitleLabel.SetSemanticFocus();
```

The **Announce** method of the **SemanticScreenReader** class can be used to instruct a screen reader to announce specified text to the user. Consider the following example:

```
SemanticScreenReader.Default.Announce("Text to be announced");
```

SemanticOrderView

There are situations when the order of elements of XAML must be changed. Probably the most common scenario is when one element, which is visually first, must overlap another. In such a case, the first element is put after the second in XAML. However, while it makes sense when someone is looking at it, it might not make sense for someone who is visually impaired and relies on a screen reader. This is where the **SemanticOrderView** control from the **Community Toolkit** comes in.

The following example shows how the semantic can be changed with the **SemanticOrderView** control:

```
XAML Markup
```

```
xmlns:mct=http://schemas.microsoft.com/dotnet/2022/maui/toolkit

…

<mct:SemanticOrderView x:Name="MySemanticOrderView">

    <Grid>

        <Image x:Name="BackgroundImage" SemanticProperties.
Description="Background image"/>

        <Label x:Name="TitleLabel" VerticalOptions="Start"
Text="Dashboard"/>

    </Grid>

</mct:SemanticOrderView>
```

Code-behind

```
MySemanticOrderView.ViewOrder = new List<View> { TitleLabel,
BackgroudImage };
```

Exclude from the accessibility tree

There are cases when it might be useful to explicitly exclude particular elements from the accessibility tree to improve user experience. For example, in the case of a complex UI, sometimes the accessibility tree generator may include redundant or decorative elements into the accessibility tree.

While most **AutomationProperties** attached properties were suppressed by **SemanticProperties**, two properties, i.e., **ExcludedWithChildren** and **IsInAccessibleTree**, can still be helpful.

The **AutomationProperties.IsInAccessibleTree** attached property of type **bool** is used to explicitly include or exclude individual elements from the accessibility tree.

The **AutomationProperties.ExcludedWithChildren** attached property of type **bool** can be attached to any UI element to explicitly specify whether the element and its children should be excluded from the accessibility tree. When the **ExcludedWithChildren** property is set, .NET MAUI sets the **IsInAccessibleTree** property to false on the specified element and its children.

The following two code snippets show how those properties can be used:

```
<StackLayout AutomationProperties.ExcludedWithChildren="true">

    <Label Text="Decorative label 1" />

    <Label Text="Decorative label 2" />

</StackLayout>
```

```
<StackLayout AutomationProperties.IsInAccessibleTree="false">

    <Label Text="Decorative label 1" />

    <Label Text="Decorative label 2" />

</StackLayout>
```

Note that in the first case, the entire **StackLayout**, along with children, is excluded from the **Accessibility Tree**. However, in the second case, **Label** elements aren't excluded from the **Accessibility Tree**.

On iOS/MacCatalyst, if the **IsInAccessibleTree** property is **true** on any control that has children, the screen reader will not be able to reach the children. This is because Apple's operating system doesn't provide accessibility features that allow navigation from a parent element into a child element.

Good practices

While Accessibility is a complex mix of attitude, systematic approach, and research, the following list of advice can help you and your UI/UX designer make your application more accessible for all users:

- Follow the **Web Content Accessibility Guidelines (WCAG)** to make your app enjoyable and easy to use for everyone. These guidelines are the go-to standards for web, desktop, and mobile accessibility worldwide.

- Do your best to create an intuitive user interface. There is nothing better than a design that doesn't require additional instructions and introductions. Make sure screen readers can access all your UI elements and add helpful text or hints when needed. For instance, add a brief description to buttons or input fields.

- Be mindful of users who prefer large fonts or high contrast. Avoid fixed dimensions for controls if possible and choose layouts that adapt to different font sizes. Test your colors in high-contrast mode to ensure that they're easy on the eyes.

- Don't just rely on sounds or color changes. Make sure your app has visual cues, like a progress bar or checkmark, and use audio or color as a bonus. When picking colors, go for a palette that works well for users with color blindness.

- Add alternate text descriptions to images and icons so that everyone knows what they represent.

- Design your visual tree with smooth navigation in mind. Pick layout controls that allow users to move between controls seamlessly, regardless of whether they're using touch or alternative input methods. Also, keep screen readers clutter-free by leaving out decorative images or redundant labels.

- If your app supports multiple languages, don't forget to localize your accessibility descriptions.

- Offer captions for videos and transcripts for audio content. It's also a nice touch to let users control the speed of audio or video and make sure they can easily find and use volume and transport controls.

- Test your app's accessibility features on each platform you're targeting.

- Invite people with impairments for a set of live app testing sessions. You will be surprised at the number of things they will bring your attention to.

Conclusion

Congratulations on completing the chapter! In this chapter, we explored the most important theoretical and practical aspects of accessibility support. We learned about the importance of accessibility support, screen readers, and semantic properties. Remember, the sooner you make accessibility support and testing essential requirements, the sooner your product can be called a world-class product.

In the next chapter, we will focus on two interesting features of .NET MAUI. Sometimes cross-platform applications are called hybrid, so one feature will allow you to make the .NET MAUI application even more hybrid. And the second will change the way you perceive in-app flow by bringing a different approach to navigation.

Points to remember

- Accessibility promotes equality and social inclusion by enabling people with disabilities to participate in various aspects of society, such as education, employment, and social activities.

- Many countries have enacted laws and regulations to ensure that digital content is accessible to people with disabilities.

- Web Content Accessibility Guidelines (WCAG) is a set of guidelines developed to help make web content more accessible to people with disabilities.

- Screen readers are usually provided by the operating system vendor and may differ in behavior and functionalities.

- When a `WebView` displays a website that is not accessible, it won't be accessible in a .NET MAUI app.

Questions

1. What are the four principles of WCAG?

2. Does the font scaling feature involve every single application installed?

3. What is a screen reader?

4. What is the difference between `Visual Tree` and `Accessibility Tree`?

5. How can we explicitly exclude elements from `Accessibility Tree`, and why should we do that?

Join our book's Discord space

Join the book's Discord Workspace for Latest updates, Offers, Tech happenings around the world, New Release and Sessions with the Authors:

https://discord.bpbonline.com

CHAPTER 9

Native Interactive Features with Shell and Blazor

Introduction

In the concluding chapter of the book, we will cover a few more interesting topics. We will write lots of code, and you will get opportunities to play around with our new solution or even make it better. By the end of the chapter, you should be ready to create MAUI Shell applications, including complex ones requiring long-term reliability. Additionally, you will get familiar with .NET MAUI Blazor Hybrid technology. See you on the other side.

Structure

In this chapter, we will cover the following topics:

- Introduction to Shell
- Shell class
- Shell life cycle
- Shell navigation routing
- Passing data
- Making Shell navigation strong

- Base ViewModels

- Bricks of Strong Shell

- Strong route registration

- ShellNavigationPathBuilder

- StrongShallNavigation service

- Shell pages

- Shall Flyout

- What is Blazor?

- Blazor WebAssembly and Blazor Server

- Blazor Hybrid

- BlazorWebView

- MAUI capabilities from Blazor code

Objectives

In this chapter, we are about to get familiar with two more ways of building a .NET MAUI application. One of them offers another way of handling in-app navigation, and the other one introduces a completely different approach that enables you to embed web applications into a native cross-platform MAUI application.

Introduction to Shell

A significant number of applications follow the same UI patterns with a flyout menu, also known as a hamburger menu, and/or tab bar. In addition, the navigation-related business logic tends to become an issue when an application grows. Imagine you have an application built around a tab bar, enabling a user to switch between different modules (for example, **Home**, **Store**, **Profile**) of an application. Each module has its own hierarchical navigation. The classic approach says you have to utilize the **TabPage** class as a main page and separate **NavigatonPages** for each tab to handle the navigation within tabs, as follows:

```
<TabbedPage xmlns="http://schemas.microsoft.com/dotnet/2021/maui"
            xmlns:x="http://schemas.microsoft.com/winfx/2009/xaml"
            xmlns:local="clr-namespace:TabbedApp"
            x:Class=" TabbedApp.MainPage">
```

```
<NavigationPage Title="Home">
    <x:Arguments>
        <local:Tab1ContentPage1 />
    </x:Arguments>
</NavigationPage>


<NavigationPage Title="Store">
    <x:Arguments>
        <local:Tab2ContentPage1 />
    </x:Arguments>
</NavigationPage>


<NavigationPage Title="Profile">
    <x:Arguments>
        <local:Tab3ContentPage1 />
    </x:Arguments>
</NavigationPage>
</TabbedPage>
```

So here, you have **TabbedPage** that handles the navigation between the application modules represented by tabs, and three navigation stacks to handle. Now, imagine the real-world scenario when you must navigate from the checkout page (assume that it's called **Tab2ContentPage5**), lying five levels deep in the hierarchy of the **Store** module, to the sign-up page of the **Profile** module (assume that it's called **Tab3ContentPage2**) and reset the navigation stack of the **Store** module to **Tab2ContentPage1** to ensure that the user starts shopping from the beginning. Then, imagine that this use case scenario is not the only one like that. Sounds fun, doesn't it? So, in the case of large and complex applications, navigation business logic might be an essential piece of complex layered business logic. Needless to say, the Xamarin community dreamed about an alternative navigation approach. Besides, developers desired an even better-optimized rendering process for complex applications in the care of overall performance.

Mainly because of those two reasons, the Shell feature was released in May 2019 as part of Xamarin v4.0.0. Since the feedback from the community was generally positive and **Shell** had become quite popular, it was moved to the .NET MAUI. In response to developer requests, Shell offers the following:

- Alternative URI-based navigation system, which simplifies navigation by allowing developers to define routes and route identifiers. It positively involves the application structure management, makes navigation business logic much simpler and more consistent, and simplifies deep linking. As a result, Shell navigation business logic code might be cleaner and more maintainable in general.

- New **Shell**-specific UI patterns like flyout menus and tab bars are included in the single consistent Shell navigation system.

- Optimized rendering and layout processes that result in faster startup times and smoother navigation experiences, especially for large and complex applications.

Shell class

The Shell class can be considered the key point of the entire **Shell** ecosystem. It enables you to describe the visual hierarchy of the app; configure the parameters of Shell, such as behavior and appearance of **Flyout** and **TabBar**; and perform navigations programmatically. From the architectural point of view, the **Shell** class derives the **Page** class and implements several interfaces.

To understand the idea of **Shell**, its advantages and drawbacks, let us turn our banking application into a **Shell** application. To do this, add the new XAML page called **MainShell** to the root of the project and make it derive the **Shell** class. Then, modify **App.xaml.cs** and **MainShell.xaml** as follows:

App.xaml.cs:

```
public App()
{
    InitializeComponent();
    MainPage = new MainShell();
}
```

MainShell.xaml:

```
<Shell xmlns="http://schemas.microsoft.com/dotnet/2021/maui"
       xmlns:x="http://schemas.microsoft.com/winfx/2009/xaml"
       x:Class="LearningMauiBankingApp.MainShell"
       xmlns:pages="clr-namespace:LearningMauiBankingApp.Pages"
       xmlns:const="clr-namespace:LearningMauiBankingApp.AppConstants"
       xmlns:localization="clr-namespace:LearningMauiBankingApp.
Localization"
```

```xml
        Shell.FlyoutBehavior="Disabled"
        Shell.NavBarIsVisible="False"
        Shell.TabBarIsVisible="True"
        Shell.TabBarBackgroundColor="{AppThemeBinding
            Light={StaticResource LightSecondaryBackgroundColor},
            Dark={StaticResource DarkSecondaryBackgroundColor}}"
        Shell.TabBarForegroundColor="{AppThemeBinding
            Light={StaticResource LightPrimaryTextColor},
            Dark={StaticResource DarkPrimaryTextColor}}"
        Shell.TabBarUnselectedColor="{AppThemeBinding
            Light={StaticResource LightSecondaryTextColor},
            Dark={StaticResource DarkSecondaryTextColor}}">


    <ShellContent ContentTemplate="{DataTemplate pages:LoginPage}"
                  Route="LoginPage"/>


    <TabBar>
        <Tab Title="{x:Static localization:Strings.HomePage_Title}"
            Icon="{AppThemeBinding Light={x:Static const:ImageId.
LightHomeIcon},
                                    Dark={x:Static const:ImageId.
DarkHomeIcon}}">
            <ShellContent ContentTemplate="{DataTemplate
pages:HomePage}"
                          Route="HomePage"/>
        </Tab>
        <Tab Title="{x:Static localization:Strings.SettingsPage_Title}"
            Icon="{AppThemeBinding
                    Light={x:Static const:ImageId.LightSettingsIcon},
                    Dark={x:Static const:ImageId.DarkSettingsIcon}}">
            <ShellContent ContentTemplate="{DataTemplate
pages:SettingsPage}"
                          Route="SettingsPage"/>
        </Tab>
    </TabBar>
</Shell>
```

Earlier, we used XAML to describe the appearance and behavior of the UI every time. The Shell subclass does not describe appearance but describes the organization of the visual hierarchy in the context of Shell. A Shell hierarchy is built of three main hierarchical objects:

- **FlyoutItem** or **TabBar** must be a child of the Shell object in the visual hierarchy. A **FlyoutItem** is used for the application that requires a flyout navigation pattern. A **TabBar**, on the other hand, is used when the bottom bar navigation pattern is required.

- **Tab** is a child of **FlyoutItem** or **TabBar**. It represents grouped content. When a **TabBar** contains only one **Tab**, the bottom **TabBar** is not shown.

- **ShellContent** is a child of a Tab. It represents the **ContentPage** objects. Besides, page objects are not passed to **ShellContent**. For the sake of better performance, the recommended way of specifying what page should be displayed within **ShellContent** is to use a built-in **DataTemplate** markup extension to set a page as a **ContentTemplate**. Thanks to this, the Shell app creates pages on demand in response to navigation. When a Tab contains more than one **ShellContent**, the top tab bar appears, providing the piece of UI that can be used to switch between **ShellContents** within the Tab.

You might notice that the **ShellContent** of the **LoginPage** was not wrapped in Tab wrapped in **TabBar**. This is because Shell has implicit-conversion operators that are applied in such a case to enable the Shell hierarchy to be simplified. The implicit conversion wraps the **ShellContent** object in a **Tab** object, which is wrapped in a **TabBar** object. So, the following markup is equivalent to what we have in **MainShell**:

```
<TabBar>
    <Tab>
        <ShellContent ContentTemplate="{DataTemplate pages:LoginPage}"
                    Route="LoginPage"/>
    </Tab>
</TabBar>
```

However, a page can also be specified as shown below:

```
<ShellContent Route="LoginPage">
    <pages:LoginPage/>
</ShellContent>
```

In such a case, the **LoginPage** object will be instantiated forcibly, along with the Shell object, instead of instantiating it on demand. It's important to highlight that it's not the recommended way as it can lead to a poor startup experience.

Another important thing here is the **Route** property. Routes can be defined on the **FlyoutItem**, **TabBar**, **Tab**, and **ShellContent** elements. The route, in a Shell world, is an essential and basic part of the navigation path/URI. For example, consider the following hierarchy (**Chapter_9/1_ShellClassSample** application):

```
<TabBar>
    <Tab Title="Furniture" Route="Furniture" Icon="furniture_icon" >
        <ShellContent Title="Kitchen"
                      Route="Kitchen"
                      ContentTemplate="{DataTemplate local:KitchenPage}"/>
        <ShellContent Title="Bedroom"
                      Route="Bedroom"
                      ContentTemplate="{DataTemplate local:BedroomPage}"/>
    </Tab>
    <Tab Title="Accessories" Icon="accessories_icon">
        <ShellContent Route="Accessories"
                      ContentTemplate="{DataTemplate
local:AccessoriesPage}"/>
    </Tab>
</TabBar>
```

Refer to the following figure:

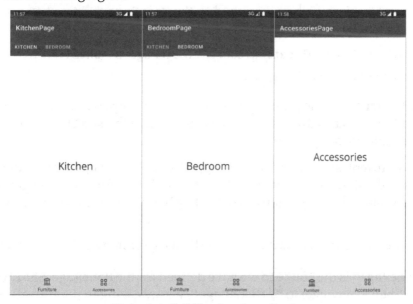

Figure 9.1: *ShellClassSample application*

The preceding application has two tabs and three pages. As you can see, Shell created two additional tabs within the **Furniture** tab. And this is how the Shell navigation routes of each page look according to what we defined in the Shell subclass:

Kitchen: "Furniture/Kitchen"

Bedroom: "Furniture/Bedroom"

Accessories: "Accessories"

While **"Furniture/Kitchen"** is a route, particular waypoints of the route like **Furniture** and **Kitchen** we will call the **RouteId**.

Let us get back to our banking app. Here, in **MainShell.xaml**, we have also configured the global appearance by applying certain values to properties like **Shell.TabBarForegroundColor** or **Shell.TabBarIsVisible**. It means those settings will be valid for all pages displayed within Shell. However, we do not need **TabBar** to be visible on the **LoginPage**. Luckily, those global settings can be overridden by particular pages, making Shell apply different configurations for different pages. So, now we can easily modify the **LoginPage** markup as follows to keep the UI as it was before Shell came in:

```
<pages:ContentPageBase xmlns="http://schemas.microsoft.com/dotnet/2021/
maui"

                        ...

                        x:Class="LearningMauiBankingApp.Pages.LoginPage"

                        Shell.TabBarIsVisible="False">
```

The **MainShell** object we have assigned to the **MainPage**, being a key point of the Shell system, can be obtained globally in two ways:

```
var currentShell = Application.Current.MainPage as Shell;

var currentShell = Shell.Current;
```

The **Shell.Current** static property returns the **Page** property value of the currently active window, which is the same object as the one that the **Application.Current.MainPage** static property returns.

Being in a current state, our banking app displays the **LoginPage** after startup because it is the first element in a Shell hierarchy. To perform the navigation to the **HomePage**, replace the navigation call in the **Login** button handler with the following call:

```
await Shell.Current.GoToAsync(new ShellNavigationState("//HomePage"));
```

Here, **"HomePage"** is the **RouteId** we have defined for the **HomePage ShellContent**. By asking Shell to navigate to **"//HomePage"**, we are asking to perform all necessary navigation actions to replace the current navigation stack and display the page associated with the specified path. So, it automatically switches to another **TabBar** and **Tab** where the specified **ShellContent** is placed.

The **GoToAysnc** method has multiple overloads. For example, some of the overloads enable you to disable transition animation and send data to the target page using a dictionary.

The **Shell** class also defines the following navigation-related properties:

- **CurrentItem** of type **ShellItem** returns the currently selected shell item, for example, **TabBar** of currently displayed **ShellContent**.

- **CurrentPage** of type **Page** returns the currently displayed **Page** object.

- **CurrentState** of type **ShellNavigationState** returns the current navigation state object; the **ShellNavigationState** class contains one public property, **Location**, which returns the URI of the current navigation stack.

- **BackButtonBehavior** of type **BackButtonBehavior** that is an attached property used to override the behavior, look, and feel of the navigation bar back button.

Shell life cycle

Shell applications fully respect the usual .NET MAUI life cycle but also raise an **Appearing** event when a page is about to appear on the screen and a **Disappearing** event when a page is about to disappear from the screen. Also, these events can be handled by pages by overriding the **OnAppearing** and **OnDisappearing** methods on the page.

When it comes to modal pages, pushing a modal page onto the navigation stack will result in all visible Shell objects raising the **Disappearing** event. Popping the last modal page will raise the **Appearing** event in all visible Shell objects.

Shell navigation routing

The Shell navigation was created to be universal and flexible, providing a better experience in the case of complex applications. However, it has its own trade-offs that become challenges in real-world applications. To better understand its capabilities and where the challenges came from, let's start with the general theory of Shell navigation.

Consider the following general pattern and example route:

```
Pattern: "//[route]/[pages]?[queryParameters]"
Example 1: $"//HomePage/TransferPage?fromCardNumber={bankCardNumber}"
Example 2: "//Furniture/Bedroom/BedsPage/ProductDetailsPage"
```

The Shell navigation path/URI can include three components: **basic route**, **pages**, and **queryparameters**. Let's describe them:

- A **route** defines the path to content that exists as part of the Shell visual hierarchy. It can contain one (**HomePage**) or a few waypoints with a single slash sign between them (**Furniture/Bedroom** where **Furniture** is a **Tab** and **Bedroom** is a **ShellContent**). The exact route config depends on **RouteIds** of specific elements of Shell.

- **Pages** are a part of the navigation path specifying pages that don't exist in the Shell visual hierarchy. Instead, the **RouteIds** of those pages are registered separately somewhere in the C# code at the start of an application. Such a page can also be called a **details page** or **global page**. A details page (**TransferPage**) or a chain of pages (**BedsPage**/**ProductDetailsPage**) creates a navigation stack similar to the one we already know from the **NavigationPage**. The navigation bars on those pages contain a back button each. A user can perform single or multiple back navigations until they reach the page displayed by the **route** part of the Shell navigation path.

- **Query parameters** (**"?fromCardNumber={bankCardNumber}"**) are one of the ways of passing simple data like short strings or numbers to the destination page object. This API is very similar to the one known from HTTP requests. Further in this chapter, we will explore why it's better not to use this way.

As explained earlier, routes of the details pages must be registered explicitly in C#; such routes are called **Global Routes**. It's usually done in the constructor of the Shell subclass. Let's get back to our banking app. First, create three new blank pages called **CustomPage1**, **CustomPage2**, and **CustomPage3** for future experiments. Then, modify the constructor of the **MainShell** class as follows:

```
public MainShell()
{
    InitializeComponent();

    var transferPageType = typeof(TransferModalPage);
    Routing.RegisterRoute("TransferModalPage", transferPageType);

    var customPage1Type = typeof(CustomPage1);
```

```
Routing.RegisterRoute("CustomPage1", customPage1Type);


var customPage2Type = typeof(CustomPage2);
Routing.RegisterRoute("CustomPage2", customPage2Type);


var customPage3Type = typeof(CustomPage3);
Routing.RegisterRoute("CustomPage3", customPage3Type);
}
```

The static method **Routing.RegisterRoute** takes two parameters: the route id string and the type of page; it then puts them into a dictionary of routes. If required, global routes can be deregistered with the **Routing.UnRegisterRoute** method.

Alternatively, pages can be registered at different route hierarchies by applying contextual navigation **RouteIds**. Consider this example:

```
Routing.RegisterRoute("Beds/ProductDetails",
typeof(BedProductDetailsPage));

Routing.RegisterRoute("Chairs/ProductDetails",
typeof(ChairProductDetailsPage));

Routing.RegisterRoute("Tables/ProductDetails",
typeof(TableProductDetailsPage));
```

Let's now get back to routes and our **SampleApplication** with furniture and accessories for a moment. It's better to read the rest of the section with the Visual Studio opened because the behavior of Shell navigation might not always seem obvious and non-intuitive. It is highly recommended to add three global pages, as we did in the banking app, and then roll up your sleeves and spend some time experimenting with different routes in different circumstances to better understand the behavior of Shell navigation.

When it comes to performing navigations, there are three URI formats that are most useful and reliable in practice:

- **//[shell route]/[optional global pages]/[optional parameters]** is an absolute route where we specify every single waypoint, starting with an element of the shell subclass that has specified **Route** properties, for example, **//Furniture/Bedroom/CustomPage1/CustomPage2**. Moreover, imagine that the current navigation state is **//Accessories/CustomPage1/CustomPage2**, and you make the **//Accessories/CustomPage1** navigation. In this case, Shell will not recreate **CustomPage1** and push it as new. Instead, it will compare the current and requested URIs and perform back navigation. However, it's important to remember that the absolute must start from the route of the Shell element. Otherwise, it will throw an exception saying that the global page can't be the root of Shell navigation.

- **[optional global pages]/[optional parameters]** is a relative format that asks the navigation service to search for the specified route among global routes. If it finds a matching page or a chain of pages, it pushes them onto the navigation stack of a current **Tab**. For example, **GoToAsync** with the **CustomPage1/CustomPage2** route from **//Furniture/Bedroom** will result in the **//Furniture/Bedroom/ CustomPage1/CustomPage2** navigation state.

- **../[optional global pages]/[optional parameters]** is a format that enables you to navigate back within the navigation stack of a **Tab**. Moreover, multiple backward navigations can be done by adding more than one **..** waypoint. In addition, we can ask to make backward navigation and then navigate to the specified route. The following navigation path will ask Shell to perform three back navigations as one and then navigate to the specified page: **../../../CustomPage1**.

There are also some other relative formats that are about to simplify navigation. However, practice says that they just add more corner cases, limitations, and risks of runtime exceptions without bringing significant value.

Although Shell is quite flexible and powerful, it comes with its own trade-offs:

- It's not strongly typed. The whole navigation system relies on so-called **magic strings**. Magic strings have no chance to be reliable in real-world applications with complex business logic. They might work well for prototypes, but such solutions always cause issues in the long run.

- There are several rules, corner cases, and limitations that must be taken into account while navigating.

- The UI of a majority of Shell elements is based on the platform controls. Many developers of complex applications say that Shell doesn't offer enough room for customization. In general, in MAUI, even *uncustomizable* things can be customized, but it requires custom platform implementations.

Passing data

As explained in the previous section, primitive data can be passed as part of the navigation URI using query parameters.

There are two ways to handle this data: the **QueryProperty** class attribute and the **IQueryAttributable** interface.

The **QueryProperty** attribute can be added to the navigable **Page** or its **ViewModel** (**BindingContext** to be precise). Consider the following code snippets:

```
Navigation request:
await Shell.Current.GoToAsync("TransferModalPage?bankCardId=16542");
```

```
TransferModalPage ViewModel:
[QueryProperty(nameof(BankCardId), "bankCardId")]
public class TransferModalPageViewModel
{
    public int BankCardId { get; set; }
}
```

In this case, the "16542" value will be assigned to the **BankCardId** property of the ViewModel by Shell during the navigation. Complex objects can also be received using the **QueryProperty** attributes. There are a few significant drawbacks to this approach. First, it relies on magic strings and the hope that no one makes mistakes. Once the URI parameter name changes or its value type changes from integer to string without modifying the ViewModel, no one will know until a QA specialist or worse, the end user gets a runtime exception and crashed application. Second, it uses reflection a lot to get class attributes and the corresponding properties in runtime. As we remember, avoiding reflection, if possible, is considered a good practice because reflection negatively impacts performance and codebase maintainability.

Fortunately, MAUI developers provide an alternative solution that can solve those issues. Consider the following code snippets:

```
Navigation request:
await Shell.Current.GoToAsync("TransferModalPage",
    new Dictionary<string, object>
    {
        { "bankCardId", 16542 }
    });
```

```
TransferModalPage ViewModel:
public class TransferModalPageViewModel : IQueryAttributable
{
    public void ApplyQueryAttributes(IDictionary<string, object> query)
    {
    }
}
```

This is what a raw solution looks like. Here, we simply pass the dictionary object to the **ViewModel** of the target page instead of using reflection. Although this solution is still not strongly typed enough, it has way better potential, and we can base more advanced solutions on it. Note that **IQueryAttributable** can also be used in conjunction with URI parameters.

Making Shell navigation strong

As we start talking about more advanced solutions, we get to the place where we are going to deep dive into coding and turn our banking app into a Shell app. We already have Shell subclass, which is assigned to the **MainPage** of the application. We just have to adapt everything related to navigation, while trying to get rid of the drawbacks of the Shell navigation and data transfer mechanisms that we talked about earlier. Further implementation cannot be a universal truth. Instead, it has to give you a solution that covers a majority of scenarios and gives an understanding of the entire concept so that you can extend or modify it according to the needs of your future applications.

Let us write down the main components and assumptions of the solution in accordance with the tasks that they will solve:

- To make the data transfer mechanism more strongly typed, we will use the **IQueryAttributable** interface and assume that only one parameter of a specific type can be passed to a ViewModel. Moreover, we make it a rule that the navigation parameter key in the dictionary is the name of a navigation parameter type. To eliminate possible mistakes, the corresponding **IQueryAttributable** implementation will be hidden in a basic ViewModel class, providing simple API for any other ViewModels that expect navigation data of a certain type.

- We also make it a rule that the **RouteId** string is the name of a **ContentPage** subclass, for example, "LoginPage". So, we will need a single source that generates unique **RouteIds**.

- Another important piece is a class responsible for building the navigation URI based on the desired type of navigation, the presence of the Shell element's **RouteId**, and global pages.

- Finally, we will need a navigation service that will provide simple, magic-strings-free but flexible enough API encapsulating Shell navigation boilerplate code and navigation URI creation specifics.

In the case of any doubts or confusion, feel free to explore the **Chapter_9/2_ LearningMauiBankingApp_Shell** application. Note that in the case of this chapter, exploring repository applications might be crucial because of the complexity of the subject we are about to dig in.

Before we start, take the following preparation steps:

1. In ViewModels and DI container, replace **INavigationService** and **HierarchicalNavigationService** with the **IStrongShellNavigation** interface and the **StrongShellNavigation** class, respectively. Keep files empty so far.

2. Override the **Shell.PresentationMode** property at the **TransferModalPage** with **"ModalAnimated"** value. This will let Shell know how navigation must be handled for this specific page.

3. Since now Shell will be responsible for page instantiating, add the following **ContentPageBase** class to the **Pages** folder. Then, make all pages inherit **ContentPageBase** instead of **ContentPage**. The purpose of this class is to ensure that the page got its **ViewModel** and to call the life cycle method of a **ViewModel**:

```
public abstract class ContentPageBase : ContentPage
{
    protected ViewModelBase ViewModel
    {
        get => (ViewModelBase) BindingContext;
        set => BindingContext = value;
    }

    protected ContentPageBase(ViewModelBase viewModel)
    {
        ViewModel = viewModel;
    }

    protected override void OnNavigatedTo(NavigatedToEventArgs args)
    {
        ViewModel.OnNavigatedTo();
    }
}
```

Sometimes, mainly in the case of modal pages, it might be useful to receive the result value from the page. For example, let's have our application show a modal page before showing the **TransferModalPage** asking for a confirmation. Let's prepare such a page by adding a new **ConfirmationModalPage** and an accompanying **ConfirmationModalPageViewModel**, and filling them with following code; this page must also inherit **ContentPageBase**:

ConfirmationModalPage.xaml:

```
<pages:ContentPageBase.Resources>
    <x:Boolean x:Key="False">False</x:Boolean>
    <x:Boolean x:Key="True">True</x:Boolean>
</pages:ContentPageBase.Resources>
<VerticalStackLayout Spacing="15" VerticalOptions="Center">
    <Label Text="{x:Static localization:Strings.ConfirmationPage_Title}"
                HorizontalOptions="Center"
                TextColor="{AppThemeBinding Light={StaticResource
LightPrimaryTextColor}, Dark={StaticResource DarkPrimaryTextColor}}"
                FontFamily="Poppins-SemiBold"
                FontSize="24"/>
    <Button Text="{x:Static localization:Strings.ConfirmationPage_
YesButton}"
            Style="{StaticResource RegularSmallButton}"
            HorizontalOptions="Center"
            Command="{Binding CloseWithResultCommand}"
            CommandParameter="{StaticResource True}"/>
    <Button Text="{x:Static localization:Strings.ConfirmationPage_
NoButton}"
            Style="{StaticResource RegularSmallButton}"
            HorizontalOptions="Center"
            Command="{Binding CloseWithResultCommand}"
            CommandParameter="{StaticResource False}"/>
</VerticalStackLayout>
```

ConfirmationModalPageViewModel.cs:

```
public class ConfirmationModalPageViewModel :
ResultingViewModelBase<bool>
{
  public ICommand CloseWithResultCommand { get; }

    public ConfirmationModalPageViewModel(IStrongShellNavigation
strongShellNavigation)
        : base(strongShellNavigation)
```

```
    {
        CloseWithResultCommand = new
AsyncRelayCommand<bool>(GoBackWithResultAsync);
    }
}
```

Base ViewModels

Let us start with **ViewModels**. Add the following classes to the **ViewModels** folder:

```
public abstract class NavigationDataViewModelBase<TNavigationData>
    : ViewModelBase, IQueryAttributable
{
    protected NavigationDataViewModelBase(IStrongShellNavigation
strongShellNavigation)
        : base(strongShellNavigation)
    {
    }


    public void ApplyQueryAttributes(IDictionary<string, object> query)
    {
        if (query.TryGetValue(typeof(TNavigationData).Name, out object
navigationDataObject)
            && navigationDataObject is TNavigationData navigationData)
            OnNavigationDataRecieved(navigationData);
    }


    protected abstract void OnNavigationDataRecieved(TNavigationData
navigationData);
}
```

NavigationDataViewModel is responsible for receiving navigation data object. It implements the **IQueryAttributable** interface, gets the navigation data parameter, and casts it to the datatype expected by concrete **ViewModel**. And if everything is OK, it passes the navigation data parameter to that **ViewModel** via calling the **OnNavigationDataRecieved** method that concrete **ViewModel** must override. Let's consider the next base ViewModel:

```
public abstract class ResultingViewModelBase<TResult>
```

```csharp
    : ViewModelBase, IQueryAttributable
{

    private TaskCompletionSource<TResult> _resultTsc;


    protected ResultingViewModelBase(IStrongShellNavigation
strongShellNavigation)
        : base(strongShellNavigation)
    {
    }


    public void ApplyQueryAttributes(IDictionary<string, object> query)
    {
        if (query.TryGetValue(typeof(TaskCompletionSource<TResult>).
Name, out object resultTscObject)
            && resultTscObject is TaskCompletionSource<TResult>
resultTsc)
            _resultTsc = resultTsc;
    }


    protected async Task GoBackWithResultAsync(TResult resultValue)
    {
        await _strongShellNavigation.NavigateBackAsync();
        SetResult(resultValue);
    }


    private void SetResult(TResult resultValue)
    {
        _resultTsc?.SetResult(resultValue);
    }
}
```

This ViewModel is supposed to be used as a base ViewModel for pages like our confirmation page, where we expect the page to be closed and the result returned to the caller. In our case, **HomePageViewModel** will be a caller that waits for the result. Note that the mechanism uses the **TaskCompletionSource** class. It's important for further explanation.

Finally, last base ViewModel is a combination of **NavigationDataViewModelBase** and **ResultingViewModelBase** . It must be used when we pass data to the ViewModel and expect some result:

```
public abstract class
NavigationDataResultingViewModelBase<TNavigationData, TResult> :
ViewModelBase, IQueryAttributable
{
    private TaskCompletionSource<TResult> _resultTsc;


    protected
NavigationDataResultingViewModelBase(IStrongShellNavigation
strongShellNavigation)
        : base(strongShellNavigation)
    {
    }

    public void ApplyQueryAttributes(IDictionary<string, object> query)
    {
        if (query.TryGetValue(typeof(TNavigationData).Name, out object
navigationDataObject)
            && navigationDataObject is TNavigationData navigationData)
            OnNavigationDataRecieved(navigationData);


        if (query.TryGetValue(typeof(TaskCompletionSource<TResult>).
Name, out object resultTscObject)
            && resultTscObject is TaskCompletionSource<TResult>
resultTsc)
            _resultTsc = resultTsc;
    }

    protected abstract void OnNavigationDataRecieved(TNavigationData
navigationData);

    protected async Task GoBackWithResultAsync(TResult resultValue)
    {
        await _strongShellNavigation.NavigateBackAsync();
        SetResult(resultValue);
```

```
    }

    private void SetResult(TResult resultValue)
    {
        _resultTsc?.SetResult(resultValue);
    }
}
```

Now you can modify **TransferModalPageViewModel** as shown here:

```
public class TransferModalPageViewModel
    : NavigationDataViewModelBase<TransferModalPageNavigationParameter>
{
    private readonly SemaphoreSlim _initializationSemaphore = new
SemaphoreSlim(0, 1);
    ...
    protected override void OnNavigationDataRecieved(
        TransferModalPageNavigationParameter navigationData)
    {
        Task.Run(async () =>
        {
            await _initializationSemaphore.WaitAsync();
            SelectedFromCard = Cards.FirstOrDefault(x => x.CardNumber ==
navigationData.FromCardNumber);
            _initializationSemaphore.Release();
        });
    }

    public override void OnNavigatedTo()
    {
        Task.Run(async () =>
        {
            Cards = await _bankCardManager.GetBankCardsAsync();
            _initializationSemaphore.Release();
        });
    }
    ...
}
```

As you can see, `TransferModalPageViewModel` still defines the expected navigation parameter type and receives it the same way as earlier. However, now we have two life cycle methods, i.e., `OnNavigatedTo` and `OnNavigationDataRecieved`, which have different responsibilities. Additionally, the `OnNavigationDataRecieved` is called only when there is some data to be applied. As you remember, the `From` card is not always preselected. So, bank cards are always retrieved, thanks to the `OnNavigatedTo` method, while the `From` card is preselected only when its number is passed. The `SemaphoreSlim` class ensures that the preselected card is applied after the collection of cards has been received. Refer to the .NET-specific literature to learn more about ways to synchronize multi-threading operations.

Bricks of Strong Shell

Before implementing a navigation service and route builder, we must address a few challenges. First of all, we have two types of pages that must be treated differently:

- **Root pages** are pages displayed by the `ShellContent` component. For navigating from one root page to another (for example, from `LoginPage` to `HomePage`), we have to use an absolute route starting with the double slash; they must be the first waypoints in navigation URIs, and their `RouteIds` should be registered by setting the `Route` property of the `ShellContent`.

- **Global pages**, or simply, pages, must be placed after root pages in a navigation URI; we can navigate to them using relative and backward navigation, and their `RouteIds` are registered in C#.

Besides, we have to keep in mind that every piece of our solution must be strongly typed so that the compilator highlights as many mistake as possible. All that means we have to find a strongly typed way to differentiate the `RouteIds` of the two types of pages in the navigation service. Consequently, we need to have a way to differentiate page datatypes so that the `RouteId` creator can create the correct `RouteId` for the specified page.

With this in mind, create two new empty interfaces: `IShellPage` and `IShellRootPage`. Those interfaces will help us determine what page we deal with and create strongly typed constraints. Now, apply those interfaces to app pages of the banking app, as follows:

```
public partial class TransferModalPage : ContentPageBase, IShellPage
public partial class HomePage : ContentPageBase, IShellRootPage
```

Next, add three new models to the **Models** folder, as follows:

```
public abstract class ShellRouteId
{
```

```
    public string RouteId { get; }
    public Type Type { get; }

    protected ShellRouteId(Type pageType)
    {
        Type = pageType;
        RouteId = pageType.Name;
    }
}

public class ShellPageRouteId : ShellRouteId
{
    public ShellPageRouteId(Type pageType)
        : base(pageType)
    {
    }
}

public class ShellRootPageRouteId : ShellRouteId
{
    public ShellRootPageRouteId(Type shellRootPageType)
        : base(shellRootPageType)
    {
    }
}
```

As you can see, the constructor of the **ShellRouteId** abstract class is a single place where the actual **RouteId** string is passed.

Strong route registration

Since we have different classes for both types of **RouteIds**, we can create the **ShellRouteIdHelper** class. So, add the following class to the **Tools** folder:

```
public static class ShellRouteIdHelper
{
    public static ShellPageRouteId GetId<T>()
        where T : IShellPage
```

```
{
    return new ShellPageRouteId(typeof(T));
}

public static ShellRootPageRouteId GetRootId<T>()
    where T : IShellRootPage
{
    return new ShellRootPageRouteId(typeof(T));
}
}
```

The only mission of this class is to prevent creating **RouteIds** for any classes but those implementing the **IshellPage** and **IShellRootPage** interfaces. With this, we guarantee that **ShellPageRouteId** will be created for the global page, and **ShellRootPageRouteId** will be created for the page from the Shell subclass hierarchy.

Let us utilize newly created classes and register types of our global pages by modifying the **MainShell.xaml.cs** constructor as follows:

```
public MainShell()
{
    InitializeComponent();


    var confirmationModalPageRouteId = ShellRouteIdHelper.
GetId<ConfirmationModalPage>();
    Routing.RegisterRoute(confirmationModalPageRouteId.RouteId,
confirmationModalPageRouteId.PageType);


    var transferModalPageRouteId = ShellRouteIdHelper.
GetId<TransferModalPage>();
    Routing.RegisterRoute(transferModalPageRouteId.RouteId,
transferModalPageRouteId.Type);


    var customPage1RouteId = ShellRouteIdHelper.GetId<CustomPage1>();
    Routing.RegisterRoute(customPage1RouteId.RouteId,
customPage1RouteId.Type);


    var customPage2RouteId = ShellRouteIdHelper.GetId<CustomPage2>();
```

```
Routing.RegisterRoute(customPage2RouteId.RouteId,
customPage2RouteId.Type);


    var customPage3RouteId = ShellRouteIdHelper.GetId<CustomPage3>();

    Routing.RegisterRoute(customPage3RouteId.RouteId,
customPage3RouteId.Type);
}
```

Being at this place of our journey, it is worth taking a look at the **ShellContent** elements routes. Currently, values are hardcoded. Since both the **ContentTemplate** and **Route** properties of **ShellContent** depend on the datatype of **Page**, we can simplify this markup and utilize your **ShellRouteHelper** to set the **Route** property value. Add the following class to the **Controls** folder and then modify the **MainShell.xaml**, as shown here:

StrongShellContent.cs:

```
public class StrongShellContent<TcontentPage> : ShellContent
    where TcontentPage : IShellRootPage
{
    public StrongShellContent()
    {
        ContentTemplate = new DataTemplate(typeof(TcontentPage));
        Route = ShellRouteIdHelper.GetRootId<TcontentPage>().RouteId;
    }
}
```

MainShell.xaml:

```
<Shell ...
    xmlns:controls="clr-namespace:LearningMauiBankingApp.Controls"
    ... >


    <controls:StrongShellContent x:TypeArguments="pages:LoginPage" />


    <TabBar>
        <Tab ...
            <controls:StrongShellContent x:TypeArguments="pages:HomePage" />
```

```
    </Tab>
    <Tab ...
        <controls:StrongShellContent x:TypeArguments="pages:SettingsPage" />
    </Tab>
  </TabBar>
</Shell>
```

Now it seems to be significantly more reliable and maintainable. Thanks to the generic type parameter, its constraint, and the **ShellRouteHelper**, we can set the critical properties of **ShellContent** while keeping the whole ecosystem strongly typed.

ShellNavigationPathBuilder

Another essential thing we have that the navigation service will definitely need is a navigation path string builder. Add the following class to the **Tools** folder so that we can discuss it:

```
public class ShellNavigationPathBuilder
{
    public const char RouteSeparator = '/';
    public const string GoBackWaypointId = "..";
    public const string AbsoluteRoutePrefix = "//";

    private readonly bool _isAbsoluteRoute;

    private Ilist<string> _waypoints = new List<string>();

    public ShellNavigationPathBuilder()
    {
    }

    public ShellNavigationPathBuilder(ShellRootPageRouteId rootRouteId)
    {
        _waypoints.Add(rootRouteId.RouteId);
        _isAbsoluteRoute = true;
    }
```

```
public string BuildRoute()
{
    var route = string.Join(RouteSeparator, _waypoints);
    if (_isAbsoluteRoute)
        route = route.Insert(0, AbsoluteRoutePrefix);

    return route;
}


public ShellNavigationPathBuilder GoBack()
{
    if (_waypoints.Any(x => x != GoBackWaypointId))
        return this;

    _waypoints.Add(GoBackWaypointId);
    return this;
}


public ShellNavigationPathBuilder Append(ShellPageRouteId
pageRouteId)
{
    _waypoints.Add(pageRouteId.RouteId);
    return this;
}
}
```

Let us take a closer look. Remember that all **RouteIds** must be divided by a slash sign and that we want to use three types of navigation paths:

- Absolute, which requires a navigation path starting with "//" and **ShellRootPageRouteId**.

- Relative, which requires only one or more **ShellPageRouteId** items.

- Back navigation, which is represented by one or more .. and optional **ShellPageRouteId** waypoints continuing the navigation path.

Here, we have two constructors: one for relative and back navigations, and another for an absolute path that requires **ShellRootPageRouteId**, which is added as the very first waypoint. The **GoBack** method checks whether **..** can be added to the waypoints list and adds ".." to the waypoints list. The **Append** method adds **RouteId** to the end of the list of waypoints. So, now our future navigation service can ask this builder to build the required path, and the navigation path string will be created with a guarantee of no runtime exceptions caused by Shell trying to navigate by invalid route.

StrongShellNavigation service

Before implementing **StrongShellNavigation**, fill the **IStrongShellNavigation** interface with the following code:

```
public interface IStrongShellNavigation
{
    Task NavigateToAsync(
        IEnumerable<ShellPageRouteId> pageRouteIds,
        object navigationData = null);

    Task<TResult> NavigateToAsync<TResult>(
        IEnumerable<ShellPageRouteId> pageRouteIds,
        object navigationData = null);

    Task NavigateToAsync(
        ShellRootPageRouteId rootPageId,
        IEnumerable<ShellPageRouteId> pageRouteIds = null,
        object navigationData = null);

    Task NavigateBackAsync(
        int numberOfGoBacks = 1,
        object navigationData = null);

    Task NavigateBackAndPushAsync(
        IEnumerable<ShellPageRouteId> pageRouteIds,
        object navigationData = null,
        int numberOfGoBacks = 1);
```

```
   Task NavigateBackToAsync(
      ShellPageRouteId searchableRouteId,
      object navigationData = null);
}
```

As you see, our service will contain one method (with three overloads) for forward navigation, two methods for navigations that affect the root page, and three methods for backward navigation to handle different cases. For example, it offers the **NavigateBackToAsync** method to navigate to the page with a specific **RouteId**. Spend some time exploring this interface, since the next step is service implementation, for example, note that **RouteIds** of global pages are passed as a collection, since, as you remember, we can push more than one page to the navigation stack.

Fill the class with the following code:

```
public class StrongShellNavigation : IStrongShellNavigation
{
    public async Task
NavigateBackAndPushAsync(IEnumerable<ShellPageRouteId> pageRouteIds,
object navigationData = null, int numberOfGoBacks = 1)
    {
        await NavigateBackInternalAsync(pageRouteIds, navigationData,
numberOfGoBacks);
    }

    public async Task NavigateBackAsync(int numberOfGoBacks = 1, object
navigationData = null)
    {
        await NavigateBackInternalAsync(null, navigationData, numberOfGoBacks);
    }

    public async Task NavigateBackToAsync(ShellPageRouteId
searchableRouteId, object navigationData = null)
    {
        var navigationStackWaypoints = Shell.Current.CurrentState.
Location.OriginalString
            .Replace("//",String.Empty)
            .Split('/')
```

```
            .ToList();
        var waypointIndex = navigationStackWaypoints.
IndexOf(searchableRouteId.RouteId);

        if (waypointIndex < 0 || navigationStackWaypoints.Count ==
waypointIndex + 1)
            return;

        var numberOfGobacks = navigationStackWaypoints.Count - 1 -
waypointIndex;
        await NavigateBackAsync(numberOfGobacks, navigationData);
    }

    public async Task<TResult> NavigateToAsync<TResult>(
        IEnumerable<ShellPageRouteId> pageRouteIds, object
navigationData = null)
    {
        var route = GetNavigationToRoute(null, pageRouteIds);
        return await NavigateToInternalAsync<TResult>(route,
navigationData);
    }

    public async Task NavigateToAsync(IEnumerable<ShellPageRouteId>
pageRouteIds, object navigationData = null)
    {
        var route = GetNavigationToRoute(null, pageRouteIds);
        await NavigateToInternalAsync(route, navigationData);
    }

    public async Task NavigateToAsync(ShellRootPageRouteId rootPageId,
IEnumerable<ShellPageRouteId> pageRouteIds = null, object navigationData
= null)
    {
        var route = GetNavigationToRoute(rootPageId, pageRouteIds);
        await NavigateToInternalAsync(route, navigationData);
    }

    private string GetNavigationToRoute(ShellRootPageRouteId rootPageId,
```

```
IEnumerable<ShellPageRouteId> pages)
    {
        var routeBuilder = rootPageId is null
? new ShellNavigationPathBuilder() : new
ShellNavigationPathBuilder(rootPageId);

        if (pages is not null)
            foreach (var pageRouteId in pages)
                routeBuilder.Append(pageRouteId);

        return routeBuilder.BuildRoute();
    }

    private async Task
NavigateBackInternalAsync(IEnumerable<ShellPageRouteId> pages, object
navigationData, int numberOfGoBacks = 1)
    {
        if (numberOfGoBacks < 1)
            throw new
ArgumentOutOfRangeException(nameof(numberOfGoBacks), "Value must be
greater than 0");

        var routeBuilder = new ShellNavigationPathBuilder();
        for (int i = 0; i < numberOfGoBacks; i++)
            routeBuilder.GoBack();

        if (pages is not null)
            foreach (var pageRouteId in pages)
                routeBuilder.Append(pageRouteId);

        var route = routeBuilder.BuildRoute();
        await NavigateToInternalAsync(route, navigationData);
    }

    private async Task<TResult> NavigateToInternalAsync<TResult>(string
route, object navigationData)
    {
```

```
        var pageResultTsc = new TaskCompletionSource<TResult>();
        var navigationParameters = new Dictionary<string, object>()
        {
            { typeof(TaskCompletionSource<TResult>).Name, pageResultTsc
}
        };


        if (navigationData is not null)
            navigationParameters.Add(navigationData.GetType().Name,
navigationData);


        await Shell.Current.GoToAsync(new ShellNavigationState(route),
true, navigationParameters);
        return await pageResultTsc.Task;
    }

    private async Task NavigateToInternalAsync(string route, object
navigationData)
    {
        var navigationParameters = new Dictionary<string, object>();


        if (navigationData is not null)
            navigationParameters.Add(navigationData.GetType().Name,
navigationData);


        await Shell.Current.GoToAsync(new ShellNavigationState(route),
true, navigationParameters);
    }
}
```

The entire magic happens in private methods. The **GetNavigationToRoute** method prepares the navigation path string for forward navigation calls, and the **NavigateBackInternalAsync** method configures back navigation; both use the **ShellNavigationPathBuilder** class. The **NavigateToInternalAsync** methods perform the actual navigation. They call the **Shell.Current.GoToAsync** method and pack the optional navigation data into the navigation parameters dictionary. Take a closer look at the **NavigateToInternalAsync<TResult>** method. It works similar to non-generic overload of the method. However, here we use the

TaskCompletionSource object, which is passed to the page's ViewModel as a query parameter. After performing navigation, we wait for the **TaskCompletionSource** result, which is set by the ViewModel. Once ViewModel sets the result, **TaskCompletionSource.Task** finishes and the result is returned to the navigation caller.

Now, it is time to crank it up. Make sure all DI registrations were made and replace all navigation calls in **ViewModels** using our new navigation service. Follow the examples below to make navigations:

```
await _strongShellNavigation
    .NavigateToAsync(ShellRouteIdHelper.GetRootId<HomePage>());


await _strongShellNavigation.NavigateToAsync(
    new List<ShellPageRouteId> { ShellRouteIdHelper.
GetId<TransferModalPage>() },
    new TransferModalPageNavigationParameter(bankCardNumber));


await _strongShellNavigation.NavigateToAsync(new List<ShellPageRouteId>
    {
        ShellRouteIdHelper.GetId<CustomPage1>(),
        ShellRouteIdHelper.GetId<CustomPage2>(),
        ShellRouteIdHelper.GetId<CustomPage3>()
    });
```

As a final step, modify the **OnBankCardSelectedAsync** method of the **HomePageViewModel** as shown here to make the confirmation modal page appear before the transfer modal page:

```
private async Task OnBankCardSelectedAsync(long bankCardNumber)
{
    var isConfirmed = await _strongShellNavigation.NavigateToAsync<bool>(
        new List<ShellPageRouteId>
            { ShellRouteIdHelper.GetId<ConfirmationModalPage>() });

    if (isConfirmed)
        await _strongShellNavigation.NavigateToAsync(
            new List<ShellPageRouteId>
                { ShellRouteIdHelper.GetId<TransferModalPage>() },
            new TransferModalPageNavigationParameter(bankCardNumber));
}
```

Thanks to separating areas of responsibility, each component of our mechanism is pretty small and decoupled. In addition, we were able to make the shell navigation strongly typed. However, it does not mean it is perfect. Of course, experienced developers can find what can be improved. This solution can also be extended or modified to serve the needs of your specific real-world application.

The task for you: Use buttons on the home page, navigation service, and empty pages we've added to play around with Shell and our navigation service. Debug it step-by-step to understand it better. **Explore and debug applications from the repository for better understanding.**

Shell pages

As you already know, **ContentPage** is the core class when it comes to displaying content. Although the **ContentPage** is used in both Shell and non-Shell navigation concepts, it has some specifics and additional features when it is used with Shell.

For example, setting the **Shell.PresentationMode** attached property on a **ContentPage** changes the way Shell shows the page. The **PresentationMode** flags enumeration has the following members:

- **Animated** means the page will be displayed with an animated transition. This is the default value of the **Shell.Presentation** attached property.

- **NotAnimated** indicates that the navigation to a page will be performed without animation.

- **Modal** means the page will be displayed as a modal page.

- **ModalAnimated** is a combination of **Animated** and **Modal** members. A page will be displayed as a modal page with an animated navigation transition.

- **ModalNonAnimated** is a combination of **NotAnimated** and **Modal** members. A page will be displayed as a modal page but without an animated transition.

As we just learned, the navigation bar can be disabled thanks to **Shell. NavBarIsVisible** attached property, its color can be changed with **Shell. BackgroundColor**, and so on. Besides, thanks to the **Shell.TitleView** property, we can also put any UI control or layout view replacing the title, as follows:

```
<ContentPage xmlns="http://schemas.microsoft.com/dotnet/2021/maui"
             ...>
    <Shell.TitleView>
        <Grid ColumnDefinitions="1*,1*"
              VerticalOptions="Center" HorizontalOptions="Center">
```

```
    <Label Grid.Column="0" Text="Put anything here"
           VerticalOptions="Center" HorizontalOptions="Center"/>
    <Button Grid.Column="1" Text="Click me"
           VerticalOptions="Center"
HorizontalOptions="Center"/>
      </Grid>
    </Shell.TitleView>
</ContentPage>
```

It's recommended to specify the **WidthRequest** and **HeightRequest** properties, or **HorizontalOptions** and **VerticalOptions** within your custom title views.

Shell Flyout

The concept of Shell's navigation is built around TabBar and Flyout. Flyout is a side view of an application accessible through an icon in the top-left corner of the screen or by swiping from the side of the screen. Flyout offers several customizing opportunities; the appearance of the Flyout, its elements, and its behavior can be easily customized.

Here is a list of the most important flyout-related properties of the Shell class that define the Flyout's general appearance and behavior:

- **FlyoutIsPresented** of type **bool** enables you to open and close Flyout programmatically from C# or via Binding.

- **FlyoutIcon** of type **ImageSource**. By default, the built-in so-called "hamburger" icon is used for the navigation bar button that opens Flyout.

- The **FlyoutWidth** and **FlyoutHeight** properties can be used to customize the **Width** and **Height** of the **Flyout**.

- **FlyoutBehavior** can be in one of three states: **Disabled**, **Flyout**, and **Locked**. The **Disabled** value disables the **Flyout**, the **Locked** value prevents the **Flyout** from being closed, and the **Flyout** value is in the default state of **Flyout** in which it can be opened and closed normally.

- **FlyoutBackdrop** of type **Brush** defines the appearance of the **Flyout** overlay.

- **FlyoutBackground**, **FlyoutBackgroundImage**, and **FlyoutBackground Color** introduce background customizations.

- **FlyoutVerticalScrollMode** changes the behavior of the **Flyout** scrolling. By default, this property has the **Auto** value set. It means that the content of the Flyout can be scrolled vertically when content doesn't fit in the **Flyout**. The **Disabled** value disables scrolling. The **Enabled** value makes scrolling be enabled all the time.

The Flyout can be visually and logically split into three areas: **Header**, **Content**, and **Footer** (*Figure 9.2*):

Figure 9.2: Flyout areas

Flyout **Header** and **Footer** areas are optional areas that can be filled up with any content using the **FlyoutHeader** and **FlyoutFooter** properties, as follows:

```
<Shell.FlyoutHeader>
    <Grid HeightRequest="100" BackgroundColor="LightBlue">
        <Label Text="Header (optional)" FontSize="25"
                VerticalOptions="Center" HorizontalOptions="Center"/>
    </Grid>
</Shell.FlyoutHeader>
<Shell.FlyoutFooter>
    <Grid HeightRequest="100" BackgroundColor="LightCoral">
        <Label Text="Footer (optional)" FontSize="25"
```

```
        VerticalOptions="Center" HorizontalOptions="Center"/>
    </Grid>
</Shell.FlyoutFooter>
```

Alternatively, the content of the **Footer** and **Header** can be set with **FlyoutHeader Template** and **FlyoutFooterTemplate** using **DataTemplate**.

By default, the **Header** is fixed and the content can be scrolled. This behavior can be changed by setting the **FlyoutHeaderBehavior** property to one of the enumeration members:

- **Default** means the default behavior for the platform.

- **Scroll** means the **Header** area will be scrolled along with the content.

- **CollapseOnScroll** means the Header will collapse to a title only during scrolling.

- **Fixed** indicates that the Header will remain visible all the time.

The **Content** area can optionally be used to display any content thanks to the **FlyoutContent** property, just like in the case of Header and Footer. This is super helpful for developing applications with a fully custom UI. However, in the universe of Shell, the main purpose of the content area is to display **FlyoutItems** and **MenuItems**. In all fairness, however, it should be said that both the elements also have good customization capabilities.

FlyoutItem is an element that wraps the **Tab** in the Shell hierarchy. For example, the following code shows the Flyout alternative of the Shell subclass for the sample app from the beginning of this chapter:

```
<Shell xmlns="http://schemas.microsoft.com/dotnet/2021/maui"
       xmlns:x="http://schemas.microsoft.com/winfx/2009/xaml"
       x:Class="ShellMauiSample.AppFlyoutShell"
       xmlns:local="clr-namespace:ShellMauiSample"
       FlyoutBackdrop="#99000000"
       Shell.TabBarIsVisible="False">


    <FlyoutItem Title="Furniture" Icon="furniture_icon" >
        <Tab Route="Furniture" >
            <ShellContent Title="Kitchen" Route="Kitchen"
                          ContentTemplate="{DataTemplate
local:KitchenPage}"/>
```

```
        <ShellContent Title="Bedroom" Route="Bedroom"
                        ContentTemplate="{DataTemplate
local:BedroomPage}"/>
        </Tab>
    </FlyoutItem>
    <FlyoutItem Title="Accessories" Icon="accessories_icon">
        <Tab Route="AccessoriesTab">
            <ShellContent Route="Accessories"
                        ContentTemplate="{DataTemplate
local:AccessoriesPage}"/>
        </Tab>
    </FlyoutItem>
</Shell>
```

MenuItems are similar to **FlyoutItems** in the way they are displayed in the **Flyout**. However, they do not contain **ShellContent**. **MenuItems** enables you to add an item that looks and feels like **FlyoutItem** but performs your custom action by clicking on it. It has the **Clicked** event and the pair of **Command-CommandParameter** properties for your custom handlers. Here's an example:

```
<MenuItem Text="Terms and Conditions"
        IconImageSource="info_icon "
        Command="{Binding LaunchCommand}"
        CommandParameter="https://mycompany.com/terms-and-conditions" />
```

The **MenuItem** element's position on the Flyout list depends on its declaration order, for example, **MenuItem** put between **Furniture** and **Accessories** (see the preceding code snippet) means **FlyoutItems** will be displayed between corresponding UI elements on the Flyout.

The appearances of **FlyoutItem** and **MenuItem** can be customized using the **ItemTemplate** and **MenuItemTemplate** properties with **DataTemplates**. Besides, the appearance can be changed by style. Shell includes three built-in style classes, which are automatically applied to **FlyoutItem** and **MenuItem**. So, specifying your custom styles with a predefined class name, shown as follows, will customize the appearance of the **Label**, **Image**, and **Layout** of each item. Here's an example:

```
<Style TargetType="Label" Class="FlyoutItemLabelStyle">
    <Setter Property="TextColor" Value="{StaticResource BrandBlack}" />
    <Setter Property="HeightRequest" Value="50" />
</Style>
```

```
<Style TargetType="Image" Class="FlyoutItemImageStyle">

    <Setter Property="Aspect" Value="Fill" />

</Style>

<Style TargetType="Layout" Class="FlyoutItemLayoutStyle"

        ApplyToDerivedTypes="True">

    <Setter Property="BackgroundColor" Value="{StaticResource
BrandBackground}" />

    <Setter Property="Padding" Value="20,5" />

</Style>
```

What is Blazor?

Let's get familiar with another way of creating .NET MAUI applications: Blazor hybrid applications. But what is Blazor? In general, Blazor came up as an answer to the requests of developers who desired to build web applications without JavaScript. Blazor is a framework developed by Microsoft that allows developers to build web applications using C# instead of JavaScript.

Traditionally, web applications consist of a server side (written in C# and other languages), and a client side (typically written using HTML/CSS and JavaScript). However, despite its popularity, using JavaScript might be less convenient or beneficial for developers and companies preferring the use of another technological stack like .NET with C# as a main programming language. Blazor was created to change this, and it offers the conjunction of C#, .NET, and HTML to build interactive web UI.

Blazor WebAssembly and Blazor Server

Web applications with C# became possible thanks to two technologies: Blazor WebAssembly and Blazor Server.

Blazor Server is a technology where the Blazor app runs on the server on top of the full .NET runtime. All UI interactions and updates are handled over a real-time SignalR connection. When an event occurs, like a button click, the information about the action is sent to the server over the SignalR connection. The server handles the event and returns the required UI updates to the client. Although this solution has advantages like full access to server resources and performance of the .NET Core server, it also comes with trade-offs. The Blazor server requires an active connection between client and server, and network latency has a significant impact on user experience.

Blazor WebAssembly, on the other hand, enables any modern web browser to host the .NET runtime. In this model, the Blazor app, along with its dependencies and the WebAssembly .NET runtime, is downloaded to the browser. It works offline and is very responsive. However, such an application is restricted to the browser's capabilities, and when using WebAssembly, the .NET runtime operates in the interpreted mode, which isn't as performant as .NET running natively.

From the coding perspective, embedding C# into HTML became possible thanks to Razor markup syntax, which is shown as follows:

```
<h3>@message</h3>


@code {
    private string message = "Hello, World!";
}
```

Blazor Hybrid

Blazor Hybrid takes **Blazor** technology a step further, allowing it to run **Blazor** web applications directly on the operating system. This technology, in conjunction with MAUI, enables developers to build native cross-platform web applications with .NET MAUI that are distributed as normal applications. Moreover, in a .NET MAUI Hybrid application, we can mix both approaches, embedding the Blazor web application into views written in XAML.

When it comes to the Blazor universe, thanks to MAUI, such a web application gets full access to the capabilities of the device it's running on. This means it can access the file system, use device-specific APIs, and generally do things that web applications cannot. Besides, it doesn't require an active connection with Blazor Server and doesn't use interpreted mode. It works as a device-native app.

BlazorWebVeiw

BlazorWebView control put in a markup of an application view is an actual way to host a Blazor web application into a MAUI application. Take a look at the following XAML markup:

```
<BlazorWebView x:Name="blazorWebView" HostPage="wwwroot/index.html">

    <BlazorWebView.RootComponents>

        <RootComponent Selector="#app" ComponentType="{x:Type
local:Main}" />

    </BlazorWebView.RootComponents>

</BlazorWebView>
```

The **HostPage** property is used to specify the HTML page, which will bootstrap the Blazor application. In the preceding code snippet, a Blazor component defined by the **Main** type is being rendered in the **app** element of the **wwwroot/index.html** page.

The **BlazorWebView** control has three events:

- The **UrlLoading** event is called when **HostPage** is about to be loaded and can be subscribed to change link handling behavior.

- **BlazorWebViewInitializing** is raised before the web view is initialized.

- **BlazorWebViewInitialized** is raised after the web view is initialized but before any component has been rendered. The event arguments provide the instance of the platform-specific web view control.

MAUI capabilities from Blazor code

Razor Components serve as the fundamental building blocks of a Blazor application, made up of reusable UI pieces implemented in .razor files. Each .razor file defines a component containing HTML markup and associated processing logic written in C#. This processing logic can be located inline in the @code block or in a separate code-behind file.

Parameters, or properties that are decorated with the **[Parameter]** attribute, allow data to be transferred from parent to child components.

Components can handle user events, perform complex rendering, and fetch data in response to events.

In a .NET MAUI hybrid application, Razor components can be utilized in the same way as in any other Blazor application. In .NET MAUI, for example, we can inject services into the Razor components. Consider the following service registered in the MAUI DI container:

```
public interface IDeviceInfoService
{
    DisplayMetrics Displayinfo { get; }
}


public class DeviceInfoService : IDeviceInfoService
{
    public DisplayMetrics GetDisplayMetrics => DeviceDisplay.
MainDisplayInfo;
```

```
}
```

`MauiProgram.cs`:

```
builder.Services.AddSingleton<IDeviceInfoService, DeviceInfoService>();
```

This simple service is a wrapper for the **DeviceDisplay** static class. **DisplayInfo** returns the characteristics of a runtime device. This is how this service can be consumed in the **Razor component**:

```
@page "/deviceinfo"
@inject IDeviceInfoService DeviceInfoService

<h3>Device Information</h3>

<p>Height: @displayMetrics.Height</p>
<p>Width: @displayMetrics.Width</p>

@code {
    private DisplayMetrics displayMetrics;

    protected override void OnInitialized()
    {
        displayMetrics = DeviceInfoService.GetDisplayMetrics();
    }
}
```

We've injected our service with the **@inject** directive and then handled the **Razor component** life cycle method using C#.

Conclusion

Shell is an advanced, powerful, and flexible technology offering lots of useful features, but it also has its own drawbacks. And its magic-string-based navigation with several rules and corner cases is the main one. Now you know how to make Shell strong once and for all.

Blazor Hybrid applications, in turn, can be a good solution for a company that has a big web application that needs to be turned into a native application quickly. Or it can be an attractive option for someone who has extensive web development experience and wishes to use it in native application development.

Points to remember

- Shell applications may follow **Flyout** or **Tab bar** UI patterns.
- Shell has additional life cycle events: **Appearing** and **Disappearing**.
- Shell title can be replaced with a custom **TitleView**.
- Shell **Flyout** can have fully custom content.

Questions

1. Why did Shell have an alternative navigation concept introduced?
2. What is the main purpose of the Shell subclass?
3. What are ways to reach Shell class instances globally?
4. What are the differences between ShellContent pages and global pages?
5. What are differences between Blazor WebAssembly, Blazor Server, and Blazor Hybrid MAUI App?

Join our book's Discord space

Join the book's Discord Workspace for Latest updates, Offers, Tech happenings around the world, New Release and Sessions with the Authors:

https://discord.bpbonline.com

Index

Made in United States
Troutdale, OR
04/03/2024

18913191R00210